MOJA

MOJADA

Memoir of a Honduran Immigrant

KEYLA SANDERS

McFarland & Company, Inc., Publishers

Jefferson, North Carolina

Library of Congress Cataloguing-in-Publication Data

Names: Sanders, Keyla O. (Keyla Osiris), 1984– author.
Title: Mojada : memoir of a Honduran immigrant / Keyla O. Sanders.
Other titles: Memoir of a Honduran immigrant
Description: Jefferson, North Carolina : McFarland & Company, Inc., Publishers, 2023 |
  Includes bibliographical references and index.
Identifiers: LCCN 2023031584 | ISBN 9781476691992 (print) ⊗
  ISBN 9781476649856 (ebook)
Subjects: LCSH: Sanders, Keyla O. (Keyla Osiris), 1984– | Honduran Americans—
  Washington (D.C.)—Biography. | Women noncitizens—United States—
  Biography. | Noncitizens—United States—Biography. | Illegal immigration—
  United States. | Human smuggling—Mexican-American Border Region. |
  La Entrada (Honduras)—Biography. | United States—Emigration and
  immigration. | Washington (D.C.)—Biography.
Classification: LCC F201.3.S36 A3 2023 | DDC 304.8/7307283092 [B]—dc23/
  eng/20230712
LC record available at https://lccn.loc.gov/2023031584

British Library cataloguing data are available

ISBN (print) 978-1-4766-9199-2
ISBN (ebook) 978-1-4766-4985-6

Front cover artwork by the author

Printed in the United States of America

McFarland & Company, Inc., Publishers
  Box 611, Jefferson, North Carolina 28640
  www.mcfarlandpub.com

To La Hita (my grandmother, María Olanda Alas)
and to my mom, Telma Yolanda Alas.
To my mom for giving me life,
and to my grandmother for raising me.
Las quiero y las extraño.

Also to my husband for his infinite support throughout
the writing of *Mojada* and throughout our years of marriage,
and to my kids, Isaac, Isabella, and Sabina,
whom I love so much and who I hope will live their lives
to their full potential and never stop dreaming.

mojada: |moh-HAH-dah|—n. A Spanish term used by the Spanish-speaking immigrant community to describe an immigrant who entered the United States without going through an official immigration checkpoint. *No le digas a nadie que eres mojada.* (Never tell anyone that you are a *mojada.*)

—adv. A Spanish term used to describe the manner in which an immigrant has crossed the border. *¿Ella vino mojada o con visa?* (Did she come *mojada* or with a visa?)

Table of Contents

Acknowledgments

Thank you to Miguel Aguilar Rodriguez for helping me to organize my thoughts and memories into a book, for pushing me to keep writing, for your guidance as an author and for your expertise in our shared *patria* Honduras.

Thank you to Moises González for your monumental effort in working on the Spanish version manuscript and the translation into English. Additionally, thank you for visiting Honduras to learn and experience where I came from and why La Entrada will always be in my heart.

Thank you to my book agent, Leticia Gomez. You are an inspiration to me and you have believed in me and my story from the beginning.

Thank you to my husband, Mark, for your continuous help with the book. *Gracias* for reviewing the translation and correcting all my mistakes in this second language. Thank you for all the long days and late nights, and putting so much time, effort, and emotion into fulfilling my dream.

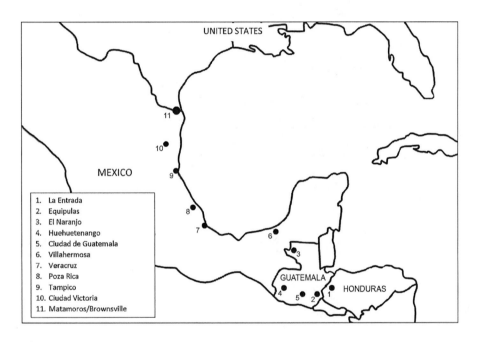

Keyla's journey to the United States.

Preface

In the pre-dawn hours of November 25, 2000, accompanied by my younger sister, I left my hometown in Honduras with a book-bag, two sets of clothes, and a dream. We both were anxious to be reunited with our family, who were all living in the United States. I did not have a visa to enter this country, and so I had to find an alternate route. I had a dream of a safer place to live, a dream of expanded opportunities, a dream of a better life. I was starting on what I knew would be a difficult journey but one that I hoped would be worth it in the end.

In the past several years, the topics of legal and illegal immigration, immigrants, asylum, refugees, and caravans have become major news stories and political talking points. Too often, the voices that are missing from this discussion are the voices of the immigrants. Some reporters provide quick sound bites and anecdotes, while others just echo politicians as they decide the motivations, intentions, and values of those risking their lives to come to this country.

This book is the voice of one immigrant. The following chapters are an account of my life growing up in a small town in Honduras and my overland trip to the United States as an unaccompanied minor. In addition, my story shows my journey through the United States immigration system, all while dealing with the tears, pains, traumas, joys, laughter, and happiness that are a part of both life and the struggle to fulfill my version of the American Dream.

It is my hope that through my story you may be able to see past the stereotypes and media portrayals of undocumented immigrants and see me for who I am—a human being with flaws and virtues, with successes and failures, and someone who, like you, wishes to better herself and provide a better future for her children. If you can see that humanity in me, an undocumented immigrant—a *mojada*—I pray that you

1

can see all immigrants for who they are and not for what documents they may or may not have.

While many migrants who travel through Central America and Mexico on their way to the United States go through similar events and challenges, this book is specific to my life and my journey. Each immigrant's experience is individual, and one blanket narrative should not be applied to all. What should be universal is the value and worth of every human soul and everyone's right to the *pursuit of happiness.*

Author's Note

All but a handful of the names in this book have been changed, as many people who are and have been in my life are undocumented immigrants or the family of undocumented immigrants. In addition, I am here to tell my story and my truth. I believe that each person should be given the opportunity to tell their own truth in the way and to the people they choose.

Prologue:
Her Last Breath

La Entrada, Copán (Honduras)

I remember it was a hot afternoon. I was only three years old. I was walking along the hallway of my house when I noticed that my older brother, Alexander, was hiding in a corner between the fridge and the wall. He was crying with his back to me. It was clear that he did not want anyone to see him. I observed him but did not speak. I listened to his moans and watched him cover his face with both hands. I could not understand why nobody came to comfort him.

In that moment, my house felt strange. There were so many people walking everywhere. I didn't know who everyone was. "Keyla, come to the room right now," I heard someone say. I wasn't sure who had called me.

While watching everyone around me, I walked toward the only bedroom in the house. It was the one I shared with my siblings, cousins, and grandmother. I looked up and could see the bunk bed where I slept and the single bed at the end of the room. On my left-hand side, next to the door, my mother was lying on a double bed.

My grandmother was standing behind me, and my two-year-old sister Gabriela—whom everyone in the family called Gaby—was on my right side. A hand beckoned me over to where my mom was. I grabbed Gaby by the hand, and we walked slowly toward her. My mom's face was whiter than usual, and she had tears in her eyes. The sheet was pulled up to her chest. Her head was lying on a gray pillow, and a cloth was covering part of her forehead. I raised my eyes toward the "window"— in reality, just a hole cut into the wall—and saw two neighbors crying on the other side. One of them waved her hand to encourage us to touch my mother's forehead. I moved closer to the bed and grabbed my mother's hand that was resting on the edge of the bed. The neighbor kept insisting that we touch my mom's forehead. So I moved even closer, along with my sister, and we both gently caressed our mom's face. Tears flowed down her cheeks, and she could barely manage to turn to look at my sister and me. She opened her mouth but could not speak. She tried to utter something a second time, but she couldn't catch her breath. The sobbing of everyone in the room grew louder.

After that moment with my mom, everything felt even stranger in my house. The removable divider wall used to form an additional room had been removed, and the living room had doubled in size. The furniture and dining table had been removed as well. I was walking down the hallway, silently and without fully comprehending what was happening, when my cousin Ritza grabbed me by the hand and took me to the backyard. She undressed me, made me sit on a stool, and started cleaning me with a wet washcloth. Bathing while having a deceased person in the home is considered unhealthy because of the *ijillo*: a popular belief in my hometown says that people are more susceptible to falling ill during a vigil, due to the fumes released by the deceased's body.

My cousin was crying and wiping me off as fast as she could. It was as if she was trying to hide her face from me. I couldn't understand what was going on. So I just stared at her carefully and curiously. Upon finishing, she dressed me in a light blue nightgown. Then, she walked me back to the house.

I walked into the living room. I don't know how much time had passed while I was outside. Then, right in the middle of the living room, I saw a casket. I had never seen anything like it before, and I felt a powerful desire to find out what was inside, but it was so high that I couldn't reach it. Four tall and thick poles were being used to support the wooden box. There were lots of flowers hanging on the walls around it. There were lit candles on top of four tall and thin candelabras that stood at each corner of the casket. The smell in the room was strong and unpleasant.

I began to jump up while trying to reach out with my hand, but I still couldn't reach the top of the casket. A niece of my grandmother's named Soledad, who lived in San Pedro Sula—a two-hour bus ride from my hometown—brought me a stool to stand on. I finally got to see what was inside the casket: it was my mother. Her body was wrapped in white cloth, and there was cotton stuffed inside her eyes, nose, and mouth. A white veil covered her head. Her body lay motionless; she looked stiff. I didn't cry; I wasn't afraid. I still didn't fully comprehend what was going on.

My grandmother and aunts didn't stop crying all night. The following day, someone closed the casket, and four men carried it on their shoulders from our living room to the cemetery. We all walked slowly behind them. We arrived at the hill where the only cemetery in town was located. There were crosses and graves all over the place. Several people were waiting around a deep hole that had soil on either side. The four men placed the casket on the ground, right next to the freshly dug hole. I knelt because I wanted to see inside; I felt curious.

"Open the casket!" I heard someone yell as they were getting ready to put my mother inside that hole.

My grandma could not speak; she only cried. Her eyes were red and swollen. Someone opened the casket lid, and I saw my mother's face, just as I had seen it in the living room of my house. My grandma threw herself on top of the casket and sobbed incessantly, moaning in pain. I took a closer look inside. I did not cry, but I knew I wanted to do so. Instead, I felt an overwhelming sadness deep inside my heart and something shattered inside of me. It was then that I knew what was happening. I would never get to see my mother again. She was gone.

Years later, I was curious to know exactly when my mother had died. My grandma told me that she passed away as my sister and I were touching her face that afternoon while she was lying on the bed.

My mother's name was Telma Yolanda Alas, and she died of ovarian cancer at the age of 26 on July 7, 1988. Most of the memories I hold of her are

My mom, Telma Yolanda Alas, around 1982 (A. Ghasani).

from the day she died. But there is one that I treasured in my heart and mind so much that, for many years, I thought it may have been just a dream. I was about two years old. I was in the eatery where my grandmother used to sell soda and food. I was sitting at a table waiting for my mother, who was coming by bus from San Nicolás, a town near La Entrada. I saw her get off the bus, and I rushed out to hug her and asked for the grapes she had promised she would bring me. I had been waiting for her impatiently for hours. I'm sure I asked more than once when she would get there. Grapes were considered a delicacy in my hometown, especially if they were the big red ones with seeds (they are my favorite to this day). As if it were yesterday, I remember the excitement of seeing my mom and how happy we were. The rest of my memories of her began when I caressed her forehead and ended at the cemetery, seeing her for the last time.

As I grew up, I felt the loss of not having my mother around. Her abrupt passing became the source of much of my sorrow as a child and during my adolescence, yet I never imagined that I would miss her the most as an adult. From a very young age, I got used to going to bed crying over her absence.

1

La Entrada

I grew up in La Entrada, a town in Copán, one of Honduras's 18 departments. It is situated in the western part of the country, near the borders of El Salvador and Guatemala. My house was in a neighborhood known as El Triángulo.

El Triángulo was a typical small-town neighborhood. It was always covered in dust, and most streets were unpaved dirt roads. Only the main roads and the two 2-lane international highways that went through the town were paved. I spent most of my days watching cars and buses go back and forth between the smaller towns and La Entrada.

The name "El Triángulo"—which means triangle—derives from the fact that the area was formed by a fork in the international highway that runs from San Pedro Sula, the largest city in Honduras, to La Entrada. The highway divides in two, with one way heading toward Copán Ruinas, one of the largest Mayan archaeological sites in the world and close to the border with Guatemala. The other way heads to Ocotepeque—a department that borders El Salvador. Along that highway, you will find Santa Rosa de Copán, the capital of the department of Copán, and the place where I was born because La Entrada had no hospital.

The international highway ran in front of my house and was where buses came back and forth from San Pedro Sula to Copán Ruinas because it is a favorite spot among tourists. From my front door, I was able to watch people from the United States and from all over the world come and go. Near the road used to be a guava tree where I hung upside down and watched people go by. The tree was planted in a ditch that used to flood during rainy days. I loved to make boats out of newspapers and entertained myself by watching them float along with the current.

From right in front of my house, I could see the best-known parts

La Entrada, Copán, around 1990 (family photograph).

of El Triángulo: the Texaco gas station, a small supermarket called El Triángulo, and Helados Nanny, the only ice cream parlor I knew of and where I got to enjoy an ice cream cone a couple of times a year. All these businesses were owned by the same woman, whose son lived close by. His house was one of the best houses in the whole neighborhood. It had miniature-sized coconut palm trees and a manicured lawn, which was rare to see in my town.

On the other side of El Triángulo—on the highway to Santa Rosa— was the bus terminal where my grandmother for a time owned a small café, where she used to sell food and soft drinks. One day, when I was about four years old, I was walking home and I fell on the dirt road that we used as a shortcut to cross from my grandmother's café at the bus terminal back to my house. I cut my right leg so severely that it would not stop bleeding. My cousins were scared because they thought my grandma would punish them for not taking proper care of me. They blamed each other for not paying attention to me while I was walking. I do not remember my grandma scolding my cousins for not taking care of me. No one took me to the doctor to get stitches, even though I did need them. Over time, the wound healed, but it left a large scar and was a reminder of that experience.

I lived in a humble house with a rough cement floor that was cracked and needed patches in more than a few places. The front facade was turquoise blue and had only the front door and a small wooden window that we rarely opened. The house was connected to the neighbors' houses on both sides. It was an older style of house and it had been built by my great-grandmother. My cousins and I were the fourth generation to live there.

The main part of the house consisted of a living room, two bedrooms, and a long hallway that ran from the living room to the back of the house. The smaller bedroom, where my aunt Laura slept, was part of the living room and was created by a removable divider wall. The other bedroom, where my grandmother, cousins, and I slept, was just off the hallway.

Our house had a roof made from ceramic tiles, which was quite common. There was no interior ceiling, and you could see the underside of the tiles. Occasionally, the roof leaked because kids from around the neighborhood would throw rocks at it, which would cause the clay tiles to break. My grandmother would have the tiles replaced as soon as she could. In the meantime, we would have to use *panas*—small plastic containers—to collect the water when it rained.

The exposed rafters in our house gave the grown-ups an additional space to hide things from us kids. My cousin Ritza, who was an older teenager, used to confiscate our basket of toys and place them in the rafters of our bedroom as her own form of punishment. But I always found a way to get them back down, using a broom or the long stick we kept on hand to get rid of the spiderwebs. Once I succeeded in recovering my toys, I was happy to host my own tea parties with my favorite set of small ceramic plates and cups.

Located at the back of the house was the *solar*—a large tract of land—that ran the length of the block to the next street over. There, on the right-hand side and connected to the back wall of the main house, were two rooms made of adobe, both painted with whitewash. Some of my older cousins slept in one of those rooms. The other one was the kitchen, where the women of the house spent the day cooking on a woodfire stove made of hard clay. I can clearly remember the smell of the simmering beans and fresh tortillas that were made there every day.

Attached at the end of the rooms was the *pila*—a large, deep cement tub containing the water we used for bathing, washing, and cleaning. Most houses in Honduras have a *pila*, which also has a flat stone slab connected to the large tub where you can wash dishes or clothes.

Water scarcity was a common issue in my town. We did not have constant running water. The municipality would usually turn on the water service two or three times a week, but sometimes we would go several days or even a week with no water. The *pila* near the bathroom was a lifesaver. Every time the water service was turned on, we would open the tap on the *pila*, as we tried to keep it full. This was necessary, as there was no set schedule for the water service. The problems came when we completely emptied the *pila* because the water service was out for too long.

The *solar* behind our house had several trees. In front of the kitchen was a large tree that grew a black fruit with a green seed that we used to make soap. We also had a small coffee plant that always bore lots of fruit despite its small size. In the backyard, we had a tamarind tree and five sour orange trees—I always enjoyed eating the oranges with salt and cumin. Additionally, we had two izote trees, a tall plant with fan-shaped branches and highly fragrant white flowers. My grandma used to cook eggs with the flowers, though I never liked the bitter taste they left in my mouth.

There were three large oak trees that shaded a big part of the backyard. I used to pick up the acorns that fell from them and use them as spinning tops. It was fun to make them dance with the perfect quick spin. In the middle of the backyard and under the oak trees, there was an old, empty *pila*, which we frequently used as a makeshift swimming pool when we had enough water.

The block where I lived consisted of nine connected houses, all of a similar plain construction, simple in design, with a front door and a window or two. They all belonged to hardworking and humble people. None of the families were rich, nor would we have been considered poor compared to others who lived in other sectors of my town.

Our town had a mix of types of houses. Most common were houses, like those on my block, made from adobe: a sun-dried brick made of clay that was sometimes mixed with straw. Those not able to afford much would build their houses out of a combination of sheet metal roofing, scrap wood, and nylon tarps.

The two houses on one side of mine were cantinas/bordellos and used to sell alcohol. On the other side of my house was a shed that my grandmother used to rent to an upholstery business owned by Don Samuel, who was from San Nicolás and would commute to La Entrada every day for work. Don Samuel was a kind man. He was *chele*—a nickname for people with white skin. He also spoke surprisingly fast, and sometimes it was difficult to understand everything he was saying.

La Entrada was a small town, but it was the commercial and transit hub for all the small villages nearby. People living in the mountains came to La Entrada to work, study, sell their crops, and buy groceries and supplies. Despite being the largest town in the area, there was still no electricity. I will never forget the day when they started digging the holes to install the posts for the power lines all along the main road.

At home, we used a kerosene lantern for light. To iron clothes, my grandmother used a hollow metal iron that she filled with embers from the stove. To cook, we used the woodfire stove and occasionally a small gas stove. We had to always have firewood and *ocote*—a type of tree bark used as a fire starter. Every morning, my grandma would light the fire in the stove as soon as she woke up in order to make some coffee and reheat the beans. We had a gas-powered refrigerator, but when we got electricity in the town, we bought an electric one.

At nights, the gas station's lights, which had their own generator, served as a type of night-light that illuminated our house for free. I would sit on the sidewalk with my cousins and aunts to tell scary stories like *La Llorona* and *La Siguanaba*.*

Before La Entrada had electricity, all my family had was a battery-powered radio. Once the power lines were installed, my grandmother purchased a small television. My cousins and I enjoyed watching *pichingos* (cartoons). With electricity and the TV, we were able to enjoy the Mexican *telenovelas*, which everyone at home, including children, watched at night. At times, our house turned into a small movie theater when neighbors and other family friends would come to watch TV. They did not come inside the house; they just stood in the doorway or window to watch the *telenovelas*.

My family didn't have much money, but we were able to afford some of these small comforts thanks to the family members who sent money from the U.S. My aunt Rafaela emigrated to the United States when I was a baby, and sent us money regularly. After my mom's death, my aunt Míriam, then only 19 years old, also emigrated to the United States so she could help my grandmother with the cost of raising us.

---

* *La Llorona* (*The Crying Woman*) is a traditional Latin American folktale about a woman's ghost who wanders at night crying for her dead children. *La Siguanaba* is a traditional Central American folktale from Mayan mythology about a mythical shapeshifting creature that attracts her victims by appearing as a beautiful woman and then shifting to her true form to scare them to death.

Aunt Míriam did it because when my mother found out that her cancer was terminal, she asked Míriam to take care of us. Aunt Míriam believed that working in the U.S. would be the best way to help my siblings and me so that we could eat and study. Thanks to the help we received from the United States, my grandmother was able to afford hiring a *muchacha* (maid) to help around the house. It was typical for even lower-income families like ours to have someone to assist us at home. It was cheap to hire additional help, and there were always people with very little income who needed to work. The *muchacha* would sleep and eat in our house, which was a benefit for her, as she might not be able to eat three meals a day back in her village. The *muchacha* helped my grandma with the housework. It wasn't easy to cook and clean for so many people or to hand-wash the laundry in the *pila* or by the river.

My grandmother, who all the cousins called "La Hita"—a derivative form of the Spanish word *abuelita* (grandma)—looked after my sister Gaby, my brother Alexander, and me after our mother died. She also took care of my cousins when their mothers emigrated to the United States. For everybody else, my grandmother was "Doña Yolanda" or "Doña Yoli," but for my cousins and me, she was La Hita.

La Hita cared for me immensely. She always looked after me, protected me, and loved me in her own way. In my family, we have never been into hugging. We never said "I love you." As a child I never got used to that. I don't remember being hugged by my grandmother or anyone in my family throughout my childhood and adolescence. I knew La Hita loved me, because she didn't punish me as severely as she punished my older cousins. Sometimes she didn't even ground me when I misbehaved or threw myself on the floor in a tantrum.

My grandma was a woman with a rare beauty that everyone admired or envied and wondered from where she had inherited it. La Hita was of average height for a woman in Honduras (a little more than five feet), with light skin, light brown hair (although it was already a bit gray), and her eyes were as blue as the sky in springtime. Few people knew, but my grandma wasn't Honduran; she was born in El Salvador. Even in her old age, it was clear that La Hita had been a knockout in her youth, because of her small waist combined with curves, wide hips, and thick legs.

Her most beautiful characteristic wasn't her physique but her huge heart and tremendous desire to help us, her extended family, and her friends and neighbors. La Hita didn't have much in terms of a formal education, yet she always found a way to support her family. She was an active businesswoman and entrepreneur. For a time, she ran a small café at the bus terminal. When she was no longer able to do that, she looked for other ways to make money, whether it was selling cheese, cheese curd, or cottage cheese that she made at home. She also sold bread and food, and frequently traveled to El Salvador and Guatemala to buy candies to sell back in La Entrada.

Every morning, she woke up very early to milk a cow we had in the backyard. One day, someone stole the cow, and my grandmother was forced to buy milk from a family that owned a pasture beyond *La Tranca*—a police checkpoint on the outskirts of town. I remember going with her a couple of times. We used to leave so early that it wasn't even dawn when we returned home after buying milk.

La Hita also raised pigs, chickens, turkeys, ducks, and almost any animal that could be sold or used as food at home. Fresh eggs and freshly made cheese curds were always on hand for us to eat. One day when I was six years old, my grandma sent me out to sell cheese curds with my sister Gaby and Camila, a neighbor whom La Hita regularly hired. Unluckily, when Gaby was carrying the tray with the food, she dropped it on the ground. We cleaned the dirt from the cheese curds with our hands as best we could and continued selling them as if nothing had happened. We thought no one would know we had dropped them, but we weren't very successful with the sales that day. So, just before the sun went down, we headed back home. On the way home, I couldn't stop thinking about the punishment the three of us would face for the incident, but my grandma never made mention of it.

La Hita was very restless and always moving. At home, she was always in the kitchen preparing something, even with both the older women of the household and the *muchacha* there to help her. When not at home, she was running errands around town or at the market where she bought meat and vegetables. Occasionally, she visited her friends, who were about the same age as her. I could tell by their gray hair. We were a Catholic family, and on Sundays we went to a church located in the neighborhood of El Centro, right at the top of a hill. As with all Honduran towns, the church was next to the town's central square.

One day, while visiting one of her friends up in the nearby mountains, La Hita broke her leg, and the doctor had to put it in a cast. I don't remember hearing my grandma ever complain of any pain. The most challenging thing for her was having to stay at home and move around on crutches for some time.

Having La Hita was extremely important for me during my childhood. I could cry and complain to her when my cousins bothered me or when I felt lonely. I always knew where to find her. If I didn't see her at home, I would go to the neighbor's house down the block or to the river where she used to do laundry.

My grandma told me that when my mother knew she was going to die, she asked God to please allow her mother to have a long life so that she could look after us. According to La Hita, a few days before she passed away,

La Hita, my grandmother, 2002 (A. Ghasani).

my mom dreamed that God was expecting her in 15 days. My mom asked God to allow my grandmother to live long enough for my siblings and me to grow up and earn a living. My mom died two weeks after that dream, and La Hita raised my siblings and me, and she did it without complaining.

My grandmother was the best role model I could ever have asked for in my early years. Even though I didn't know it at the time, she played a critical role in my future. She made me who I am, and her love and dedication in raising me were more than any daughter could ever wish for in a mother. I will never forget her smile, her sparkling eyes, her tears over my mother's death, and how much she loved me and cared for me. María Olanda Alas will forever be La Hita and my heroine.

2

Zapatos Rotos

My siblings and I grew up without knowing what it was to have a father—or at least not one who lived at home and played with us every day. Not one whom I could ask for advice or complain to when one of my cousins was annoying me. I never knew what it was like to wait for a dad to return home after work. Someone who would come in the house with a bag full of food as I laughingly hung onto his legs. My mom was a single mother, and as far as I remember, my father never much concerned himself with taking care of us.

My mother gave birth to my brother Alexander when she was only 16 years old. During his childhood, my brother had long, straight hair in a mushroom-shaped haircut, and the people in our family always said that he looked a lot like my mom. He was short like his father. I knew that because I remember seeing his dad on one occasion when he visited my brother at our house. Alexander had a temper: he was always angry, and it was common to see him fighting with my cousin Fabricio.

Gaby and I had a different father than Alexander. I have no memories of his hugs or attention, much less of him supporting us financially. My father's name is Carlos Humberto Green. His last name was a little out of the ordinary in Honduras, but it was also what helped me find him 18 years later. My father didn't come to my mom's funeral. I did get to see him a couple of times after that, though, when he came to visit us in town. There was also a time when we dared to visit him at his job in San Pedro Sula.

I don't remember exactly how much time had passed after my mother's death when my father visited us. It was about a year or so later. I was old enough to have a more precise recall of that day. I knew in advance that my father was coming over. I felt excited, or at least I thought I was supposed to feel that way. When the day came, I was confused when I saw him. My feelings for him seemed odd. He was a

15

Zapatos Rotos (K. Sanders).

complete stranger to me. If he was my father, why did I feel that way? Why did I feel I could not trust him? I went over to him and felt embarrassed as I hugged him.

I was still little. I barely came up to his knee. My father was tall, long legged, dark haired, slim, and a well-dressed man. On that day, he was wearing slacks, a button-down shirt, and well-polished black shoes. He parted his hair to one side. It was thick, black, and wavy. I had seen his face before in an old picture my family had of him in the stacks of photos they kept. It was a photo taken at my aunt Míriam's high school graduation. My family always said how much I looked like him. I was also tall for my age, slim, long legged, and dark skinned, with wavy black hair. I didn't inherit his eyes, but I did inherit his face, and his *chocoyos*: dimples.

On one occasion, La Hita told me that my dad was an engineer and worked for the National Electric Energy Company—known by its acronym in Spanish as ENEE—the only electricity utility company in Honduras. When he came to visit us, the first thing he did was order us to bathe.

"The two of you, go and take a shower!" he ordered Gaby and me.

That was what I thought fathers were supposed to do. They would educate, scold, give orders, and we were supposed to obey. I thought dads weren't as loving as moms. Nearly all my friends with fathers were constantly terrified of being scolded by them. They always preferred to be reprimanded by their mothers.

Even still, it seemed odd to hear him ordering me to take a shower. I wondered why a stranger, whom I barely knew, would come to my house and order me to shower. The only reason I knew he was my father was because La Hita kept telling me, "Your dad is coming!" But he was a total unknown to me.

That visit was short lived. He just walked in, sat down on the couch in the living room—which then seemed much smaller because of the removable wall we were using to create an extra room—and ordered us to take a shower. Gaby and I rushed to the *pila*, where we always bathed because we hardly ever used the main bathroom. Without running water, a "shower" consisted of scooping water into a *pana* and dumping it on your head. It was easier for me to scoop water out of the *pila* as opposed to the water barrel that we maintained in the cramped bathroom. Close to the *pila*, I took all of my clothes off except my underwear, grabbed the *pana*, poured water from the *pila* onto my head, and starting scrubbing with an extremely hard natural loofah that scratched my skin.

By the time we had finished taking a shower, he was gone. I thought I saw him walking toward the main street. I ran out in search of him and went to the *pulpería*—a small neighborhood convenience store—on the right-hand side, three houses down from mine. I passed the almond tree near the bus stop for the buses that went to Copán Ruinas. I looked everywhere, but I didn't have any luck. He didn't even say goodbye to my sister and me.

The following day, I woke up and noticed that my dad was sleeping in the extra room next to the living room. I approached quietly. He was so tall that all I could see were his feet dangling off the bed. That day, he helped my grandmother with the measurements for a house that would be built on the plot beyond the oak trees. The house where we lived at the time—and where my mother died—wasn't ours. When my great-grandmother passed away, Mario—one of her grandsons—inherited the house and the front half of the property. La Hita inherited the back half of the property so that she could build a house of her own there in the future.

The house that my father was helping to plan would be the house where we would live years later. We didn't know exactly when we would move in because it was being built slowly. In Honduras, houses were built over time, as they had to be paid for and getting a home loan from a bank was not possible for most Hondurans.

There was another occasion, about a year later, when my father came to visit us, and on that day his visit turned out to be a gift from heaven. We had not had water service for several days prior, and La Hita was worried because the *pila* was completely empty. We didn't have any water for cleaning or bathing. My dad arrived with his friend Luis in a white pickup truck that belonged to the ENEE. Some of my cousins and I went with them to Los Llanitos, a natural mountain-water spring. They drove to the outskirts of La Entrada—about five minutes by car, but it seemed farther away to me when I was a child. When we arrived, my cousins and I jumped in and bathed right there, under the stream of water flowing through the steel pipes.

We always used *tambos*—large five-gallon plastic barrels used to sell paint—to collect water and carry it to the house. The water flowing from the mountain poured through two pipes from which we would fill the *tambos*. On that day, we were able to bring back enough water for household chores and for bathing.

After that day in Los Llanitos, we didn't see my father again for a long time. We were so short on money that La Hita felt somewhat desperate and decided to visit my father at his workplace in San Pedro Sula. I was six years old, and I remember that trip clearly because it stuck in my mind for many years.

Every time we would go to San Pedro Sula, we would stay at Soledad's house. She knew the city best, so she was the one who helped us find the place where my father worked.

"Go ahead, Keyla, and ask your father for *pisto*," she said to me in her boisterous tone.

Pisto is a slang term for money in Honduras. La Hita was bringing me there to ask him for money because I needed new shoes, and my grandmother was not able to buy any. The only shoes I owned at the time were white patent leather with straps that tied near the ankle. They were cheap and would scuff easily. Because they were my only pair of shoes, I wore them everywhere and had worn them out. The shoe I was wearing on my left foot had a hole in the front. It was so big that I could see my toe. I wore white socks to match the shoe, hoping to make the hole less visible. In Spanish they are called *zapatos rotos* (ripped shoes).

On that day in San Pedro Sula, we got lost for a while: we wandered several streets and walked into several buildings, but we couldn't find the right place. After a couple of hours, we finally managed to find where my dad worked. It was a towering building, and from the outside, it glowed like a big lighthouse because of the glass reflecting the light. The place was very upscale, clean, and air-conditioned. Being in an air-conditioned room was unusual for me. The building was more upscale than those in my hometown. There, the houses were made of cement blocks, bricks, and adobe, and there were no large multistory buildings. We walked in and took the stairs to the second floor. We entered an office on the left-hand side, where we saw a secretary and a waiting room. La Hita asked for Carlos Green, and the secretary took our names.

"On behalf of Doña Yolanda and his daughters," replied La Hita.

The secretary called him on the intercom and announced that we were there. A few minutes later, my dad came out, looking astonished, as it was evident that he wasn't expecting us. He seemed to be financially stable. He was wearing nice clothes, and the place was much more than I could ever have imagined. That day, he was wearing dress pants and a dress shirt, similar to when he visited us in La Entrada. He also had his own office, into which he invited us. It was spacious, and there was a large desk on the left-hand side that seemed only for him. I didn't see any other desks or anyone else in there. La Hita, Soledad, my sister, and I walked in. He sat behind the desk, and La Hita and Soledad sat in the chairs across from him.

My sister walked over to greet him, and I stayed behind my grandmother, as far away from him as possible. I didn't want to get close because of my *zapatos rotos*. I felt so embarrassed—I didn't want him to see me like that.

My dad noticed that I hid behind my grandmother, and he tried to spot me with his eyes while I hid even more.

"Why are you so shy, Keyla?" he asked me gently.

Slowly, and with my head down, I walked toward him so that he could hug me. I stiffened and didn't return his embrace. He asked me again why I was so shy, but I didn't respond. On that occasion, he never knew why I didn't want to get too close.

It was my turn to ask my father for money, but I couldn't do it. I didn't dare to ask him for anything. I was too shy. To me, he was a complete stranger, and I didn't trust him. I have never dared to ask for money or help from people I don't trust, even in my most desperate times. I knew Soledad would scold me later, but I didn't care. If it had been up to me, I would never have even said hello to him. I was so embarrassed to be in that place with my *zapatos rotos*. I didn't want him to see me like that. As I stood next to him, all I could think about was the hole in my shoe and how to hide my feet from my father so he wouldn't see it.

We left my father's office the same way we had walked in. As I walked out, I still thought it wouldn't have been appropriate to ask him for money. It was his responsibility as a father to support my grandmother in raising us. She was the one who was watching over my siblings and me. A father should know that his children needed clothing, schooling, food, and medical care. I can't imagine the pain my grandmother felt when she couldn't get me new shoes. I spent several more weeks wearing my *zapatos rotos* until La Hita was finally able to buy me a new pair of shoes when one of my aunts in the United States sent us some money.

That was the last time I would see my father during my childhood. He never again came to visit us in town, and we never again went to see him. On several occasions, we tried to track him down, but we had no luck. Over the years, I kept wondering where he could have gone and why he never wanted to see us.

When I was 10 years old, my father's friend Luis came to live in La Entrada. My grandmother used to sell him food for lunch, and he would come to our house every day. When he first saw me, he told me that I was very tall and looked like my father. He also said I bore a strong resemblance to my other sister, my father's daughter with another woman. We asked Luis about him, and he told us that my father lived in Comayagua—a city located in the country's central region—and that he had two other children. Luis said that he would tell him that he had seen us. Weeks later, Luis gave me my dad's phone number, but I don't know if it was correct because the calls never went through. Luis told us that he told my father he had seen us, but my father still never came to visit. I could never understand his indifference and unwillingness to see us. Particularly knowing that my mom had passed away, and that my grandmother was getting older and wouldn't live forever.

Many nights I cried, asking God why He took my mother and why my father didn't want to see me. I never understood what I had done wrong to deserve the life I had.

3

The Pain of Growing Up

Growing up, I grieved over my mother's death and my father's abandonment with endless nights of tears, but those weren't the only reasons for my suffering as a child. My earliest memories are tinged with sorrow, questions, and confusion. When I realized that I didn't have a father or a mother, like some of my cousins, I thought I was fated to be unhappy for some reason I could not figure out.

I thought I wasn't special. I felt like the ugly duckling. I was always too skinny, too tall, and too dark. I believed that put me at a disadvantage compared to others. To make matters worse, I felt rejected by some members of my family. Gaby and Alexander were both always spoiled by one adult or another in my family. But I was in the middle. I wasn't the eldest or the youngest. I was just the middle child, the darkest one, the one who resembled Carlos Green who never showed up to say hello, much less take care of his children.

Any time my aunt Laura and my cousin Ritza would go on outings and take some of my cousins along with them, they would never invite me. I really wanted to go; no matter where they would go or what they would do, I just wanted to get out. Instead, they always chose Gaby, the most pampered in the house. I always assumed it was because of my physical appearance: that I wasn't that pretty, and perhaps they were ashamed of me. I didn't have any self-esteem. On one occasion, they decided to go on a trip to the beach and took only Gaby with them. They left me at home with the rest of my cousins. She was able to see the beach, which I had longed to visit ever since I knew it existed. It was not until I was a teenager that I was able to see the ocean for the first time.

At times, there were so many of my first and second cousins living in the house that the adults couldn't care for everyone. I was alone and unattended sometimes; therefore, others saw me as easy prey.

One day when I was four, I was playing hide-and-seek with my cousins, and I happened to hide under the crib that was in the front bedroom where my aunt Laura slept. My cousin Mario—Aunt Eunice's son—had the same idea as me, and we both went right under there. I expected it to be the perfect hideout, even though the space was so small that we were very close and facing each other. After a while, he pulled down my panties. He took out his penis and rubbed it against my vulva. I remained silent. I didn't know whether I should say something or keep quiet. I don't remember how much time passed, but my aunt Laura eventually came into the room. With his finger, Mario motioned for me to remain silent. I obeyed him. I didn't know what else to do.

I was too frightened to leave, but I didn't want to stay under there with him either. I seized the first opportunity I could to get away from my cousin. I sat on the side of the bed behind my aunt. My aunt was getting ready for work and was so busy that she didn't notice when I came out. She continued to look at herself in the mirror on the dresser. Upon leaving the room, she locked it from the outside, as she normally did, so that no one would enter. I panicked when I heard the door lock. I didn't want to be locked in there with Mario after what had just happened. I couldn't help but scream and cry out of despair, fear, and confusion. My aunt rushed back and found me shaking on the bed.

"I didn't know you were here, Keyla!" said my aunt as she grabbed my hand and led me out.

I didn't tell her Mario was under the crib—he didn't dare venture out either. I never knew how he got out of there. It has been almost impossible for me to forget the trauma and pain of that episode. Years later, it still triggers anxiety and fear every time I recall that day. I have always had a good memory, and my mind seems to recall my most painful experiences the most vividly. Months later, Mario emigrated to the United States with his mother, and I didn't see him again for more than a decade.

On another occasion, I was four or five years old or so and taking my afternoon nap. I was wearing a long, light blue nightgown, the same one I had on when my mother died. I wasn't wearing underwear because I only had a few pairs. My grandma had washed them and hung them out to dry while I slept. I don't remember how long I slept, but I suddenly felt a hand with thick fingers touching my vulva. I sat up in bed and immediately moved the hand away from me. It was Don Joche—my aunt's father—whom I had loved and treated like my own grandfather. I couldn't believe what had just happened. He had lain down in the same bed as me after I fell asleep.

Don Joche didn't live in our house. He only came two to four times a year to visit La Hita and his grandchildren ... at least, that is what he said. Whenever he would come to our house, he would always bring us bunches of plantains and small bananas that I loved. Moreover, he would give some money to La Hita and all of us too. Don Joche was known as a hardworking, kind, and loving man. He worked driving tractors and earned enough money that he could spend most of his salary on alcohol. That, however, was his problem: whenever he got drunk, his kindness would fade into something dark.

I felt dirty. I felt I was to blame for what happened. I hadn't been wearing underwear. What was going on in my head when I decided to go to sleep with no underwear on? I blamed myself repeatedly. If I had been wearing more clothes, perhaps Don Joche wouldn't have done that. "Yes, this is my fault," I kept repeating to myself. He couldn't be that sort of man, especially with me. I loved him so much. He never attempted anything like that with me again, and I managed to quiet my mind by thinking it was likely he had been unconscious or drunk at the time. I continued to feel shame for many years. I thought I was a sinner and was afraid to talk about it with anyone, so I chose to bury the whole thing and lived in silence for years.

I recall one specific day when I was five years old and at the river washing clothes with La Hita. It was during one of the times when we didn't have water service in town for an extended period of time. We used to go to a deep pool in the river called El Ceibón. The river was only a 10-minute walk from our house, and we went there for chores and a little fun. It was there where my cousin Kevin taught me how to swim after nearly making me eat a *pichira*—a small fish—because, according to him, that is how I would learn to float.

On that day, while playing shirtless along the river, I looked up and right in front of me on a hill, I saw a man staring at me. When he realized I was watching, he took his penis out of his pants and started jumping up and down while grabbing it with his hand. I lowered my head and felt petrified. The guy started beckoning me with his hands so that I would go to where he was. I felt like I was running out of strength, and my legs began to tremble; it was hard to move. La Hita was close by, but at the time, she seemed so far away. I managed to find my strength and walked back to where she was. I couldn't speak. I disguised my fear as best I could. I didn't say anything to her. I felt too ashamed, and I convinced myself that it was my fault, for walking shirtless and half naked along the river.

After that, I was afraid to go back to the river. I no longer felt as excited as when I used to go with my cousins to swim during hot afternoons or in times of water shortages. I couldn't help but remember that strange man I saw on that hill whenever I went there. I wondered what might have happened to me if my grandmother had not been around.

As a small child who had been through what I had, I became sexually curious at a very young age, and I did inappropriate things with my friends. I wanted to know what it was to feel pleasure, to rub, to touch. I didn't have somebody to guide me, to tell me what was right or wrong. La Hita didn't talk about that kind of thing, much less my aunts. I began to play an inappropriate game of "house." I would take off my underwear and ask my friends to take off their underwear and rub their private parts against mine.

By the time I was six years old, I could already interpret the sexual intentions of others. One of Alexander's friends—who I knew had matured because I had seen him swimming naked in the river and saw that he had pubic hair—called me over near the hallway of my house.

"Keyla, do you want to be my girlfriend?" he whispered in my ear so no one would hear.

I immediately moved my body backward in denial.

"I'm going to tell my brother!" I replied.

He got scared and begged me not to say anything to anyone. I never said anything about it to anyone, nor did I ever intend to. I had learned to defend myself with the threat of talking. I knew my threat of telling would keep him away from me. I never heard from him after. I didn't know who his parents were. I only knew that he didn't live in town, that he was a *vago*—a street kid—and would occasionally come to play with Alexander.

Gradually, and on my own, I moved away from everything that led me to do inappropriate actions. I stopped the indecent and inappropriate play with my friends. Something inside me told me I should stop. Perhaps it was the Church's teachings or an unconscious defense mechanism of a girl trying to figure out the world on her own. I started to identify when my conscience told me that something was right or wrong.

Even still, I was left with a lot of anger that would come out at times. One day, when I was a second grader, a classmate tried to play a joke on me. He stole a love letter I had written to the cutest boy in the classroom. I got so angry that I grabbed a freshly sharpened pencil and got ready to stab him in the face. I don't remember who stopped me;

I was blind with rage. It was either the teacher or the child's screams against such a threat that alerted everyone. I didn't understand such aggressiveness in me; I didn't know what was happening to me.

At age 11, as was customary in a Catholic family, I was to receive the First Communion. As part of the preparation, I had to confess my sins to the town priest. When the day came, I couldn't do it. It was so hard for me to trust men, and besides, the priest looked at me in a way that made me wary. I had learned to read men's intentions at an early age; it was my defense mechanism. Even though I often doubted it, or it might have been merely a fantasy in my head, I had learned to follow my instincts whenever they would sound the alarm that I was in danger.

At the age of 12, I started to have boyfriends. I had two in my neighborhood at the same time and kissed them both on the mouth. I don't remember the circumstances of my first kiss with either of them because neither kiss was special to me. I had been kissing other kids since I was five years old. I don't even remember who the first one was. I grew up with a such a distorted sense of sexuality. In middle school, I used to give boys lessons on how to kiss. I didn't know what it was to respect myself.

I became a teenager, and my body began to change little by little. I was getting taller and taller—but only that. I felt like I was growing like a palm tree: only upward, not to the sides or front. As a teenager, I failed at attracting boyfriends because I was Keyla, "the palm tree," "the coconut tree," "the long-legged giraffe."

Years later, during one of our town's celebrations, someone grabbed my crotch while I was walking. There were so many people, that I never knew who groped me. Never again did anyone assault me. Perhaps it was thanks to the fact that I learned with honed accuracy when someone had malicious intentions. I turned into a rude, angry adolescent, ready to fight anyone who would mess with me. I would no longer let anyone ever dare to hurt me again.

When I was 14, I had a boyfriend who was much older than me. One day while we were arguing, he raised his hand and threatened to hit me.

"Come on! I dare you to hit me. I want to see you hit me!" I looked him in the eyes defiantly.

Deep down I wanted him to do it. I wanted to feel pain and have an excuse to attack him too. I needed to vent my anger and rage on someone.

After that relationship, my life changed completely. I stopped dwelling on what had happened to me in the past and instead tried to live one day at a time and focus on my future.

I focused on my dream of going to college. I wanted to wear a white dress to my wedding: a dream that La Hita had for me, and what my mother would have wished for if she were still alive.

4

Immigrants

My grandmother was born in Las Flores, Chalatenango, El Salvador. She was descended from a light-skinned, blue-eyed family of Spanish ancestry. Although I never had the opportunity to go to El Salvador to visit that part of my family, I certainly would have loved to do so. In the late 1940s, La Hita and her mother decided to emigrate from El Salvador to Honduras. Her uncle had been murdered, and her father had received death threats.

My grandmother's father—Don José Alas Castillo—had already emigrated to Honduras before them because he had been threatened with death. Don José fled with no word on where he would go or how they could locate him. He had vanished for many years. It wasn't until he was on his deathbed—in a hospital in San Pedro Sula—that his family was able to locate him. My great-grandfather had spent all those years living in the department of Colón in the northern part of the country. Those in the family who had known La Hita's father claimed that she had inherited his looks. He was very tall, light skinned, and had light-colored eyes.

My great-grandmother's decision to emigrate to Honduras wasn't due to a lack of resources; on the contrary, her family was wealthy and quite well off. When I was a child, my aunt Rafaela told me that when my great-grandmother emigrated to La Entrada, she was carrying two sacks of money on a donkey. She also carried a large clay jar with old silver coins known as *bambas*.

La Hita told me that her mother owned many businesses in La Entrada. She used to sell everything from food to gold and ran a small boarding house where she would rent out the rooms like a hotel. I wish I had known her, but she died many years before I was born. Her name was María Isabel López. Though I only saw her in a photo, I loved the legacy of values she instilled in La Hita, which helped her be an honest and hardworking woman.

My great-grandmother's final years were somewhat sad. As she aged, she became ill with diabetes. Her health gradually failed, and she had to spend a lot of money on hospital bills. She lost her right leg and shortly after that, she passed away. My grandmother suffered a lot after her mother's death. She had learned a lot from her mother, especially her determination to get ahead. After her mother's death, La Hita began to face many challenges. The money was gone. She only had the plot of land inherited from her mother, where she built her house some years later.

La Hita had four daughters: Rafaela, the eldest; my mother, Telma; Míriam; and Laura, the youngest. My aunt Rafaela was one of the first to emigrate to the United States, following the path of her aunt Norma, who emigrated years earlier. My aunt Rafaela had three children: Ritza, Kevin, and Fabricio, who remained under my grandmother's care when my aunt left for the United States in pursuit of a better life. My aunt Rafaela came back for my mother's funeral, and shortly afterward, she returned to the U.S. and took my aunt Míriam with her.

My aunt Laura was pregnant with her first child when my mom died. A few months later, she also decided to emigrate to the United States, as she was pregnant again. Life would have been challenging for her as a single mother if she'd stayed, given the limited opportunities in La Entrada. Sadly, she had to leave her first child Isaías, just a baby, with La Hita when she decided to go. All my aunts—including my mom—were single mothers. It was common for men not to take care of their wives and children in my town, which was the case in my family.

La Hita was also a single mother for most of her life. She left her first husband after he made her life impossible. She had found brief romance with other men and had children with them, but in the end, they ended up letting her down in one way or another. La Hita lived by the phrase in Spanish, *Mejor sola que mal acompañada* (Better alone than in bad company).

"Never marry a jealous man, Keyla! My first husband was a terribly jealous man!" La Hita advised.

I first met my grandfather when Alexander, Gaby, and I visited him at his workplace. His name was Ramón Paredes, and he was born in Copán Ruinas. I don't remember his face clearly, as I only saw him once. Years later, La Hita told me that my grandfather had committed suicide. I never knew how or why. That was all I was ever able to learn about him.

By 1990, all my aunts had emigrated to the United States, and La

Hita was responsible for raising her grandchildren who had remained in La Entrada. My aunt Laura's room became Ritza's room. In the other room, where my mom had passed away, the rest of us slept. There were three beds and additional mattresses on the floor. La Hita's grandchildren, and those of her sister Noemí, loved her very much because my grandmother had helped raise many of them. A little while later, even more people came to live in our house: other cousins moved in from San Pedro Sula after their parents also emigrated to the United States.

For her part, Soledad—my great-aunt Noemí's eldest daughter—was left in charge of a lot of her nieces and nephews for many years. Her favorite hobby was watching *telenovelas* and raising all the *cipotes* left under her care by their parents. *Cipote* is what we call children in Honduras. Like my grandmother, Soledad also had a golden heart and an infinite amount of patience. I imagine it wasn't easy to take care of so many children at the same time.

La Hita always looked older than she really was. It wasn't an easy task for one woman to look after so many children. With the financial help that her daughters sent her from the United States La Hita finished building her house on the plot of land she inherited from her mother.

In June 1992—when I was eight years old—my aunt Rafaela came back from the United States to collect her children. Years before, she had married my uncle Don Javier, who was a U.S. citizen and was able to get her citizenship as well. It was then possible for her to bring her children to the U.S. with *papeles* (visas).

After they left, the house felt empty. The one I would miss the most was my cousin Fabricio. We always used to play together. He would help me with my homework and helped me improve my reading when I was a first grader. Thanks to his support, I became the second-fastest reader in my classroom. When Fabricio left, never again did I have any help with my homework. I loved to read, but it wasn't the same anymore. Beside the fact that I had no books, there was also no library to go to. As a child, I only had the Bible to read.

Fabricio was different from my other cousins. He had a unique sensibility and was very special to me. Whenever we played, he liked to wear my dresses, and he was so creative that he found a way to place a wire inside to make them look puffier. I always hated it when the other kids made fun of him for being different. Fabricio was effeminate and was often bullied by kids in town.

I recall one morning when Fabricio went to the bakery to buy bread. La Hita would send my cousins to buy what was called *pan quebrado* (broken bread) because it was sold at a reduced price compared to the whole loaves. On the way back home, a group of *vagos* (street children) began to tease him, pushed him, and then punched him in the face several times until he fell on the ground and all the bread ended up ruined in the dirt.

Some time later, my cousin Kevin—Fabricio's brother—worked in that same bakery. Kevin was never a huge fan of school and decided to work instead of study. The good thing about it was that we got more bread than usual thanks to his job at the bakery. Sometimes, Kevin would get a bag of bread for one lempira—Honduras's currency—and on rare occasions, it would be given to him for free.

Whenever my aunt Rafaela came to town, she would bring her son Milton, who had been born in the U.S. He was a brat. One time he threw me to the ground, grabbed me by the neck, and tried to choke me. He was spoiled and always claimed to be right.

One day an older cousin Ana, who was visiting my house, reprimanded me and told me that I had to learn to use silverware, just like Milton did. Growing up, no one had ever taught me how to use a fork or a knife. I was used to eating like all my other cousins: grabbing bites of food with a piece of tortilla. I hated being compared to others and constantly heard complaints from everyone: "You have to be more like him," or "Learn from your cousin Milton; he knows how to do this or that." I always felt different from the other members of my family.

"Keyla, although you're dark skinned, you're not ugly!" Ana once dared to tell me.

Before my aunt Rafaela left, I begged her to take me to the hairdresser for a haircut. I wanted a trendy haircut, and as my aunt was in town, it was the perfect opportunity for me. We went to the hairdresser's, but it was closed. I wanted my new haircut so badly that I insisted, and we ended up going to a barber. The stylish haircut then was a short bob, and I wanted my hair to reach a little below my ears. I guess the barber didn't understand anything I said, and I ended up with a boy's haircut. My hair had never been that short, not even when I got lice, which used to happen every year. I cried all the way from the barbershop to the house. I walked with my head down, trying to hide my tears. When I arrived, everyone in the house laughed at me, and that made me feel even worse.

The day before my aunt Rafaela and her kids were to leave for the United States was difficult for me. Ritza was crying and wanted to stay, but she knew it wasn't her decision. Her mother had made so many sacrifices for her, and obtaining legal residency in the United States was the dream of many.

The following day, we went to the airport in San Pedro Sula to say goodbye to my aunt Rafaela and my cousins. When I saw them get on the airplane at the San Pedro Sula airport, I cried even more than I did at my mother's funeral. A big part of me left with them.

Upon our arriving back home from San Pedro, Mario's mother, Eunice—who had just arrived from the United States—argued with La Hita and kicked us out of the house where I had lived for the first eight years of my life. Mario had inherited that house from my great-grandmother, and then Eunice took advantage of the fact that he was in the United States to kick us out.

"Get these filthy stuffed animals out of here!" she said contemptuously and then handed me the few stuffed animals I owned.

We had no other choice but to grab our belongings and move into our new but still unfinished house. We had to sleep in a house with a leaky roof and no glass panes in the windows. The first night we moved in, it rained all night long; water was leaking everywhere, and the thunder and lightning frightened me to death.

Although La Hita was always a strong woman, I saw a deep sadness in her eyes that day. Most of her family was gone, and she didn't know when she would see them again. La Hita, Gaby, Alexander, Isaías, and I were the only ones left. It wasn't all bad, though; thanks to that unexpected move, it was easier for me to get used to not having my other cousins around. Sooner than expected, living with just the five of us seemed like the norm.

On the following day, with the sun shining, things looked better. Even though our new house was unfinished, it was much nicer than the previous one that faced the international highway. We had new neighbors, whom we already knew but now we were able to see them with more regularity. The neighbors were also very friendly, and in times of need, when my grandmother wasn't able to make ends meet with the money my aunts sent her from the U.S., she could go to her neighbor across the street. She was my grandmother's *comadre*—a close friend. My grandma could borrow a cup of sugar from her or anything else that was needed. We helped each other out, and we always loved to help our neighbors when we had the chance.

When I was 10, another meaningful change took place in our family. My aunt Laura came back from the United States and lived with us for a few months. I didn't realize that her idea was to take Isaías and Alexander to the U.S. with her when she returned. My aunt didn't tell anyone about her plans because whenever someone emigrated to *La USA*—as we all called it in town—they didn't tell anyone beforehand. Most of the time they did this to avoid having to say goodbye and making their friends sad. Everyone used to leave without saying a word, although it wouldn't be long before everybody in town would find out. In our small town, all the neighbors were especially talkative.

The day my aunt and cousins left, I was asleep in my room when I heard noises in the house. I opened my eyes, but I stayed in bed. I saw Alexander walking into the room. He approached quietly and thought I was still asleep. I closed my eyes and pretended to be. He carefully lifted the pillow and left me five lempiras. He then turned and left the room. I didn't know when I would see him again. I felt sad, took a deep breath, and fought back my tears. Our family kept getting smaller. Only my grandmother, my sister, and I were left at home.

5

Childhood

The backyard at my old house was my favorite playground. I could spend days and nights there, playing with the few toys I had and climbing the different trees. The tamarind tree next to the *pila* was tall and had a lot of large branches that gave us shade and a cool place to rest on hot afternoons. Every afternoon at five o'clock, my grandmother ordered Fabricio and me to collect the hens so that they would go up to sleep in the branches of the tamarind tree. I enjoyed climbing to the top of the tree, where I could see the roof tiles and the main road from there.

In a neighbor's yard beyond the fence grew a mango tree that bore fruit every year, from February to April, and on which I used to climb during the fruiting season. I would eat the green mangoes with salt, cumin, and sometimes with *chile* (spices). I used to fill a bucket with mangoes, take them with me to the old *pila* in the middle of the backyard—which was out of use—sit down next to where we did the laundry, and peel them. Then, I made myself comfortable and would eat as many mangoes as I could.

One day, Fabricio and I climbed the tree, and while collecting some green mangoes and throwing them on the ground, we saw three drunk men arrive. We used to call them "*los pachangueros*" (party animals) because they were always drunk. Both my cousin and I were afraid of being seen by them—in particular, by *Ojo de Pollo* (Chicken Eye), an elderly man who used to pass by our house with a sack on his back. The adults used to tell me that if I misbehaved, he would put me inside that bag. Whenever I saw him pass in front of the house, I would run to the backyard and hide. That day, we stayed up in the tree for quite a while. We didn't make any noise until the men were finally gone and we could climb back down.

When birds would build their nests in the oak trees, I would climb up to grab and smash the eggs they had laid. My cousins and I also used a sling to try to kill birds while they flew through the air. My cousin Kevin hit one once, and we had a delicious meal that day. Once, I threw small rocks at a beehive in one of the coconut trees beyond the oak trees. The moment I did it, I knew it was a bad idea, but I was hoping that the bees wouldn't do anything to me. I was wrong: they started chasing me, and I ran as fast as I could to the *pila* by the tamarind tree and stuck my head in the water. I had at least a dozen dead bees on my scalp, and it hurt. My quick idea of submerging my head underwater helped to soothe the pain faster because the bees died amazingly fast. After this experience, I never again killed any birds or threw rocks at beehives.

From the age of four, I used to go by myself to the *pulpería* to buy mangoes or candy. La Hita would send me to buy coffee and would give me a *tostón*—a 50-cent coin—and I would even bring back 20 cents in change, because a small bag of coffee was only 30 cents. My grandmother always preferred the coffee El Indio Lempira over other brands. Back in those days, one dollar equaled seven lempiras, and with just one lempira, you could still buy a lot at the store. Also, when I went to school, La Hita would give me 15 cents, which I could use to buy a snack at recess. I used that money to buy a *topogigio*—a treat made of frozen fruit juice in a small, clear plastic bag with a knot on top. In addition, I could buy a bag of *tajadas*—fried plantain slices with cabbage and salsa.

Growing up, my favorite time of the year was Christmastime. In Honduras, we celebrate Christmas on the night of December 24 because it was customary to celebrate Baby Jesus's birth at midnight. The most important thing on December 24 wasn't the toys, but the *estréno* (new set of clothes) that my aunts used to send us from the United States to wear on Christmas and New Year's Eve. I was thrilled to know that I would have new clothes and could show them off in front of the neighbors. It was rare for us to receive new clothes during the rest of the year. Sometimes my aunts would send a box of used clothes and other stuff. Also, on certain occasions, my aunt Rafaela or another relative came would come to visit, and other family members would take the opportunity to send us some things, but that wasn't always the case.

Every time I thought about the United States and my family who lived there, I felt that I would go there one day too. I loved my life in Honduras with La Hita, but I knew she wouldn't be with me for the

Gaby (two) and Keyla (four), 1988 (family photograph).

rest of my life. Something was telling me that my future was tied to the United States. I was always talking to my friends about moving to the U.S. Then María, one of my best friends at the time, asked me when I would be leaving.

"You always talk about leaving, but I still see you here!" she exclaimed.

I explained that it all was up to my aunt Míriam. She was fixing her *papeles* (legal immigration status in the U.S.), and once it was all in place, I would be able to leave. She also promised me that whenever she got her papers, we would go to Acapulco, a beautiful port that we had seen in Mexican *telenovelas*. The thought of going to the U.S. with my family gave me a thrill, though I knew it wouldn't be easy.

My first attempt to obtain a U.S. visa was when I was five years old.

Keyla and Gaby at the kindergarten Independence Day celebration, 1990 (family photograph).

My aunt Rafaela came to visit and took me to San Pedro Sula to get my first passport. (To this day, I still keep the photo of that passport in my album of treasured memories.) Then we went to the U.S. Consulate in Tegucigalpa, the capital of Honduras. We also went with my grandmother, my sister, and my brother on that trip. We stayed in a hotel just a few blocks from the consulate. Our room was air-conditioned, and it was one of the first times in my life that I experienced it. We also had hot water because the weather in the city was a lot cooler than in La Entrada. I still remember how different and amazing the sensation of the warm water felt on my skin. On the following day, we went to the consulate, awaited our turn, got interviewed, and then were told that our visa application had been refused.

We got home and continued with our lives as if nothing happened. But I kept dreaming that one day I would travel to the U.S. I wasn't even thinking about what career I wanted to study in Honduras because I felt it wasn't necessary. I knew I didn't have to worry about that.

In La Entrada, kindergarten was held in a separate building from the regular elementary schools. I attended the kindergarten Profesor Erasmo Aquino, which was the only one in the El Triángulo neighborhood and was about seven blocks from my old house. In the beginning, when I was younger, my cousins or my brother would walk me there, but by the third year, I used to go by myself. *Kinder* (kindergarten) was supposed to be for two years, but I somehow started early. After finishing my second year, I wasn't accepted into first grade because I was still six and I needed to be at least seven—so I ended up going to *kinder* for a third year. Classes ran from 7:00 a.m. to 12:00 noon, Monday through Friday from February to November.

My grandmother raised me Catholic. After my mother's death, both my sister and I were baptized in the Catholic Church because it had been one of my mother's last wishes before she died. Alexander was baptized years before us when my mother was still alive. Our godmother and godfather were the owners of a pharmacy and hotel that was close to the house. They were always good to us, and whenever my grandmother sent me on an errand to the pharmacy, my godmother would say to me:

"Keylita, you're so grown up! Take care and behave yourself."

I listened to her carefully and said to myself: "I will, godmother; I will!" I liked her advice because I knew she appreciated me, although she would never come to the house. She sent one of her employees with presents for us on New Year's Eve or *Día de los Reyes Magos* (Three

King's Day). Her attention and love always made me feel special, even if it was only once a year.

La Hita would take me to church, although I never liked it because the Mass was too long, and most Sundays I ended up falling asleep under the pews. At times, we didn't attend because my grandma was sick, but if she was up for the walk up the hill to the church, we were there. I completed my First Communion at age 11, and I nearly completed my Confirmation. I did like the Church and its teachings because I have always been attracted to spiritual teachings. I learned the Lord's Prayer and the Hail Mary by heart. My grandmother always took me to religious celebrations, and during the Easter Holy Week, we used to pray the rosary. From a very young age, I learned to pray and read the Bible.

La Hita only completed three years of elementary school because that was the highest level of education offered in her town; she could barely sign her name. She couldn't write, but she could read, although with some difficulty. Every afternoon, she would sit in a hammock or in a chair under a tree, read the Bible, and occasionally take a nap after reading. She read most of the time quietly, but I would hear her trying to pronounce the words from time to time, though she struggled a bit.

The Bible was the only book I had ever read, and I really enjoyed it, mainly the Psalms. In school, we had no books of our own to read. Only the teachers owned the books, and all students had to take notes during class to study later at home.

After turning seven, I transferred to first grade at the local elementary school. It was called Daniel Cruz Berríos. It was the same one my aunts and my mother had attended until the sixth grade. Now, my siblings and I were studying there. Back then, Isaías was a baby and had to stay home with La Hita, as he didn't even go to kindergarten yet.

I would go to school until noon, although sometimes I had to go to the afternoon shift. I had a couple of friends with whom I got along very well. At the beginning of each school year, I always had to share a desk with someone different, and that is how I would make new friends. María and I remained friends over the years and studied together starting in the second grade. As the years went by, she often came to my house and got along very well with La Hita. My grandmother was very fond of her and would even let me visit her too. Our friendship has endured over the years.

In school, there was a time when they would serve us a daily glass of a very creamy and tasty milk, very similar in consistency to oatmeal. All the children were required to bring their own glass and a spoon. It was then common to see us all sitting in the school hallways, eating with our spoons the creamy milk. This aid was from the "Alliance for Progress" program, a U.S. economic, political, and social aid program for Latin America. In fact, a couple of times I also received from the program a pair of "*paredes*" shoes—that is what we all called them in town—which were black with black shoelaces and very comfortable. That program lasted only for a couple of years, until the incentive stopped. By the time I was in sixth grade, the 15 cents my grandmother gave me to buy some snacks at recess wasn't enough. She used to give me five lempiras, with which I would buy a Coke and a snack.

We also received assistance once a year, but in order to be granted financial aid, it was necessary to meet with the school director to have my need assessed. Only once was I lucky enough to qualify for a 75-lempiras bonus, as my situation didn't normally fit the category of extreme poverty because I had family in the United States. Although, for some reason that I never understood, my sister Gaby managed to receive more bonuses than me.

I liked sports and played soccer or basketball, although Gaby and Alexander were much better at sports than I was. My brother was naturally talented at soccer and was part of the national teenage minor league team in San Pedro Sula. He even traveled to El Salvador for a competition and was featured in a national newspaper. As for Gaby, she used to play soccer every afternoon in front of our house with the children of the neighborhood; that was her favorite pastime. The *muchacha* always complained that my sister's shorts and shirts were dirtier than the rest of our clothes.

I loved to draw, do craft projects, and make art. In school, I had a fine arts class once a week. It was my favorite class! At times, we would paint, carve wood, or do some embroidery. They weren't always masterpieces, but most of the time, I was happy with the results of my art projects.

I also really enjoyed reading and writing. One day, at the age of 11, I decided to write a book. With a notebook and pencil in hand, I climbed into the empty old *pila* in the middle of the *solar* between my old and new houses and sat down in one of the corners. I grabbed my pencil and paused to think. Surprisingly, I didn't know what to write! I didn't have any ideas. My head was completely blank. I couldn't even write a single syllable. Ever since that moment, I've felt I needed to write a book. I kept that idea in my head for 15 years, until I knew what the book would be about.

Moving to our new house came with another added benefit—our new house faced a small neighborhood street instead of an international highway. During the afternoon or evening, I would spend time in the street playing with my neighbors. Depending on the day, we would play either soccer with a plastic soccer ball or baseball with a broken broomstick. We also liked to play hide-and-seek. Sometimes, there were as many as 10 kids playing in the neighborhood streets. That was the common playground for my childhood friends from the neighborhood and me.

Our kitchen was small but very nice. My grandmother had the cedar cabinets and tile countertops custom made. We owned a cedar dining table that my grandmother also had custom made and that she placed in the dining room, which was in between the kitchen and the living room. The table was beautiful, and we never removed the plastic tablecloth, so that it wouldn't get scratched and we could keep it in good condition. The *pila* was outside, but by then we had a water reservoir on the roof to store more water. However, it was challenging to make the water reach the bathroom and kitchen because there wasn't enough water pressure. We had several plumbing malfunctions in the new house, and the water and electricity would go in and out as usual, but we were used to that being a part of life. We always made sure to clean the *pila* and keep it filled whenever we had water service.

My new house had three rooms. Gaby used to sleep with my grandmother, in the same bed. I slept in another bed, but in the same room because I was afraid to sleep alone. My brother Alexander had his own room, and there was an extra one that was occasionally occupied when one of my cousins from San Pedro decided to come to visit us.

In my new windowless house, I celebrated my ninth birthday on December 21 because that was the day my grandmother had told me was my birthday. It wasn't until I learned to read and found my birth certificate that I discovered that I was actually born on December 4.

La Hita bought me a cake; we invited a few children from the neighborhood, and they sang Happy Birthday to me. I still keep a picture of that day as a souvenir, and I can see my hair was growing back after the short haircut. Although I wouldn't say I liked my hair, because it was still too short, I knew it wouldn't be like that for the rest of my life.

I used to walk around town a lot when I had to run errands for

Gaby (12) and Keyla (14) at the back of new house, 1998 (family photograph).

my grandmother. We didn't have a car, so we had to walk everywhere: even on Sundays, when we went to Mass, we walked up the main street. I enjoyed going to the market with La Hita to buy the day's groceries, particularly when buying the ingredients for the weekend's *sopa de res* (beef soup). Everything was fresh, and we didn't usually keep food in the refrigerator. In fact, the fridge was always empty and smelled funny because there was nothing inside. It was so small that, after a couple of years, I had already grown taller than it.

Our neighbor around the corner, Doña Carmen, owned a *pulpería* and used to sell essential food items. She would help us from time to time by lending us eggs, lard, and anything else we needed. La Hita often found it challenging to make ends meet with the money my aunts sent her, because the cost of living was increasing as time went by. I knew that because Doña Josefa—my grandmother's friend, who also baked bread to sell—used to help La Hita write the letters she sent to the United States. My grandmother always complained about the lack of money, telling my aunts how expensive a *quintal* (a unit of measurement) of corn and beans was.

When I got a little older and could write better, I began to write my grandmother's letters to her daughters. Her concerns were always about the rising cost of living, because a bag of coffee, for example, no longer cost 30 cents but had gone up to one lempira. As a child, I wasn't aware of my grandma's struggles because she made sure that my siblings and I were as comfortable as possible, regardless of our lack of resources. She always did her best to make us happy and made every sacrifice possible to achieve this.

Despite our needs, I still enjoyed the unpaved street in front of my new house and the trees and flowers that my grandmother had recently planted. We went on with our lives as normally as we could. I grew up happy in my new home despite the significant changes in my life. I always woke up feeling joyful, ready to go to school every morning and play with my friends every afternoon.

As I grew older, I became taller and skinny. It seemed like I was all knees and elbows. When I turned 11, I was the same height as my grandmother; at 12, I was already taller than her. Everyone commented about my height. I wasn't even in middle school yet, but it seemed very soon I would have to duck to fit through the door, just like my father.

I was skinny due more to genetics than a lack of food because, thanks to my aunts in the U.S., we always had the essentials. Our diet was based mostly on fried plantains, beans, eggs, cheese, and cream—and, of course, tortillas with every meal. For lunch, we had spaghetti with sauce and white rice. On Saturdays, we used to eat meat or chicken—or on Sundays, with *sopa de res*—but only if we had enough money to buy the meat, which wasn't always the case.

Thankfully, we were also able to supplement our diet with food grown in our *solar*. Occasionally, when my grandmother was in good health, she would plant corn and beans in the backyard. Cassava and tomatoes grew naturally. We had two patches of sugar cane plants and a guava tree that bore pink guavas every year. It was sometimes so full of fruit that we had to give them away to keep them from going bad. Two palm trees also grew in the backyard, but their coconuts were useless. They always came out small, and the coconut milk never tasted good. Other trees were still growing, such as the avocado tree, but I wasn't around long enough to try their first fruit. La Hita was very fond of plants, especially flowers; she had two rose bushes and took great care in tending them.

Keyla in 6th grade, 1997 (family photograph).

Once a year, my siblings and I would help my grandmother clean the backyard. I loved the smell of the damp earth. It was such a pleasant aroma that I even felt like eating it, though I never did. La Hita would tell me to paint with whitewash a few stones, and we would place them in a circular shape around all the trees in the backyard. By the end of the day, we had a completely new backyard. It was charming and clean.

After we moved into the new house, we didn't have as many animals as before. La Hita only had a coop for the chickens and maybe one or two roosters. My grandmother was getting older, and there were only the four of us to help her. We had a gas stove, but La Hita still preferred to cook on a woodfire stove. When the new house was being built, she had the crew build her an adobe woodfire stove with a shelter over it right outside in the yard. With the shelter overhead, she could be outside cooking in sunshine or rain. Next to that outdoor stove, she had a large adobe-brick oven to bake quesadilla bread (a sweet bread with cheese in the dough), *torta* bread, and rice bread from time to time. She would occasionally sell the bread, but she ended up giving it away to her neighbors and friends most of the time.

Gaby (12) and Keyla (14) in a guava tree in the *solar* of the new house, 1998 (family photograph).

La Hita always woke up early to cook beans and make fresh torti-llas. I was in charge of going to the mill to grind the corn used to make tortillas two or three times a week. I loved it when La Hita made hen soup. I used to eat it with fresh tortillas. But I never liked it when I was put in charge of plucking the chicken. My grandmother would grab the chickens by the neck, twist them, and then hang them on the fence so that the blood would run down to their heads. It was hard for me to watch such torture—though I never complained when having a delicious bowl of hen soup.

We would go to the cemetery to bring flowers to my mom's grave from time to time. La Hita also brought flowers to her mother, her father, and those buried in the same place. One of her sister Elvia's sons was murdered months after my mother's death. He died young; I don't remember getting to know him, and Elvia died a year later at 62. Every time I went to the cemetery, my grandmother would cry in front of my mom's grave, which made me feel sad.

After my aunt Laura left with Alexander and Isaías, we had to get used to our new smaller household of just La Hita, Gaby, and me. Things worsened with La Hita. She got sick and suffered three heart attacks in rapid succession. Gaby and I were terrified. At times, I thought it was going to be my grandmother's time to join my mother. Those were difficult years for me; I was only around 10 years old. One day, while standing in the kitchen watching my neighbors help my grandmother, I asked God to please not to take her yet. I recalled La Hita telling me about the dream my mother had before she died.

"God, please don't take my grandma away; You promised my mom You would let her live until we grew up!" I begged, in tears.

I wasn't ready to lose my grandma and be left without anyone to take care of me. I was still a little girl, and I wasn't yet ready to work. We had a big scare the day of La Hita's first heart attack. My grandmother didn't die, but she remained bedridden and sick for a long time.

Gaby was very attentive in looking after La Hita. She would stay up all night and give her water and medicine. I, on the other hand, was never able to help her during late nights. I was such a heavy sleeper that I would be sound asleep until the following day. My cousin Ana—who was already 18 years old and lived in San Pedro Sula—moved in with us for a while. She helped us a lot with La Hita and took care of her when my sister and I were at school. With Ana there, we didn't feel so alone and unprotected.

La Hita was always very protective of me. At the age of 12, I got my first period. I went to tell my grandmother, and she got mad at me. I didn't understand why. I imagine that she was concerned that I might make a mistake and end up pregnant. She never talked to me about menstruation, puberty, or the changes I would experience as a teenager. I only knew about it because my classmates and I would talk about menstruation and puberty at school. I was afraid and embarrassed to tell my grandmother that I'd gotten my period, but I needed pads, so I had to tell her. Her first reaction was to get angry. Then her expression immediately changed, and all I could see was concern on her face.

During puberty, I became rebellious. I didn't like to be scolded, much less spanked—although my grandmother rarely spanked me. Once, when I was six years old, she knocked me to my knees after I rudely talked back to her. Another time, when I was older, she hit me in the legs with an extension cord. It really hurt! On another occasion, I yelled at my grandmother, so she grabbed a *chancla* (sandal) and threw it at me, but I managed to dodge it and ran away. After that she never hit or spanked me again.

I do remember being scolded and punished for being rebellious and unruly. My sister would often tell my grandmother all the things I would do with my friends in the neighborhood, which resulted in me receiving several sermons from my grandmother.

I was rude to everyone, my insults cut deeper, and I got angry quickly. Through most of my difficult preteen years, La Hita was sick a lot, and all I did was constantly give her reasons to worry. In my head, it was simple defiance: I didn't want to follow what an adult told me to

Keyla and Gaby (12) on Keyla's 14th birthday, December 4, 1998 (family photograph).

do. I knew I wasn't doing anything wrong, and I wasn't looking to get in trouble, but my grandmother didn't like it when I wasn't at home.

On my worst days, I would complain to my grandmother about my mother's death. Angry and sad, I would ask La Hita why my mother had to die so young. La Hita cried whenever anyone would bring up my mom. She was never able to accept the loss of her daughter. I would run to my room and sob. I knew that La Hita would also make her way to her room to cry, and knowing that caused me even more pain.

6

New Beginning

In Honduras, we have the following educational levels: *kinder*; *primaria*, which ranges from first through sixth grade; *colegio*, from seventh through ninth grade (also called first, second, and third *curso* or *ciclo común*); and then *bachillerato*, from 10th through 12th grade. Back when I was a child, finishing the sixth grade was considered "an education" to a lot of people in La Entrada because it meant that you could read and write.

One of my dreams as a young child was to study and become a bilingual secretary like my mother. After giving birth to me, she finished her *bachillerato* and worked in the best school in town, Bernardo Galindo y Galindo. She went to San Pedro Sula to continue her education, because *colegio* only went up to the ninth grade, and there was no *bachillerato* in our town then. This was the reason my great-aunt Noemí left La Entrada and took her children to San Pedro Sula. She realized that the educational opportunities were far better in the city. My grandmother and her other sister Elvia opted to stay in La Entrada.

I finished the sixth grade when I was 12. La Hita refused to enroll me in the *colegio* Bernardo Galindo, where most of my friends were going to go. In her opinion, El Galindo (as we called it) had too many bad influences, and she thought studying there could lead me astray. Instead, with the help of my aunts in the U.S., she enrolled me in a small private evangelical school called Ministerio Arbol de Vida/Plan Escalón in a neighboring town called La Laguna, 15 minutes up the highway on the way to Copán Ruinas.

I loved studying at Plan Escalón (as we called the school). I learned to enjoy the prayer devotionals held every morning, and it was there that I found one of my lifelong best friends. Being there was an important first step in my spiritual growth.

My grades at Plan Escalón were bad, though I was able to pass each year I was there. Despite my grades, La Hita was glad that I continued there, because she knew it was the perfect place to help shape my attitude and behavior. Recalling my days as an *escalonera* (what we students called ourselves) still fills me with emotion. I will never forget the trees around the school, the soccer field, the benches, the yellow bus—which would pick me up every morning under an almond tree on the main road—my teachers, my classmates, the classrooms without windowpanes or doors, and the morning prayer devotionals to praise God before classes started. And finally, an endless number of memories that I thought I would make, but never got to live because I left Honduras before finishing school.

Plan Escalón was founded by American pastors who provided social aid in Honduras. The school had two types of students. I was a day student, which meant I attended classes during the day, but I would return home every afternoon. The others were boarding students who stayed there at the school during the school year. Most came from low-income homes. Their families paid what they could afford, and the school provided them with classes, housing, and food and supplemented the difference through donations collected back in the U.S.

Whenever I heard that an American was coming to visit the school, I got excited. I really loved meeting Americans, especially the ones who were my age. Oh, how I wished to be able to speak their language, even if only a little bit. At school, my English classes were basic, and I never retained very much. In fact, I learned more from a small English book that La Hita bought me for only three lempiras than I did in the school. The day my grandmother gave me the book, I was so happy that I started to study it almost immediately. I began to learn basic phrases, numbers, the alphabet, and sentences such as "My name is Keyla" and "Nice to meet you!" I also learned a little grammar and some pronunciation, though pronunciation was always the most difficult for me. Knowing that someday I might express myself and communicate in another language was enough motivation to keep me going.

The school year began in February and ended in November. Every school year, it was essential to get the financial support of my aunts for Gaby's education and mine. It was only through their help that we could pay our tuition and buy the necessary school supplies needed during the year. Their help always arrived from the United States, and thanks to them, I always had a new bookbag—sent from *La USA*—every year, which was considered a luxury. La Hita was able to pay the school fees on time most months, but occasionally she would get behind if money was tight.

During my third year of *colegio* (ninth grade), one of my neighbors mentioned to me that her daughter Leticia hadn't passed her second *curso* (eighth grade). I was so enthusiastic about my new school that I took that opportunity to tell her about all the wonders of Plan Escalón. Apparently, my sales pitch worked, because Leticia ended up at the same school, in the grade below mine. This wasn't a complete loss, as she was in the same class as my sister.

Leticia was one of my best friends from my previous school, Berríos. I was so glad that we were together again, because most of my former Berríos classmates had ended up at different *colegios*. Leticia and I became neighbors when I first moved to the new house, because the house where she lived was right next to where mine was built. We always got along well, even though her beliefs differed from mine. My family had always been Catholic, and she and her family were members

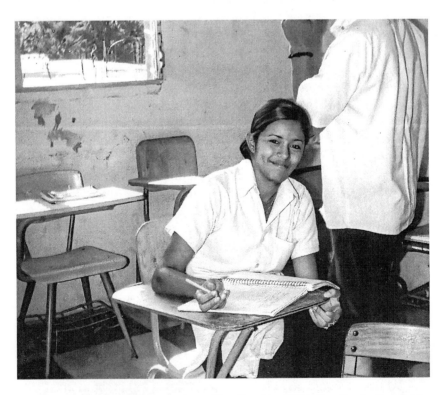

Keyla in her 9th-grade classroom at Plan Escalón, 2000 (family photograph).

of The Church of Jesus Christ of Latter-day Saints, commonly known as Mormons.

My family always thought Mormon beliefs were a little strange. Leticia's family didn't drink coffee for breakfast like we did; instead, they drank something called Postum, a dark and nearly tasteless beverage. On several occasions, some missionaries from her church had come to our door. But to us, someone who didn't drink coffee was strange, so we preferred to close the door and pretend that no one was home.

I was 15 when Leticia and I began to attend the same school, and we grew closer day by day. On one occasion, she invited me to attend church with her. I felt a little awkward about her invitation. At that time, I was preparing for my confirmation in the Catholic Church. Moreover, La Hita was very Catholic, and I was sure she wouldn't like me to attend other religions' activities. In the end, I accepted Leticia's invitation because the Mormon chapel had a basketball court, and I wanted to play there.

After that first visit, Mormon missionaries called elders came by my house to chat with me a little about their beliefs. Before starting formal lessons with them, I first wanted to make sure that, as a condition of receiving the lessons, I wouldn't be required to be baptized in their religion. Leticia told me that wasn't the case, which was a relief because I wasn't being pressured to do something I may not want to do. The idea of converting to a new religion other than the one I had been taught since I was a child was frightening in several ways. I was sure my grandmother would be against it as well.

The missionaries started coming to my house to teach me about their religion. I paid close attention to everything they said in each lesson. Their names were Elder Keyser and Elder Lux, from the United States and Guatemala, respectively. I learned the meaning of *elder* and understood that certain people received that title in their religion. After the first lesson, they gave me a copy of the Book of Mormon, a sacred scripture of their religion. I accepted it with trepidation but also with a desire to read it because I loved to read, even if I didn't understand everything. I would read it in the evenings, and even La Hita started to join me in reading the book from time to time. She always treated the missionaries well, although she kept telling me that she didn't want them in the house.

At first, I would go to the Mormon church to play basketball with Leticia and the other girls, and in a short amount of time, I found myself going because the church became a second home for me. I began to attend not just the activities but also the Sunday church services, and I started to feel like it was the place for me. After more than several visits with Leticia and the elders, I came to the conclusion that I should be baptized. I knew it was the right thing to do at that point in my life. For the first time, I felt with all my heart that it was the church where I belonged. It wasn't an easy decision for me to make. It would go against what my grandmother had taught me and above all, against my mother's wishes before she died. I thought long about it until I decided to stop attending my Catholic confirmation classes and be baptized a member of the Latter-day Saint (LDS) religion. Even though La Hita disagreed with my decision, she told me that she would accept it if it was what I honestly wanted.

On the day of my baptism, my grandmother begged me not to go through with it and, in tears, reminded me that my mother's wishes were that I remain a Catholic. I also cried there with her. While I was sad because my grandmother disagreed, I was at peace with my decision. There was no turning back.

I headed to the chapel with Gaby and a friend on Sunday, May 14, 2000. Never in my life had I felt closer to God. I felt His spirit telling me that all was well. That afternoon, I left my house wearing a skirt and blouse—my typical Sunday church attire—but I changed to a set of all-white clothes at the church. Upon arrival, seeing several others in white clothes, I realized that I wasn't the only one to be baptized. My turn came last. I stepped down into the baptismal font when it was my turn, and in the name of Jesus Christ, Elder Keyser gently submerged me in the water. Upon leaving the font, I felt a deep inner peace; the influence of the Spirit that I felt at that moment was so intense that it is impossible to describe. My heart was full of joy, tears flowed uncontrollably, and I understood that it was one of the best decisions I had made in my life to that point.

For the very first time, I felt that all my sins had been forgiven, even though I was only a teenager. Conversion to a new religion also meant a significant change in my lifestyle. I tried not to swear, even though it was hard not to at first. I was determined to be worthy of God's love, even though, at times, I felt I didn't deserve it. It wasn't easy to change, but the church's teachings gradually nourished my soul and filled me with the love and insight I needed to make better decisions and do better day by day.

I loved going to church because going there had an impact on my life in different ways. I learned important values and how to better manage my anger. I began to see chastity differently, and wearing white at my wedding was more important to me than ever. And I discovered that someday I could also marry a man who was worthy of me. I also learned that fasting is helpful whenever something big is happening in our lives and we want God's help and spiritual guidance.

In June of that year, my aunt Rafaela came to visit with her husband Don Javier, my cousin Fabricio, and his half-brother Milton. I always had a wonderful time with Fabricio whenever he came. On that occasion, his visit was especially welcome because he arrived just in time to help me decorate an outfit I needed for the school's *India Bonita* Pageant that was held every year. That year—and in previous years—I had been chosen as the *La India Bonita* nominee for my grade level due to my dark complexion and the fact that I was the one considered to have the most Indigenous-looking traits.

This contest was part of a larger celebration held every June to commemorate the *Indio* Lempira—a national hero, and the namesake of and image on the Honduran currency. We didn't have regular classes during that week. Instead, the school hosted activities to recognize the Indigenous heritage of Lempira and the Lenca people. One activity was building *champas* (traditional Lenca dwellings) out of straw, sticks, and coconut palms. Each class built their own, and whichever one was judged to have the best *champa* was declared the winning grade. During the week, we used to make and sell traditional dishes such as *ticucos*—a popular dish from the country's western region—and *riguas*—thin, tender corn cakes baked inside banana leaves. We also made *tamales*, corn, and other more typical Honduran dishes.

As a part of the *India Bonita* Pageant, I had to design and make an Indigenous-looking dress that incorporated traditional food and plant elements important to Mayan and Lenca culture, like corn, coffee, and cacao. I enlisted the help of a friend of mine who was also particularly good at designing. Together with my "design team" of my cousin, my friend, and his friend, we created a beautiful dress for the *India Bonita* contest. I was ready for the first part of the competition, which was modeling regular clothes, and I loved it. I was tall and long legged, and several people had told me I could be a runway model.

On the day of the competition, things began to turn in my favor. One of the other contestants wore a very low-cut top as a part of her first outfit. The judges—who were some of the teachers—believed that the top wasn't modest enough for a school activity. Modesty was an important value at my private Christian school. My first outfit was very modest, but my *India Bonita* dress not so much. My original design would have been disqualified as well because the top was cut short to show off my stomach. Thanks to a last-minute ingenious idea of attaching strings of corn kernels across the midriff of the dress, it wasn't disqualified.

The second part of the competition was an oral essay on why I should be selected as the winner. I had written my response beforehand and had gone over it so many times that I knew it by heart. I was able to stand in front of everyone and give my speech confidently and without stammering or stumbling. I was confident I would win.

The winner of the final element of the pageant was determined by which contestant had the most support from the students. Students would buy one-lempira tickets to support their favorite. That year, the winner would come down to whoever had the greatest number of tickets. My classmates were all behind me and bought as many as they could. They were so dedicated to helping me that they ended up using the money from the profits of the traditional food we had sold that week. Thanks to them I won and was named *La India Bonita* of my school.

My joy at winning *La India Bonita* of the year 2000 soon faded after the pageant. My cousin Fabricio ended up returning early back to the U.S. His sudden departure was disappointing to me, but I understood that his life was there and not in Honduras.

My aunt Rafaela, for her part, stayed an extra month in order to help La Hita apply for a visa to be able to travel to the U.S. To begin, they first had to travel to El Salvador to obtain a passport for my grandmother. Even though my grandmother had lived in Honduras for nearly 50 years, she had never applied for Honduran citizenship. Once the two of them had returned from El Salvador with the new passport, we all made the eight-hour bus trip from La Entrada to Tegucigalpa.

The Sunday before leaving, I fasted and prayed and begged God to help my grandmother if it was His will. All of La Hita's family, except Gaby and me, were living in the U.S. It had been years since she had seen her family, including those grandchildren whom she had raised, and she was anxious to reconnect with them. While my aunt Rafaela, her children, and a couple of my cousins born in the U.S. were able to visit, the rest of the family was not able to return to visit. At that point, they had been granted Temporary Protected Status (TPS) by the U.S. government. They could not come to Honduras unless they were willing to embark on that long and dangerous journey of an undocumented immigrant through Guatemala and Mexico back to the U.S.

Early Tuesday morning, we returned to the compound where the U.S. Embassy and Consulate were located. This time around, only my grandmother was applying for the visa. Security informed us that only one person was allowed to accompany the applicant inside, and my aunt decided I would go in with La Hita. As we walked in, I continued to pray silently, begging God that everything would go as He wanted it to. I was sure that whatever happened there would be best for all of us. My aunt Rafaela was able to join us later because she was a U.S citizen and could enter the building without a problem. I stayed next to La Hita until she was called to be interviewed and my aunt joined her at the window. I had to step aside, and I could barely hear what the officer on the other side of the window was asking. After a few questions about her documented family in the U.S and their job status, I heard it.

"Your visa has been approved, congratulations!" I heard the agent say.

It was an exciting moment. My grandmother could finally travel to the U.S. to see her family. We went back to La Entrada and stopped across the street and asked to borrow our neighbor's phone to call my aunts in the U.S. They were all happy with the news. Just a few days later, La Hita left with my aunt Rafaela. Gaby and I stayed home, as it was August and the middle of the school year. The *muchacha*, who was a grown woman, was living in the house with us. In addition, our next-door neighbor, who was La Hita's best friend, kept an eye on us and stopped in from time to time to make sure we were okay.

During those days, Gaby and I continued our lives as usual. In the mornings, we would go to school. In the afternoons, I normally would go play basketball at church with my friends. On Sundays, I would go to sacrament meetings and Sunday school. We weren't sure of the date when my grandmother was supposed to return. We assumed that she would only be gone for a few weeks because we knew that she didn't want to leave us alone for too long.

By September 15—Independence Day in Honduras—we were still alone at home, and we still didn't know when La Hita would be back. As a part of the Independence Day celebration, I would be participating in the annual parade because I was *La India Bonita* of my school. Leticia was also going to be in the parade, as she had won the Miss Independence Pageant for the school. She and I helped decorate the float that we would ride on to represent our school in the parade.

In October, we received a call from my aunt Rafaela: the family wanted Gaby and me to come to the U.S. as *mojadas*; that is, we would travel by land to the U.S-Mexico border and cross without a visa. For both Gaby and me, that decision came as a shock. Apparently, my grandmother was on a trip to New York City and had run into a neighbor from La Entrada who was a *coyote*—the name given to those who help smuggle undocumented migrants to the U.S. She was the same *coyote* who had helped my aunts when they had gone to the U.S. She was a very persuasive person, and convinced La Hita that crossing the border without a visa was our best option, and that La Hita should hire her to bring us to the U.S.

We didn't know when we would leave; we just knew it would be soon. I was nearing the end of my school year, and it was difficult to focus on my classes, so I stopped trying. I had assumed that I didn't need to worry about school because I would no longer be in Honduras by the time final grades came out. By the end of the year, my grades had fallen to the point that I was not going to pass the school year. I wasn't proud of my grades, and I felt terrible about quitting on this last year. It was the first time that I was going to fail the school year. There wasn't going to be a saving miracle like my first year at Plan Escalón, when, after the destruction left by Hurricane Mitch in 1998, all students were promoted to the next grade, regardless of their grades.

In November, my aunt Rafaela arrived to help us get ready. In an effort to make our journey a little easier and less dangerous, we went to San Pedro Sula to get our Honduran passports and apply for a Mexican visa. Having a Mexican visa would allow us to travel through Mexico without having to worry about being arrested and deported by the Mexican Federal Police. However, we didn't have any luck, as the Mexican Embassy rejected our visa application.

My aunt began to sell or give away everything from our house. I packed a suitcase with most of my clothes, which my aunt Rafaela would take with her to the United States, although it wasn't much. I also packed two sets of clothes in a backpack that I would carry with me on the long road ahead.

I was not supposed to tell anyone I would travel as a *mojada*, but I didn't care. I wanted to say goodbye to my friends. I told my church family that I would be gone soon. Before I left, they came to my house to see me off. They sang me a song whose lyrics I still remember: "God be with you 'til we meet again." It was a bittersweet evening, and many people there, including me, cried as I said goodbye to my friends from church. In our conversations, I told some of them that I would travel as a *mojada*, that my *Coyota* would be Doña Roberta, and her daughter would be going with us.

I told a family friend named Virginia that Doña Roberta was our *Coyota*. She became extremely concerned when I told her who was transporting us. She told me that she didn't understand why my family would agree to hire the same woman who had left one of my aunts stranded years ago when she tried to cross the border. Virginia told me all the horror stories she had heard about Doña Roberta from other people as well. I didn't understand why either, but I also knew it wasn't something I needed to worry about. I was a child and was supposed to follow what the adults had decided. Besides, all I could think about at that point was getting to the United States because I would see my brother, whom I had not seen for almost six years. I would also see my cousins again, and above all, I would be with La Hita again. I knew my future belonged in the United States.

7

Our Departure

The night before I left, I snuck out of the house. I went over the fence because my aunt Rafaela had locked the gate. I walked through the dark toward my friend Leticia's house to say goodbye. As we cried and hugged each other, I was comforted by the hope of one day being able to see her again. She said that in case I didn't make it across the border and had to return to town, she would sing me a song that says:

Por allí vienen los inditos por la cuesta del Picacho con su carga de frijoles para vender en la ciudad....[*]

It is a song deeply rooted in the memory of Hondurans, which reflects the life of those who get up with the sun to sell the products they harvest themselves. We laughed, hugged, and cried one more time.

To me, Leticia was like an angel sent from heaven. She had shown me a different world. One full of love and healing, rescuing me from the pain I once felt. Thanks to her, I found a new way of living life. Thanks to our friendship, I was no longer the "rebellious Keyla" I had been. I stopped complaining about the things God had taken away from me and stopped asking why I had to go through so much at such an early age. Now, I wasn't afraid to look forward, to imagine a future filled with love and happiness.

I walked back home in the darkness and hurried my pace because it was extremely late. That night, I was supposed to have gotten a good night's sleep because we would wake up early in the morning, before the roosters started crowing, to start our journey.

"It's time to leave, Keyla!" announced my aunt Rafaela well before dawn.

---

[*] That's where the Indians come up the Picacho hill with their sacks of beans to sell in the city...." *This line is from a Honduran folk song referring to the Honduran people who get up early in the morning to harvest.*

A representation of the day of my departure from the bus terminal in 2000, with my daughter standing in for me, 2021 (K. Sanders).

I dressed in jeans, a shirt, and a light gray sweater because it was already late November, and it was starting to feel a little chilly. I wore black lace-up sneakers, and I carried two more sets of clothes in my backpack. I had no room for a blanket or stuffed animals: just enough clothing for three days. My aunt suggested that I bring sanitary pads;

I listened to her, but according to what I estimated, I didn't need them. I had calculated that I wouldn't get my period again until I crossed to the U.S., which I thought would be in a maximum of 12 days. I was supposed to arrive around my 16th birthday, and I was extremely excited about that.

When you turn 15 in Honduras, traditionally your family throws a big party. The previous year, I didn't get a celebration for my *quinceñera*. I had heard that in *La USA* you get a big party when you turn 16. In my head, it felt like things would work out in my favor so that I could celebrate my sweet 16 with La Hita and the rest of my family.

On November 25, 2000, we set off early in the morning before the town woke up. Together with my aunt Rafaela, we headed for the Guatemalan border, less than three hours away from La Entrada. Gaby, Dunia—the *Coyota*'s daughter, whom I already knew—and I left together. As we started walking toward the bus terminal, I took the time to look around my town and began to replay in my mind everything I had experienced there. We walked past my grandmother's old café. We passed the bus stop where I had waited for my mother to arrive on the bus with a bunch of grapes so many years ago. I had no idea if I would ever return to my hometown; I only knew that leaving was the right thing to do, and that God had a future full of blessings planned for me.

It hurt to leave my friends, but I no longer had any other close relatives in La Entrada. Ever since La Hita left in September, I had been alone with my sister. My dog Rinti was hit by a car while I was in San Pedro Sula trying to obtain a Mexican visa. I was sad when he died, but at the same time, I felt a sense of relief because I wouldn't have to abandon him in a place where he would most likely end up living in the streets; knowing this made my departure easier.

We didn't take the bus to the Guatemalan border as I thought we would. Instead, my aunt Rafaela arranged a ride with a truck driver who was going that way. He loaded the four of us in the sleeper cab of his tractor-trailer truck. I fell asleep during the ride, and by the time I woke up, we were already at the Guatemalan border checkpoint.

My aunt got off to have our passports stamped. We were allowed to stay 90 days in the country as tourists, and I remember thinking that I would be in the U.S. by then. I imagined that I would be enjoying a different atmosphere, full of hope and opportunities. After Guatemala, Mexico was our next destination. My aunt gave us $20 each and told us to keep the money safely inside our bras and to not let Doña Roberta know that we had it.

Once we were past the checkpoint, we took a local micro-bus to Esquipulas and got there in less than 30 minutes. That municipality is part of the department of Chiquimula, located in Guatemala's central-eastern region. It wasn't the first time I had visited Esquipulas. Three years before, I had gone there with La Hita; we brought candles to the Virgin Mary inside a beautiful, large Catholic church. On that trip, my grandmother bought me some *conservas de coco*—a local dish made from coconut—that was served in a pink basket made of palm leaves.

We arrived at an ugly, rundown motel where the *Coyota* was waiting for us. Doña Roberta was short and stocky, with brown skin, short wavy hair, and a mole on the left side of her lip. In contrast, her tall daughter had a sweet voice, light complexion, small eyes, and shoulder-length hair, bearing little resemblance to her mother. A few of her people, who would be part of our group of *mojados*, arrived at the motel.

That same day, my aunt Rafaela went back to La Entrada. I felt alone, unprotected, and surrounded by people I didn't know. I was wearing a bit of makeup, which made me feel more confident because it helped me to look older. Being tall had its advantages: many people thought I was up to three years older than I really was. I also felt that I could go under the radar as a *mojada* in those places if I wore makeup.

That first night, we went for a walk and bought a few things to eat. We spent the night in that motel as we waited for the rest of the group, which included Dunia (18 years old) and Gaby (14 years old), and me (15 years old).

That night, the next part of our group arrived at the motel. This included José David, aged 23, and his niece and nephew—Noemí and Daniel, aged 16 and 17, respectively—who came from San Pedro Sula. José David was young, slim, and of average height. He had a long nose and curly hair. Noemí was a little shorter than me. She was of average build, had slightly curly hair, dark brown skin, thick lips, and hazel eyes. Her brother Daniel was also curly haired and had dark brown skin, and was shorter than the two of us.

Rebeca, a 32-year-old woman, also joined the group. She was tall, of a thick build, had short shoulder-length hair, small lips, and a soft voice. Rebeca told me that she had left her teenage daughter in Honduras. She had decided to go to the U.S. to provide her daughter with a better quality of life. The only valuable thing Rebeca carried with her was a small bag of soil from the cemetery where her grandmother was buried. Full of faith, she believed that her grandmother's soul would help guide her to her destination.

José David left a younger son behind. Before leaving for the United States, he had worked in a *maquila* in Honduras, but according to him, a good position within the factory still wasn't enough to make a living. His niece and nephew decided to accompany him because their parents were already in the U.S. and wanted to be reunited with them.

I also met Óscar; he was 28 years old and very tall, dark skinned, and had straight hair combed to the side. He looked a lot like my cousin Kevin, who had been in the United States for quite some time. Óscar was also Honduran and had an uncle waiting for him in the U.S.

On the second day, two older women joined the group: Nancy, who was short, had curly black hair, and wasn't very friendly. Roxana was tall and cinnamon skinned and was much nicer. Both women were around 40 years old and from Guatemala.

We were 10 *mojados* and one *coyota*. Some of us were from Honduras and others from Guatemala, but we all had a common destination. While our individual aspirations varied, there were many overlapping motivations guiding our journey to the United States: to be reunited with family, to find a decent job, to be able to help our families back in

A *mojada* ready for the journey, my daughter again standing in for me, 2021 (K. Sanders).

Central America, and maybe one day, to be able to go back to the place where we were born.

For my part, I wasn't sure I would ever return to La Entrada. At that point, I didn't have anyone else left in Honduras. So, for me, there was no turning back. I knew I had to make it to the United States. I would miss my hometown, but nothing was holding me to the place where I had lived for 15 years.

8

Forced Stop

The neighborhood where the motel was located was a rundown part of town, and the motel fit right in. Dunia, my sister, Noemí, and I went for a walk around the area. Doña Roberta had warned us to take certain precautions while on the trip so as to not draw attention to ourselves. We tried not to speak out loud around others so people wouldn't notice our accent and tell where we had come from (and where we were headed). We weren't supposed to walk in groups of more than three people, so we split up to walk in pairs.

We found a place to exchange our lempiras into quetzals—Guatemala's official currency—to buy some candy. We didn't have much money, but it was enough to stock up on snacks for a few days.

Gaby and I had been told that we would not have to worry about food or lodging because Doña Roberta would take care of our expenses with the money our family had already paid her. The *Coyota* had promised my aunts and grandmother that she would charge them less to bring us compared to her usual rates because she knew my family.

That first night, we went out to the market and bought a few lovely handmade bags. I didn't feel like we were *mojados* at all, but rather on vacation discovering new places. Up to that point, a *mojada*'s life didn't seem so bad, but I didn't know what awaited me in the days to come.

With such a large group, we had to share rooms. My sister, Dunia, Doña Roberta, and I spent the night in the same room. The rest of the group also shared rooms between them. Dunia became very attached to Gaby and cared for her like a younger sister. I spent more time with Noemí and talked to Rebeca and the boys a lot. For some reason, I always get along better with guys rather than girls. At school, I remember my friend Eda and I spent most of our time with the boys because there was a lot less drama and they always made us laugh. Because of this, many of the other girls at the school labeled us as *locas* because we were "easy" girls.

We only spent one night in that motel, and from the very moment we arrived, I couldn't stop thinking about leaving and getting on with our trip. My birthday was coming up, and my main wish was to be able to celebrate it with my family in the U.S. In my mind, there could be no better gift for me than to celebrate my 16th birthday in the country where I had dreamed of living since I was little.

On the morning of the second day, Doña Roberta announced that we would be leaving on a bus that same afternoon. My final destination felt closer and closer! We set off for the bus station, spaced out and pretending we weren't together so we wouldn't arouse suspicion. As it turned out, the bus was late, and we ended up leaving several hours late, so we had to spend most of the night on the bus.

Sometime during the ride, the bus was stopped at a checkpoint, and three Guatemalan police officers got on the bus, shining flashlights in our faces while asking for our passports. I had been fervently praying ever since we left. I prayed that our journey would go smoothly and that nothing bad would happen to us. Scared, I handed them my passport, which they returned after a couple of minutes. Unfortunately, the agents confiscated José David's passport. Doña Roberta gave José David 100 quetzals to bribe the agents. They accepted the money and handed back his passport. It was the first of what would be many frightening encounters with police officers on this journey. The bus continued its way. I had no idea where we were, nor was I interested in trying to find out. I could only think about making it to my destination.

Early the next morning, we stopped on a small, unpaved road in a small town near an open-air market. The road was dusty, and I knew we were in a remote town, because the streets were not very busy and the houses had a more of a rural look. We waited there for the next bus that could take us to our next stop, where we would spend the night. Doña Roberta split us into two groups and had each group ride a different bus. Some people went with Óscar—who seemed to be the most responsible—and I had to go with Doña Roberta, Noemí, and Gaby. Óscar told me he had previously tried to cross the border with the help of Doña Roberta, but without success, and that is why he already knew the route.

I was exhausted because I hadn't been able to sleep very much on the overnight bus ride. Thankfully, this second bus ride was shorter than the previous night's, and when I least expected it, we had arrived in another small town, called El Naranjo, in Guatemala. We got off the bus and walked to a house close by. The house was humble in design but kept in good condition.

It was the home of the González family. They were all very friendly, welcomed us with open arms, and told us they would have food ready for us soon. The older women in our group—Dunia, Rebeca, Nancy, and Roxana—were assigned to help in the kitchen. They along with the González women prepared beans, scrambled eggs, and cheese with tortillas both for lunch and later for dinner. After eating this same meal several times, I wondered to myself if the González family ate the same thing all three meals of the day.

After lunch, Noemí, Daniel, José David, my sister, and I went to the *pulpería* for chips and a Coke. In the small market, there were several stands selling candy and used clothes. We went to one of the second-hand clothing shops, though we didn't buy anything because we had limited money and even more limited space.

We returned to the house and went to an empty room that had been added on to the side of the house. It was made of wooden planks and had a single hammock hanging in the middle. José David had brought some cards with him, and we got ready to play. We had a lot of fun together. Daniel was a very funny guy and could imitate Donald Duck's voice exactly as I had heard it on TV. It was an excellent time to start getting to know each other better. I had not known beforehand with whom we would travel, and I was happy to have them as new friends.

The González family kept their house spotless and in better condition than many others nearby. The kitchen was outdoors, and the bathroom and shower were in a separate building out back. It reminded me somewhat of how I had lived back in Honduras. Even though she had an indoor kitchen, La Hita always preferred to cook outdoors and wash the dishes in the *pila*.

That night we slept in separate rooms, the women in one room and the men in another. I slept on a mattress on the floor, and others slept on beds. I admired the kindness of the family. We spent two nights in that house. On the second day, everyone began to wonder why we had to stay in one place for so long. I also was anxious to continue our journey. Doña Roberta had left on our first day there and still hadn't returned by the middle of the second day. We were starting to get a little restless and worried. Dunia, however, was still there in the house with us. As long as the *Coyota*'s daughter was still with us, I had nothing to fear. At least that's what I kept telling myself to calm down.

Doña Roberta finally returned and announced that we would be going to our next stop in the morning. Moving to another place was easy, as we had little to nothing to pack. Everyone traveled packed the same way as Gaby and me: just a backpack and a set or two of extra clothes.

Before we left, a young Guatemalan man joined the group. He was short, and his eyes were green, like two olives. A car came to pick us up and took us in groups of four to a remote intersection in the middle of nowhere. My group included Noemí, Rebeca, and Gaby. We arrived and a tractor was waiting for us. We climbed on top of the tractor and set out on what would be a two-hour ride.

The driver told us how dangerous that stretch of road was. He recounted stories of people being killed, and of the numerous women who had been raped on that road. I kept praying and asking God for protection and that no harm would come to any of us. Ever since I had left La Entrada, I hadn't stopped praying, and that moment was no exception. The road was narrow and muddy, with small trees and dense underbrush creeping in from both sides. It seemed so far from anything that could be called civilization. Had anything happened, I felt like we could have screamed at the top of our lungs, and no one would have heard us. Two hours later, we arrived at a wide *rancho* house built of exposed bricks. It looked more like a farmhouse. It had an elevated front porch that sat halfway up on four wooden posts that stretched from the ground to the overhanging roof that covered the porch. With the first group who had arrived, we sat on a low concrete wall in the front of the house while we waited for the rest of the *mojados*.

When I walked into the house, the first thing I saw was a short hallway that ended at a door leading to a backyard. On the right-hand side there was another hallway with a room at the end that was used as a *pulpería* that sold products to us *mojados*. In front of the *pulpería*, there was a window where we could buy snacks and soft drinks. There were two bedrooms close to the front door and one at the end of that hallway near the back door. On the left-hand side there was a large kitchen with a dirt floor. The floor of the rest of the house was poured concrete. It was possible to see inside the house from the porch because the bricks had been laid with gaps to allow air to circulate—although to me, it seemed more of a way to allow bugs to circulate.

The toilet was about 30 meters away from the house, near the corral where cows and horses were kept. Also behind the house was a wooden barn where I would sit and eat my snacks and hang out with my new friends.

Everyone, including Doña Roberta, arrived by the end of the day. I stopped by the *pulpería* to buy some candy and realized that they were overcharging me.

"We always overcharge *mojados!*" the guy snapped when I politely asked him why he was charging me extra.

Everything cost us 10 to 30 cents more than what they sold for to a Guatemalan. I then understood why there was a *pulpería* inside that isolated house.

On that night and the other ones to come, I had to sleep on the concrete floor, with no mattress or blanket and next to a wall full of holes. The only comfort I had was that I could use my backpack as a pillow. I thought about the dozens of insects that would be coming in and out of those holes all night long. The *Coyota* and Dunia slept in the small second bedroom right in front of me, and they invited my sister to sleep in there with them. A little while later, Dunia brought me out a blanket, as it had gotten cold in the night. She told me that she had been charged five quetzals to rent it for only that night. Noemí curled up next to me, and we slept close to each other for warmth.

As I had imagined, mosquitoes came in through the holes and bit me all over. It was tough to sleep on the floor. I heard an animal howling all night long; I didn't know what it was, but my imagination told me it was some colossal beast. I had never heard anything like that before. The following day, I woke up hungry. The women in our group and the owner of the house were already in the kitchen. They gave us eggs, beans, and tortillas for breakfast. When I finished, I went to the backyard, near a well from which I could collect cold water with a bucket for showering and for brushing my teeth. With me, I had shampoo, soap, toothpaste, a towel, and my toothbrush.

While showering, I kept looking at clouds, getting lost on the horizon, and I felt as if my life was headed in that direction. Afterward, I walked a bit further to the fence and began to pray and ask God for help. Despite everything, I was able to admire the beauty of the landscape. I missed the camera that my cousin Fabricio had given me years before. I had been taking pictures since I was 13 years old, and I wished I could have captured that scene, but all I could do was close my eyes and take a picture in my head so I would never forget.

While there at that stop, I didn't have to worry about cooking because the older women took care of it. Being one of the younger ones, I had to help wash the dishes and sweep up afterward. One night after dinner, Noemí and I were in charge of cleaning up and washing the dishes. We forgot to put a lid on the pot of beans, and by the morning, there were crickets inside. We couldn't throw the beans away because it was the only food we had. We took the crickets out of the pot and pretended like nothing had happened. While at that stop, we ate only twice a day, and it was always the same meal: beans, rice, eggs, and corn tortillas.

We had been there for two days and still didn't know when we would be heading to our next stop. We weren't told anything. By the fourth day, many of us were starting to worry. Day five came and went without word. All we could do was wait.

To pass the time, some of the members of our group and I would spend hours in the barn playing cards. Most of the time, the card group was Noemí, Daniel, José David, Gaby, and me. I didn't know about how the others were doing, but at least we were trying to cheer each other up amid such uncertainty. That barn became our happy place. There, we laughed and stayed out of the way. Even though that house was the only one for miles, we felt safe as a group. Still, we were cautious and tried not to make too much noise.

Little by little, I became closer to José David. We spent more time together. He knew me better than the others, and I knew him better. I developed an attraction toward him. One day, after we had finished playing cards with the others, we stayed behind in the barn. I was sad. José David noticed, so he came over to talk to me. I told him about my life in Honduras. Up to that moment, I hadn't realized how happy I had been in La Entrada, regardless of all that I had been through there. José David tried to comfort me and told me that he would have never left Honduras if he were me. His words encouraged me. Before I knew it, as we talked, we ended up very close to each other. We kissed. I liked his kisses, and spending time with him. When I was with him, I didn't feel as lonely. During the following days, we didn't try to hide our relationship from the rest of the group. No one seemed to be in favor of it, and everyone began to look down on us. Nothing else happened between the two of us. We only kissed and kept each other company. We never talked about the future together, as we were just living in the moment.

The whole time there, I tried very hard to look pretty. I took a shower every day and put on a little bit of the makeup I had brought with me. I would put on a silver eyeshadow pencil and some mascara. The Guatemalan woman Nancy was very critical of me. She didn't like me at all, and would tell me that I shouldn't wear makeup—let alone make out with José David—because I was a Christian. Makeup made me feel better; it helped calm my anxiety. Besides, José David's kisses and hugs gave me peace of mind.

"Feeling good is not a sin!" I replied to her.

From that day on, she stopped speaking to me. Instead, she would look at me with disgust and roll her eyes. Not only did Nancy look down on me, but others also began to treat me differently. It wasn't just because of José David, but also because I had no problem speaking my mind about the situation we were going through.

Doña Roberta found out that José David and I were making out and scolded both of us. She told us that she had promised my family she would take care of Gaby and me. As of that day, the *Coyota* began to treat me differently as well. Eventually, Noemí, with whom I spent most of my time, began to be treated differently just for hanging out with me. My sister stayed out of the crosshairs by staying close to Dunia because Dunia cared for her and protected her. Besides, Gaby was quiet and got along well with everyone, and she was the youngest in the group.

The days continued to drag on with no word and no movement. On December 4, it had been 10 days since we left La Entrada. December 4, 2000, was also my 16th birthday. I couldn't help but feel sad. Things hadn't turned out the way I had expected them to. I was supposed to spend that day with La Hita, Fabricio, and my whole family. I didn't want to accept that I had to spend my birthday in that middle-of-nowhere house in Guatemala. I was sleeping on the hard concrete floor, getting eaten mercilessly by mosquitoes, eating only twice a day, and I didn't know when I would get out of there. I couldn't hold back my tears that day and let my emotions and sadness come flowing out. Gaby and José David tried to comfort me. I felt terrible that everyone saw me like that, but I couldn't stop my tears. I missed my bed, La Hita's food, my friends, and my life in Honduras. I finished my crying and felt much better now that I had gotten it all out. On that night of my birthday, Doña Roberta returned and announced that we would finally be leaving early the following day. I was desperate to get out of there. I set my sights on the idea of seeing my family before Christmas, and that, at least, gave me some hope.

9

Lost Shoes

On December 5, we woke up at three in the morning. We were finally able to leave the *rancho* where we had been waiting for so much of our week-and-a-half journey. It was very early, but I didn't mind getting up at that hour. I was so eager to get out of there that waking up early was the least of my worries. We left through the rear of the house, through the pens where horses and cows were kept. There was so much mud that it was easier to take off our shoes and walk barefoot through the cold, wet mud. Óscar and another person were ahead of us, so they lit the road with flashlights. It took us about 10 minutes to reach the banks of a river. It was the same river that Noemí and I had discovered a few days before while exploring the area.

The river was wide, brown, and muddy, and appeared to be quite deep. I put my shoes to the side, on a stone, so that I could roll my pants up while we waited to get on a boat that would take us downriver. Moments later, when it was my turn to get in the boat, I reached for my shoes, but they were no longer there. It was very dark, and I was expecting the worst. I could feel my heart pounding and was suddenly filled with anxiety. Having to go barefoot the rest of the journey would be torture. I thought that I would have to walk barefoot for days on unfamiliar terrain. I started to ask everyone around me if they had seen my shoes, but no one had. I was about to break down crying, so I began to pray.

"Keyla, I've got your shoes here!" I suddenly heard José David's voice say.

My heart returned from my throat back to my chest, and I pulled myself together. At that moment, I knew God was with me and I knew that He was watching over me.

From the outset and through the entire journey, my faith had been a vital component that filled me with hope when I was afraid. I knew that God was by my side and saw confirmation when I least expected it. Two days before leaving the farmhouse, without even looking for it, I came across a book published by The Church of Jesus Christ of Latter-day Saints. Most shocking of all, based on the name written on the inside cover, the book had belonged to someone whom I had met in my congregation at church some time ago in La Entrada. Surely, he had also been a *mojado*, like me, and had previously traveled this same path. Coming across that book was like hearing God speak directly to me and tell me that I wasn't alone—that I had to be strong and have hope because something better was waiting for me.

I got on the boat, and José David handed me my shoes. I hugged them to me and thanked God once again. The boat started off, and in less than five minutes, it stopped near the riverbank. There was no dock or anything that would tell us we had arrived. We knew that we had arrived because the man driving the boat told us to get out. I hopped out of the boat, and the water came up above my ankles. Luckily, I had already rolled up my pants. I walked out of the river and found some dry ground where I could bend over, dry my feet as best I could by wiping off as much of the excess water off as I could, and then put on my shoes.

"We are in Mexico!" I heard someone say.

I couldn't believe it. All that time, we had been just a few yards from the Mexican border—but still, we hadn't made much progress. We had just sailed up the San Pedro River across the border. Finally, we were in Mexico!

Far off in the distance, we spotted what seemed to be a large fence with a checkpoint that read "Welcome to Mexico." It was still dark, but the sky was beginning to reveal the first rays of daylight. There were people getting ready to sell their goods at the border. We started to walk deeper into Mexico, away from the Guatemalan border and toward the highway. We walked for a few minutes, when all of a sudden, we saw the lights of a car approaching in our direction. We reacted immediately and dove into a ditch on the side of the road. The ditch was overgrown with underbrush that hid us. We lay there on our stomachs until we were sure the coast was clear and we could continue along. We crossed the highway, jumped over a waist-high wire fence, and headed into the dense jungle for what would be a long journey.

We walked the entire morning and into the afternoon. A young man with a machete guided us through the dense jungle forest. I kept wondering when we would get to the place where we would spend the night. We had been in that jungle for more than six hours, and we were allowed to sit down only a couple of times—for less than two minutes each—to drink water from the plastic bottles we had brought with us. We were not given any food, and we had not brought any in our backpacks either.

In the late afternoon, we arrived at a small, very humble adobe house. Finally, we were able to rest. We were welcomed by a young girl who I figured was the daughter of the owners and who directed us to a small room on the side of the house. It looked more like a henhouse, like the one my grandma had in Honduras. The room was built of wooden planks, and there was a hammock hanging in the middle of the room. I wanted to lay down and rest, but even more, I wanted to get something to eat. We didn't have any breakfast before we left, and we hadn't eaten all day. We were all starving, and we didn't know if the family there would feed us or not.

Our *Coyota,* Doña Roberta, wasn't there with us. She had stayed in Guatemala when we had all crossed the river. I then understood why. The trail we had hiked was rough and through so much wild brush, it would have been nearly impossible for a woman like her, over 50 years old and overweight, to make it through.

Rebeca and I went back around to the main house to talk to the owners, but they weren't there. Instead, the muchacha told us she couldn't feed us because the owners were not there. Rebeca and I begged her to give us some food. We told her we would take whatever she had to offer, even if we had to prepare it ourselves. Thankfully, she took pity on us and fed us fried ripe plantains, refried beans, and scrambled eggs. It was the only meal we ate that day. It was a simple meal, one very common in southern Mexico and Central America for people who have limited resources. However, I was so grateful to finally have something in my stomach that it tasted like the most delicious meal I had ever eaten in my life.

There in that house, we were in the middle of the jungle. There were trees of all sizes all around us. I could hear monkeys screeching somewhere in the trees, though I couldn't see them. We would spend the night there and, on the next day, continue on our way. José David and I both slept reverse (head to foot) in the hammock. The rest of the group slept on the floor. I was so tired that, after climbing into the hammock, the next thing I remembered was the loud chorus of birds in the morning. The sounds of the animals in the jungle were so loud that we didn't need an alarm clock.

We all woke up, but again we were not given anything for breakfast. We had to keep going on our journey with our stomachs empty. We got ready, but we didn't leave until around 11 o'clock in the morning. That day, we went up and down mountains and large and small hills, single file as we walked through the dense forest for several hours once again. Although we had water to keep us hydrated, it wasn't enough. The hunger pangs in my stomach increased, especially when going uphill. Gaby, on the other hand, seemed to be dealing with hunger better than I was. She had a lot more energy and went up and down the hills as if nothing was happening. I envied my sister's energy at that moment!

In truth, I don't really know how many hours we walked. With the dense jungle, hunger, and exhaustion, it was difficult to accurately track the time. At some point, I felt like I couldn't continue anymore. We were starting to climb another hill, and I felt like I just didn't have any more strength to take another step. Rebeca was walking ahead of me, and I grabbed her backpack to help me up the hill. She turned around and told me not to do so because I was slowing her down. I didn't want to keep walking any further. I was so tired. I wasn't sure if I would be able to take another step.

"Don't stop! We must keep going!" I heard the guide's voice in the distance up ahead.

Shortly thereafter, we finally reached an area that flattened out. For me, it was a huge relief. The weather was milder; I extended my arms out to my sides, and I felt the cool breeze all over my body. I started to enjoy the walk more, even with my hungry stomach, because I knew we were getting closer and because we were in the middle of nowhere. There wasn't anyone for miles. At that point, for a moment at least, I didn't have to worry about getting caught by the Mexican immigration police.

We arrived at what seemed to be the backyard of an old house. It was an isolated house without any other houses nearby, so we felt safer.

The purpose of that two-day trip was only to avoid the Mexican border checkpoint. What would have been a 20-minute trip down the highway turned into two days of hiking through a jungle. Since leaving that *rancho*, we had only eaten one meal and had drunk little water. Even with the exhaustion, hunger, and semi-dehydration, I still felt so grateful that my shoes hadn't ended up lost on the bank of the river back in Guatemala. I can't imagine making that trip barefoot on top of everything else.

10

Good and Bad People

The *Coyota* was already waiting for us at that isolated house when we arrived. We remained behind the back fence, hidden in the forest and waiting to see if the coast was clear. She waved at us, indicating that it was safe to enter, and we crossed the fence and walked toward the house. We were so sticky and gross that we kept our distance from each other. We couldn't stand our own stench, not to mention each other's. I didn't dare get close to José David, much less try to kiss him.

I was thirsty, hungry, and my appearance resembled the exact image I had in my head of how a *mojada* looked. I looked like a *vaga* (street child) with nowhere to live or shower, just like many I had seen at the bus terminal in La Entrada and the *vagos* my grandmother used to feed and clothe. My face and hair were covered in dust and grime. My clothes were filthy, as if I had rolled around on the ground.

The past two days had been an ordeal for the whole group. The young Guatemalan man who joined our group halfway through our trip through Guatemala decided to return home. The journey to this point had been much more difficult than he thought it would be. His family was still in Guatemala, and he could go back home to them. Returning to Honduras wasn't an option for me, as my whole family was waiting for me in the U.S. With his departure, we were once again 10 *mojados*.

In the backyard of the house, I found some shade under a shed where the family stored firewood, a place where I could rest. The backyard was somewhat similar to mine in La Entrada but not well kept. There were chickens and pigs walking free all through the yard. Still, at that moment, I was the most unpleasant-smelling being in that backyard. I was so desperate to take a shower, but we couldn't go into the house for fear that immigration agents would spot us. After our days-long trek through the jungle, getting caught by Mexican Immigration was what we least wanted.

I rested there in the shade for a while. I looked up at the sky. Then, after a while, I closed my eyes and tried to breathe deeply to alleviate the fear and anxiety that I had felt since I embarked on that journey.

"Immigration's coming; Immigration's coming!" I heard someone shout.

Everybody ran to hide. The men jumped the fence at the back of the yard and hid in the underbrush there on the hill. The women and I who had been resting in the shade of the shed didn't have time to run anywhere. All we had time to do was climb up on top of the pile of wood so that we would be hidden by the roof of the shed. We stayed in our hiding spaces for a while, but nothing happened. After a while, we realized it had been a false alarm.

The house where we were stayed busy. They had a small *pulpería*, and people were in and out of the house all afternoon. A few hours after the scare, one of the members of the family came to talk with us. We were offered food, and a floor where we could spend the night. I desperately wanted a shower, but that was not part of the deal, and I was forced to sleep in my filthy clothes. We had to wait for our next destination in order to be able to take a shower. That night, I slept on the ground. I was so tired that I didn't care about the bugs, rocks, or the hardness of the cold ground. I fell asleep quickly, and I slept soundly through the night.

We were set to continue our journey the following morning, deeper into Tabasco, the Mexican state that borders Guatemala. Doña Roberta began to organize us in groups of two or three so that we would stagger our travel. Noemí and I were put in the last group because we were the *Coyota*'s least favorite. Nancy had been telling Doña Roberta negative things about me for several days. By then, the *Coyota* excluded me and ignored me as much as she could. The same happened with Noemí because she spent a lot of time with me. On one occasion, Doña Roberta even told others in the group that she didn't care if Noemí or I got deported. Gaby, on the other hand, was having much better luck. Dunia continued to keep her close and protect her.

After all the other groups had gone, it was Noemí's and my turn to leave. We boarded a small bus that took us along that same road that we had briefly walked the day we crossed the river into Mexico. We didn't dare say a word to each other or anyone else on the bus so that no one would notice our Honduran accent.

In Honduras, our accent and vocabulary are very distinct and different from even the Spanish spoken in El Salvador and Guatemala, not to mention Mexico. For those in Mexico, it is very easy to recognize people from Honduras and Guatemala, just by the way we talk. After crossing into Mexico, I had to quickly learn to not talk at all in public unless it was absolutely necessary.

A few hours after arriving, the *Coyota* led us to another small village not too far from where we had been. Once again, we traveled by local buses, small groups at a time. By the time we arrived at the house where we would sleep that night, it was after dark. The structure sat on a low hill behind a larger main house and wasn't much more than a one-room shack, with a roof and "walls" made from long, thin tree branches lashed together. The room was no more than 12 feet by 12 feet. On the bright side, there was a small river with clean water nearby. The other women from our group and I immediately headed to the water to bathe in the dark. After my bath, I felt like a new person, as if the cold water had washed away all of my anxiety, stress, and fear.

That night, I got my period. To complicate matters more, I didn't have enough pads, as I had given some to Noemí and Rebeca earlier in our trip. I didn't think I would need them because, according to my predictions, I should have been in the U.S. already. I had to improvise and used folded-up toilet paper, which I had to change constantly.

Sleeping in that hut was no small task. It was cold, and the cement floor was rough. We didn't have anything to sleep on or to cover ourselves with other than a nylon tarp so old and worn that it was nearly transparent. We slept in groups of five with our bodies so close to each other that we looked like sardines in a can. Women slept on one side and men on the other side of the room. I had never longed for a bed so badly as I did that night.

The following morning, I walked down to the river. There was no bathroom in the hut where we were staying, so I had to use the river to relieve myself. While there, I washed in the river the set of clothes I had been wearing the past few days. The previous evening, when I changed my clothes, I had noticed how my pants were a lot baggier than when I had previously worn them; I had lost several pounds since leaving La Entrada. We had walked a lot and eaten very little. At that point, everyone in our group was looking skinnier to the point of appearing a little sickly. Even Dunia and Rebeca, who had started the trip with a few extra pounds, were starting to look a bit malnourished.

That afternoon and evening, someone brought us food from the main house. We were served a pot of beans, rice, and tortillas. It didn't taste very good, but it was all we had for lunch and later for dinner. During our two-night stay there, we didn't eat breakfast and they only served us two meals, if we were lucky. Before the second day was over, we talked to the owners and begged them to allow us to sleep inside their home. The previous night, we were so cold inside the hut: the air was seeping in from all sides, and we had nothing to cover ourselves with. The owners agreed and let us sleep on mats on the floor of their house, but made us pay 10 pesos to rent some blankets for each of us. I wasn't bothered by the floor's hardness, as I was growing accustomed to sleeping on the hard floor. That second night, we still had to sleep on a hard floor, but with our rented blankets, at least we slept warmer.

The afternoon of the third day, the *Coyota* came back for us, and we took a bus to our next stop. The drive was less than an hour, and we arrived in another small Mexican town also located in the state of Tabasco. Suprisingly, Doña Roberta rode with me on that leg of the trip. Even more surprising, she sat and talked with me on the bus. She told me about my family and what life was like in the United States. After our conversation (and now that we were no longer hacking our way through the jungle but moving from town to town by bus), I felt like our arrival in the U.S. was just around the corner. I just knew that soon I would see my brother, Fabricio, La Hita, and my aunts. I missed them all so much.

Once the bus arrived, we took a cab to an empty house in a residential neighborhood. The house was still under construction, and there was no furniture, electricity, or water. It had only four walls and a roof, but it was enough to spend the night in, and in truth, was better than many of the places where we had stayed lately. That night, José David headed out to buy tacos for everyone. After days of isolated ranch homes and small villages in the jungle, being there in that town made the tacos taste like a gourmet meal. More than anything, finally being in a town large enough to even have a taco vendor meant that we were in the next phase of our journey. That night, the tacos represented a new hope that this journey would be over soon.

The next day, we left the house one by one so as not to raise suspicions. Doña Roberta advised us that to avoid being noticed, we shouldn't have our bookbags stuffed full like we were traveling cross country. She told us to only take the necessities for the day and that we should leave our less important belongings there at the empty house. She told us that she would later take them to the house where we would be going next. So, I left with only the clothes I was wearing. In my backpack, I only brought my toothbrush and a towel. In the house under construction, I left my two extra sets of clothes and my sweater.

Things were looking up that day. After another bus ride without incident, we arrived at the home of Señora Mercedes. She lived with her 22-year-old daughter Dulce. Dulce was still single and living with her mother because, not too long before, her fiancé had died days before their wedding was supposed to take place. Both Señora Mercedes and Dulce were very friendly and kind-hearted people and helpful to everyone. I felt more relaxed there. It wasn't a luxurious house, but it was the most comfortable place I had been in the last few weeks. We had food to eat and a bed to sleep in and an actual bathroom where I could bathe and take care of my needs indoors rather than in a river.

I got along really well with Dulce. She even helped me do my makeup a couple of times. That same day, the *Coyota* called my family and asked them to send her more money to buy clothes for Gaby and me. I had overheard her conversations but still didn't understand why she was doing that. We shouldn't have needed more clothes. She had told us that she would later bring us the rest of our belongings. It turned out that it was part of a plan to ask my aunts for more money. I realized that Doña Roberta would not be bringing our things. Now all I had were the clothes that I was wearing. I was furious. My sweater was comfortable and warm and had been all I had to keep warm on some nights. Also, I had no way to call my aunts and tell them the reason why we needed more clothes and how Doña Roberta was only trying to get more money out of them.

My aunts sent her money, and she gave us some of it to buy clothes at the market. She kept the rest for herself. Dulce went with me to the market, but I was afraid the whole time. I didn't speak in public, so that people wouldn't realize that I was Honduran. I bought a black skirt, a purple shirt, and a pair of shoes with clear plastic toes and a small heel. The clothes weren't comfortable at all, but I bought them hoping that they would help me go unnoticed. In my mind, they would help me look more Mexican and less like a *mojada*.

Two days later, we left Señora Mercedes and headed to Villahermosa. Doña Roberta, my sister, Rebeca, Noemí, and I traveled in the same group, while everyone else would depart on the next bus. As we were traveling to a city on a busier highway, I decided to wear my new clothes and put on makeup to avoid looking like a *mojada*. I hid my passport in the waistband of my skirt. I had a bunch of coins, and my skirt didn't have deep pockets. I tried to hand them over to Gaby, but she wouldn't take them, which made me a little upset. I managed to put them in the two small pockets of my skirt as best as I could. I suggested that Gaby sit next to the *Coyota* because I felt she would be safer with her. As we had been instructed not to sit together, I sat in a seat away from the group.

As the bus made its way, I repeated in my mind what I should say in case an immigration agent asked me the city and state I was from and the town where I was going.

"*Soy de Palenque, Chiapas, y voy hasta Villahermosa*" (I'm from Palenque, Chiapas, and I'm going to Villahermosa) I repeated in my mind.

Minutes later, the bus stopped, and two officers got on to check documents. By that time, the sun had gone down and so it was very dark on the bus. The officers used flashlights to check our faces. They shined a light onto my sister's face, but they didn't ask her for anything. I knew that they wouldn't because she looked too young.

One officer approached me and asked for my travel documents. I tried to stammer through my rehearsed lines, but I was so scared that I had forgotten what I was supposed to say.

The other officer continued his flashlight review of the faces of the other passengers. He stopped and asked both Noemí and Rebeca for their travel documents. Even though we were seated separately, the three of us were taken off the bus.

Standing there in the dark of night on the side of the road, I felt more fearful with every second. Other officers arrived and continued to question us. Rebeca and Noemí were able to repeat their lines, but it only made the officers laugh. It was evident that they knew we were *mojadas*. They told us they were arresting us and that they would take us to a temporary holding cell with other detained Central Americans.

As we stood there, the bus pulled back onto the highway and continued on its route with the *Coyota* and my sister still inside. My heart dropped as I watched the bus drive away. I didn't know if I would ever see Gaby again. I had no idea how I, a 16-year-old girl, would ever be able to find her in that large and unknown country.

11

Deportation

After the bus to Villahermosa drove off, the immigration officials who had detained us escorted us into the station there at the checkpoint. We were inside a room that was a combination of an office and jail. We were led to stand in front the desk, close to the door where we had entered. The immigration officers continued to make fun of us for a while, as it was evident that Noemí, Rebeca, and I weren't Mexican. At that point, I didn't care about their jokes, nor their lack of empathy for our situation. All I could think about was the bus that had just left with my little sister on board.

The officers continued to ask me where I was from, as I still had not answered that question. Suddenly, I remembered what the *Coyota* told me to say.

"*Soy de Palenque!*" (I am from Palenque!) I answered.

One of the officers burst out laughing, as my very Honduran accent exposed my obvious lie. Still, I kept my passport tucked inside my skirt, and nothing in this world would convince me to voluntarily hand it over to the immigration officers.

Behind and to the left of the officials who were interrogating us, we could see the cell where we were going to be locked up. The cell was nearly full of both women and men. Many of them stared us down from the cell while they lobbed catcalls, obscenities, and vulgar invitations at the three of us. As I stood petrified, I silently and fervently prayed to God, asking for His help and mercy.

One of the immigration agents standing behind the desk was a tall, thin, light-skinned man with a stubbly beard and a wicked look in his eye. He tried to flirt with me and told me there was a disco nearby, and that if I wanted to, I could go with him. I didn't know what to answer. No matter how hard I tried to speak, each time I would open my mouth, I couldn't emit even the smallest sound. My dread and revulsion had rendered me mute. Without meeting his gaze, I managed to shake my head no to reject his vile invitation.

Rebeca—the eldest of the three of us—tried to comfort us. She was so afraid, that any of her words of comfort or affirmations that we would be safe seemed absurd. Noemí was also panic stricken, and I could see the alarm in her eyes.

"Please, God, don't let them hurt us," she quietly prayed out loud.

"There are too many people here; the boss said to take these three to the other facility," announced an officer.

God had heard our prayers! There were so many immigrants at that checkpoint that they decided to move us to another location.

After a few moments, a police pickup truck arrived. It had bars welded around the bed to form a cage so that the prisoners couldn't escape. The three of us were loaded onto the truck bed along with a few other people from the station. It all seemed like a bad dream, and I was so scared. Once I got into the truck bed's cage, I curled up and began to cry. I continued to beg God not to leave me alone and to protect my sister and me.

After a fairly short ride, we arrived at the immigration detention center, which was larger than the checkpoint. The cage was opened; we climbed down and were taken inside. In the cell area, there were two large rooms facing each other. The front wall of each room was made of iron bars, with a barred door, just like I had seen in Mexican soap operas. One cell was for men and the other for women. I was relieved to see that at least we wouldn't be locked in the same cell as the men. We walked one by one into that gloomy room full of nauseating smells. There were several women inside. It looked like they had been there for a couple of days already. I sat down on a cold cement bench and asked one of the detainees how long they had been there.

"We've been here for three days now," replied one of them, seemingly discouraged.

That answer shattered my little remaining hope. None of us three said a word for a while. I needed to use the bathroom, but I waited as long as I could. I didn't want to add any more horrific experiences to my current situation than were absolutely necessary. Unfortunately, I got to the point where I could no longer hold it, so I walked toward a door on the left-hand side of the cell to what seemed to be the restroom.

The room was dark, with only a dim light from a lamp in the hallway coming through the barred door. I could barely see anything, though I wasn't completely sure I wanted to. It reeked of urine, feces, blood, and an assortment of other noxious odors. You could tell that they hadn't cleaned the place in a long time. There was no seat, and to avoid sitting directly on the toilet rim, I had to hover while balancing on my legs in a half squat. Upon finishing, I washed my hands with water only, as there was no soap, let alone a towel to dry my hands.

I walked out of the bathroom and back to the cement bench. I was completely drained. I lay on my left side while staring at the main door that would lead to freedom from that place. I was a bit cold, so I tried to cover my legs using the longest part of my skirt. I curled up as much as I could, hoping to find a more comfortable and warmer position, but nothing really helped.

The men from the neighboring cell didn't stop leering at us and lobbing obscene catcalls at us all night. They shouted, "*Mamacita, mi reina, let me see your legs.*" I couldn't sleep, even though I was exhausted.

That night, some women slept on the floor, while others were standing or sitting in a corner of the cell. They all looked overwhelmed mixed with some combination of sleep deprived, filthy, starving, and hopeless. The night went by more slowly than any night I had ever known. Each hour seemed like a day in that place. I continued my silent prayers through the entire night.

Early in the morning, before dawn, two officers came over to the cells.

"It's time to go!" shouted one of them.

I felt some hope at the thought of getting out of there, though it was mixed with a dose of fear because we still didn't know where they would take us. It was still dark outside even though it felt like I had been in that cell for two full nights by then. They loaded us into a large, clean, and comfortable charter bus. I was very worried, not knowing where we would go, but at least I was no longer inside that putrid cell.

Men and women alike were loaded onto the bus. Rebeca and Noemí sat together in one row, and I ended up in the back row of seats. As I walked down the aisle, a depraved-looking man made note of me as easy prey and ogled me up and down. I sat down next to a young man, who gave me a slight smile. He asked me my name. "Keyla," I said so softly that it was almost a whisper. I was afraid to even say my name.

In what I knew was an answer to prayers, the driver's helper—a younger man who was carrying a rifle—realized the danger I was in sitting there in the back by myself. He motioned for me and told me to sit in the front of the bus, next to the driver. He also offered me his coat.

His kindness made me feel safer. Lying there on the seat while under my newfound protection, I was finally able to sleep. I slept the entire trip until the bus arrived at its destination, and we were escorted off.

Rebeca, Noemí, and I stood in the bus terminal where they had left us. Panic was starting to set in. We didn't know what we should do or where we should go. We knew we were in Guatemala, because the bus ride wasn't long enough to get us to Honduras or El Salvador, but we had no idea in what part of the country we were.

"We should find a payphone," suggested Noemí.

It was at that moment that I remembered the $20 bill that my aunt had given me before leaving us in Guatemala. I also had the coins that were still in my skirt pockets. I felt very grateful that Gaby had refused to take them back when we boarded the bus to Villahermosa. Had I given them to Gaby, we would have been even worse off.

With the coins, I was able to use the payphone, and with the $20, we ate breakfast. I dialed the number of my aunt Míriam, who lived in North Carolina with my grandmother. Before leaving La Entrada, I had memorized my aunts' phone numbers in case of an emergency. The phone started to ring and, after a couple of seconds, I heard La Hita's voice answer on the other end. On hearing her voice, I was overtaken by a feeling of deep sadness, and I wanted to cry, but I contained myself.

"I was deported, and I am back in Guatemala. I don't know where Gaby is, but she is with Doña Roberta. I'm fine, don't worry. Tell my aunt Míriam that I will call her back as soon as I can. I don't have any more coins left to call you, and the call will be disconnected soon." I hung up.

I didn't even let her talk. I didn't want her to worry, and the few coins I had were just enough for a one-minute call. I had no idea what to do after hanging up. I knew that I needed to find Gaby some way or another. Noemí, Rebeca, and I started walking away from the bus terminal, with no apparent destination in mind.

"Keyla, Keyla, Keyla!" I heard someone shouting my name from a distance.

I didn't want to turn around, but something told me that I needed to. When I turned around, I realized it was the same man who had asked me my name on the bus. He ran over to us and asked us if we knew where to go. We told him that we had no idea where we were.

"My name is David, and my cousin and I are *coyotes*. If you want, we can give you a ride in our van," he said.

"But we don't have any money," I replied.

He told us not to worry, that we didn't have to pay him. I felt relieved but a little suspicious of the offer at the same time. Rebeca, Noemí, and I quickly huddled to discuss David's proposal, and we decided to go. We walked toward the van and immediately got in. The van started, and I was forced to close the window because the dust was blowing in. I was covered in dirt and dust, and once again I was starting to look like the street kids who sell gum and trinkets in the bus terminals. My feet ached. It turned out that buying those sandals was the worst choice I could have made.

"What was I thinking?" I questioned myself.

I tried to sleep on the ride, but David sat down next to me and tried to start up a conversation, so I was unable to get any rest. David was about 25 years old, although he looked older. He asked me my age. I lied and told him I was 18. Our somewhat awkward conversation continued until, eventually, we arrived in the municipality of Huehuetenango. David and his uncle rented a room for the three of us in the same hotel where he and his group would spend the night. Beyond paying for the room, later that evening, they brought us some food for dinner.

That evening, I took advantage of the chance to take a hot shower at the hotel. It felt so good! I washed my skirt, too, and left it drying in the bathroom. I kept my shirt on and the black spandex shorts I was wearing under the skirt and got into bed to take a long nap. Shortly after I woke up, David came into the room to talk to me. I didn't know what to do because my skirt was still wet, and I didn't have anything else to wear. I stayed in the bed, under the sheets, the whole time he was there. It was becoming clear to me that David was interested in me, and Noemí and Rebeca noticed it as well. Nevertheless, he was always very respectful and polite.

David told me that he became a *coyote* after his sister tried to emigrate to the United States. Tragically, while traveling she was raped by a man with whom she had crossed paths somewhere on her journey. David told me that he dreamed of finding that man and avenging what had been done to his sister.

That is why David and his uncle, after seeing our situation, felt that they should help us as much as they could. He offered to take me with him and his group to cross the border but that it would cost me $1,500. I told him I didn't have the money, and that I couldn't go with him. Then he told me that he loved me. He said he didn't know how or why, but that's how he felt there in the moment.

"That's not possible, David. We've just met," I replied to his rash and rushed declaration.

I talked to him about my religion and my beliefs about taking care of my body, and how I believed in chastity. He understood and didn't try to push it any further. He was respectful of my beliefs and was a complete gentleman with me. Our conversation finished, and he had to leave to run an errand with his uncle.

On the following day, David and his uncle left with their group. It was a collection of seven *mojados*. I never spoke to any of them, but I did know from my conversations with David that they had all come from El Salvador.

Rebeca, Noemí, and I stayed there at the hotel. From there, we called collect to our families in the U.S. They wired us money for food and transportation to travel to La Ciudad de Guatemala, the country's capital. After calculating what we would need, we realized that there was enough extra money for us to go to a beauty salon. Rebeca got a haircut, and I decided to bleach the top layer of my hair a lighter color. I left the salon looking almost completely blonde. I had already lightened my hair to brown back in Honduras. Growing up, I had never liked my hair's natural black color.

My new look served as therapy for me. After the ordeal of being arrested and deported, the afternoon in the salon gave me a small break from feeling like a *mojada*. I was able to forget my fear and anxiety for a little while and imagine that I was visiting the town and getting ready to meet my family. I didn't feel like a *mojada* but more like a tourist, at least for that short time.

Later in the afternoon, we set off in a bus for La Ciudad de Guatemala. My aunt Rafaela and her husband would arrive on a plane from Miami that same day. My family in the U.S. was very worried about me and about what had happened. My aunts had decided that my aunt Rafaela would travel to connect with me in Guatemala. So, we embarked on a six-hour bus ride to La Ciudad de Guatemala to meet her.

Upon arriving in the city, we took a cab to the airport to meet my aunt and her husband, Javier. When I saw my aunt Rafaela, I ran and hugged her. Tears welled up in my eyes, and I started to shake uncontrollably once in her arms. I was overcome with relief and excitement when I was finally able to meet up with someone in my family. I was suddenly full of hope again that I would soon be reunited with the rest of my family.

I introduced Rebeca and Noemí to my aunt and her husband, and then we all went to a nearby hotel. My aunt rented a hotel room for my friends, and I stayed in a room with her and her husband.

"Keyla, you're so skinny; you look like a skeleton!" said my aunt upon seeing me.

She couldn't disguise her look of shock when she saw me. My legs were full of mosquito bites, and my lips were dried and cracked from dehydration and exposure to the sun. My whole family was angry at the *Coyota* for her treatment of Gaby and me. Rebeca and Noemí also shared their experiences from the journey with my aunt. They told her how Doña Roberta kept us in the same place for days while she would call to ask our families for additional money, telling them she needed more money to continue on our journey.

The following day, we would head back toward the Mexican border. We would travel back to Villahermosa to meet up with my sister and the rest of our group. This time, I felt much safer with the company of my aunt and her husband.

12

Return Journey

We woke up very early in the morning, after a good night's rest. I felt much calmer with my aunt there with me. I no longer felt like I was living a nightmare as I had just a few days before while I was in the process of being arrested and deported by Mexican immigration officials. Furthermore, my aunt was able to get in contact with the *Coyota* and determine that Gaby was safe and waiting for me. With that, I was able to move past the fear of not seeing my sister ever again.

My aunt purchased bus tickets from La Ciudad de Guatemala to El Naranjo, the town near the Guatemalan and Mexican border where we had stayed at the home of the González family back near the beginning of our trip as *mojados*. This time around, I was determined to pay more attention to our route and where we would be going, as we no longer had the *Coyota* with us to be our guide, and I was less and less sure that we should trust her anyway.

The route of the bus went east before turning north and brought us close to the Honduran border. From my window on the bus, I saw a sign indicating the direction and distance to Honduras. At that moment, it dawned on me that I was closer to La Entrada, my house, and my friends than to Villahermosa and my sister. Even still, I knew I wasn't returning to my country. I had gone through way too much to give up now. I was determined to reach my final destination and see La Hita again.

We arrived in the dusty town of El Naranjo, and to my surprise, José David was waiting there for us. He had brought the backpack that I had left behind in Dulce's home before I had gotten on the bus to Villahermosa and been apprehended. It had a set of clean clothes and my tennis shoes. I once again had something comfortable to walk in.

José David was there because Doña Roberta had sent him to bring us back to Mexico, though he wasn't too happy about it. She knew that

Noemí was his responsibility and that he couldn't say no. It would delay him in his journey and put him at greater risk of being deported just as we had been.

My aunt and her husband had come with us to El Naranjo, but they did not stay with us at the González house. Instead, they told us we would meet later near the San Pedro River and went up ahead of us.

We spent only one night there in the house with the González family. The next day, I changed my clothes, and we headed out of town toward the border. We took a small local bus and drove past the turn-off to the deserted road in the middle of nowhere that we had traveled via the tractor previously. I remembered the stories the tractor driver had recounted of rape and murder. I was so relieved that we didn't have to take that path again.

We arrived at the riverbank where my aunt told us we would meet. There were a number of small eateries and docks with boats. We had lunch and waited a few hours until José David found a boat to take us upriver near the border of Mexico and Guatemala. The four of us *mojados* would travel to the *rancho* by boat so we could cross the border back into Mexico from there.

My aunt and Don Javier didn't come with us on the boat, nor would they have to find an alternate way to cross into Mexico. They both had United States passports, which allowed them to easily move between the countries at official immigration checkpoints. My aunt Rafaela told me that she and her husband couldn't accompany us the whole way because, with their U.S. passports, they could be arrested for smuggling. She told me they would remain close by us as we traveled the rest of the way through Mexico, and she would stop by to check in on Gaby and me when she could.

We got in the boat José David had arranged for us to travel in. The boat started, and 30 minutes later we were close to the Mexican border. We got out and walked the short distance to the *rancho* house.

We arrived at the house, and I sat on the porch and recalled the bitter days I had recently spent there. My horrible birthday crying in the barn, almost losing my shoes, and the days and days of waiting. This time, thankfully, we wouldn't even be spending the night.

The *pulpería* that overcharged us was closed, and there were a few other people in the house at the time. We didn't stay for very long because we had to keep going toward the border, and the night and darkness were fast approaching. As we left the *rancho*, I almost couldn't believe we had gone from La Ciudad de Guatemala to the Mexican border in less than two days. In our first attempt, it took us 10 days to leave the *rancho* on the way to the border.

The looks on José David's and everyone else's faces weren't very excited. We were all tired and angry over the situation we were in. We had to get to the Mexican border, and we knew it was nearby. We didn't go by boat that time, but we hiked along a small and rough dirt road that passed near the *rancho* and continued across the border. We had seen numerous groups of people with bookbags take that same path heading toward Mexico. After about 20 minutes of walking, we were stopped by a trio of Guatemalan immigration officers and asked for our passports. We were not worried, because we were still on the Guatemalan side of the border, and thanks to the visa stamps in our passports, we had legal status to be in the country. They checked the visas in our passports and let us go. A few minutes later, that legal status ran out as we arrived at the big "Welcome to Mexico" sign.

Both sides of the border were full of local residents selling food, souvenirs, and any number of other things from booths and makeshift stands. When we arrived, the sun was already setting, and the merchants were packing up their stands to head home. We were able to persuade one of the vendors, on his way home to a town further into Mexico, to give us a ride in the back of his truck. Riding in the back of the pickup was faster than walking. I would have loved to continue this "shortcut" all the way to the town, but we could not because there was a Mexican immigration checkpoint on the road, before arriving at the man's town.

In Mexico, the borders are fairly easy to cross, as the main immigration enforcement happens at checkpoints that are along main roads and highways several miles inland from the actual border. On our first trip through, the multi-day hike through the jungle was to avoid one of these checkpoints. This time, it appeared that we would be able to avoid that nightmare of a hike through the hot and humid forest.

Before sending him back to get us, Doña Roberta had instructed José David on where to go and with whom to stay. Before reaching the checkpoint, the truck stopped near a large, leafy avocado tree, and we all got off there. We expressed our gratitude to the vendor. Noemí, Rebeca, and I stayed under the tree while José David decided to talk to the owner of the house where the *Coyota* had told us to stay. After about 15 minutes, José David came back with sad news. The owner wouldn't let us stay there. According to her, the *Coyota* repeatedly failed to pay her when she had allowed previous groups to stay in the house, and the owner of the house was no longer willing to accommodate Doña Roberta or the people who traveled with her.

Rebeca was very nervous. It was getting dark, and none of us really liked the idea of spending the night outdoors, with no roof over our heads. I leaned against the tree and asked God for help once again. At that point, I had lost count of the number of times I had asked Him for His help and protection during the trip.

Rebeca decided to talk to the owner. She explained that she was traveling with two teenage girls and begged her to let us spend the night. After Rebeca's tearful begging, the owner of the house took pity on us; she agreed to let us sleep inside a small storage room outside of her house. We had to sleep on the hard ground, and we had nothing to use to cover ourselves. However, it was better than sleeping outdoors, at risk of being harmed by a dangerous animal or a person.

That night, I slept next to José David. I hugged him and kissed him a lot. I didn't care what my aunt would think if she found out. It was cold and dark, and I felt lonely, but the warmth of José David's body and the softness of his lips made me feel better.

"A tarantula! There's a tarantula! Kill it, please!"

We all woke up suddenly to Rebeca screaming. In a corner of the room close to where Rebeca had been sleeping, we saw a tarantula that was bigger than my hand. I was very scared. José David grabbed his shoe and got up to kill the spider. It took a few minutes, but he finally succeeded, and we were able to go back to sleep, the four of us side by side on that cold floor.

The following morning, I awoke to hear the *Coyota*'s voice in the distance as she spoke to the owner of the house. I didn't understand exactly what they were talking about, but I could tell that it was Doña Roberta who was there. When we joined them, the *Coyota* told us that she had arranged a guide to walk us back to the house with the firewood shed.

We were told we had to leave right away, so we didn't get anything for breakfast that morning. We ended up walking for about four hours, with only the water bottle that we were carrying. I was starving, but there was nothing I could do about it. At least this time we didn't have to go up and down the steep hills. We were walking closer to the road and not deep in the jungle, because the terrain was much flatter. When we arrived at the house, Doña Roberta was already there waiting for us. Without giving us much time to rest, she led us to the bus stop, where we took a small local bus to our next stop.

We got off the bus, crossed a red metal fence, and walked for about two minutes until we reached an old house. A couple welcomed us with a plate of beans and eggs. It was very simple meal, but after walking all morning without anything to eat, my stomach was grateful for that food.

After we ate, Rebeca, Noemí, and I went to take a shower in a metal *pila* in the front yard. We were outdoors, so we left our underwear on to shower. Rebeca told us that young women shouldn't let anyone touch their breasts, because they will become soft. Rebeca and Noemí both asked me if anyone had ever touched mine, and I denied it.

Maybe it was partly because my breasts weren't as firm as they thought they should be, but mostly they asked because they wanted to know what kind of relationship I was having with José David, and they didn't dare ask me straight out.

Only once as a teenager had someone touched me on my breasts. It was a boy I liked, but it was traumatic, as he did it without my permission. I didn't say anything to him because I was so shocked by his actions, especially because he was a Christian. After that, I never let a boyfriend or a friend touch me there again.

After showering, we waited in the house for a few hours, ate again, and then took a bus to the house of Doña Mercedes. I was excited to get going because it meant that we wouldn't have to spend the night again in the wooden hut. Everything on the trip went smoothly, as no immigration officers stopped us.

Doña Roberta had us travel on small local buses to avoid immigration stops and checkpoints. Small buses that used local roads to go from town to town weren't inspected as much as the larger buses that went directly from city to city. Even still, we felt lucky that during this leg of our trip, no one stopped our bus.

We arrived at Doña Mercedes's house, where she lived with her daughter Dulce. I was happy to greet them. It was a pleasant but unexpected reunion because when I had last left their house, I never thought I would see them again.

Also, to my surprise, Nancy and Roxana were still living there in the house. They had decided they would stay in Mexico long enough to obtain visas to remain in the country. That way, it would be easier for them to travel through Mexico to the U.S. border.

The reunion with Nancy was far less pleasant, as we still weren't on good terms. True to form, she didn't wait long to criticize me and to tell Rebeca that her new haircut didn't look good.

We spent one night there, and the following day we took another local bus. This time, we avoided the checkpoint where I had been detained and deported to Guatemala. We arrived at a small, makeshift bus terminal with food vendors and rested a little while the *Coyota* found a ride to Villahermosa, where the remainder of the group was waiting on us.

While waiting, right next to where I was sitting, I saw an *esperanza*—a type of small cricket that doesn't jump as high as a grasshopper. In Honduras, we have a belief that seeing one of these is a sign of upcoming good luck or fortune. The name *esperanza* literally translates to *hope*. I smiled and said a quick, heartfelt thanks to God. I was sure that this was one of His signs of comfort.

The *Coyota* came back with someone who would give us a ride. We rode in the back of a cargo truck, and I was feeling more confident. Something inside was telling me that the journey would be easier. No one stopped us, and we made it to Villahermosa safe and sound. We headed toward the area in the city where Gaby and the others were staying. I was so happy to see my sister again, and we hugged each other tightly like we hadn't done in a long time.

"You're so thin, Keyla! You look like a walking skeleton!" Gaby exclaimed.

13

Christmas Day

The *Coyota* brought José David, Noemí, Rebeca, and me to the house of Don Francisco, located in a nondescript neighborhood in the city of Villahermosa. Francisco was a kind and generous man. He was always carrying a Bible under his arm, so I knew he was a devout Christian. His house was humble, and he always kept it clean and tidy. He had a metal barrel filled with water in front of the main door and a washing rack to do the laundry next to it. I thought it was curious that they didn't have *pilas* there, like the houses in Honduras did.

My sister continued to tell me how thin I looked. To me, it also looked like she had lost weight, but not as much as I had. Throughout the entire trip, we hadn't eaten enough. During my second trip up from Guatemala, I had even less to eat than the first time through. Luckily, I didn't have to walk as much compared to the first time. When I left Honduras, I used to wear size three pants. That day when I saw my sister again in Villahermosa, my size three jeans were so big on me that I had to use a shoelace as a makeshift belt to keep them up. I tried not to focus on it, but deep down I knew that we weren't getting enough food and that we wouldn't last long like this.

I didn't give Gaby a lot of details about everything that happened after I was arrested and we were separated, and she didn't ask. On a trip like ours, sometimes the easiest thing to do was to focus on the goal and try and forget the rest. Even with Rebeca and Noemí, I didn't talk about all that we had gone through and seen. Even good people like David weren't mentioned again.

During our return trip, Gaby and Dunia had gone through their own difficult time. They had been staying together for most of that time in a rundown motel in a rundown part of the city. There had been more than one day when they went without eating. I didn't see the motel where they spent the week, but based on my sister's expression as she remembered the place, I thanked God that they had moved over to Francisco's home by the time we got there.

We were beginning to realize the *Coyota*'s true nature: she was a heartless woman focused only on how she could get more money, and not even her own daughter could be saved from her greed. For the entire trip, she had consistently been calling our families, asking for more money, claiming that it was needed for food, lodging, and transportation. (This was on top of the thousands of dollars that had already been paid for each of us.) Whatever message was being given to our families, our lived experience was much different.

Transportation on the local buses was literally the cheapest option except for walking, which we also had done a lot. Our food was basic and limited. We were mostly fed by the owners of the homes where we were staying. Unfortunately, some of those people had been the victims of the *Coyota* as well. More than once we were told by Doña Roberta to get up and leave before dawn, fairly sure that we were skipping out on the bill. On more than one occasion we had to go an entire day without any food.

It was getting harder for me to hide my contempt for Doña Roberta. She was the exact opposite of La Hita. When I was growing up, my grandmother had taught me to always help those who were in need. If someone was hungry, she would always give that person something to eat, even if it meant taking it from her own plate.

As time went by, Doña Roberta didn't care to hide how much she disliked me and, because she was my friend, Noemí as well. She only put up with us only because we represented money to her. I never knew what she did with all the money that our family sent her, because we were increasingly in need. As the days passed, she was less willing to do much to help improve our situation, though she took every opportunity to complain to us that the money our families were sending wasn't enough. On top of that, every setback and stated need (replacing clothes that were lost or left behind, feminine hygiene products, etc.) she used as an excuse to call and ask for more money.

Don Francisco welcomed us into his home. On top of that, he cooked and served us food from what little he had. Doña Roberta met him working at the motel where my sister and the rest of the group stayed while waiting for the rest of us to return after our deportation to Guatemala. He knew that a group of *mojados* staying long term in a motel would arouse suspicions and that someone could easily call the immigration authorities. By staying with him in his home, we would be a lot safer from the risk of being deported back to Guatemala, or worse, back to Honduras. Doña Roberta didn't think twice about taking advantage of this man's Christian goodness in order to save more money.

At Francisco's house, we ate a little more regularly, but not always. We knew that he didn't have the money to feed an entire group of people three times a day, and it wasn't his responsibility to do so either. The *Coyota*, who handled all the money and who did have the responsibility to get us food, was never around. During the four days or so we were there, we barely saw her. We were starving and desperate and decided that we would have to go out to beg for food in the street.

There in Villahermosa, like the rest of the places where we stayed in Mexico, we didn't go out or get to know the city we were in. With our Honduran accents, being out in public and talking to people would make us easily recognized as *mojados*. Being a *mojada* is not like being a tourist. For us, our priority of getting through the hundreds of miles north to the U.S. was far more important than some simple sightseeing. We decided we would have to venture out this time, however, because our short-term goal of not starving was more important in that moment.

We found a small church not far from Don Francisco's house, and we decided to go there to ask for food. We sat on a short fence across the street while we planned how, when, and who we should ask for food.

It was Christmastime, and people in that part of Mexico would serve roasted lamb as a Christmas tradition. To the side of the church, they were roasting the lamb and serving plates to members of the congregation. My stomach was churning and aching, and the smell of roasted lamb completely hypnotized me. I'm not sure if it was our scraggly (and now baggy) clothes or our worn and hungry faces that gave us away (or maybe both), but one of the churchgoers approached us and asked us if we would like some food. All of us nodded vigorously, and they brought a plate of food for each one of us. It was a feast fit for a queen.

While in Villahermosa, I was able to see my aunt and her husband again. They had told me they would be close by, but I hadn't seen them since the river trip at the Guatemalan border. I knew they were around, but it made me sad that they couldn't be with us all the time because it would be too dangerous for everyone. The larger our group was, the more it would arouse suspicion. At the same time, if immigration officials found people with U.S. passports with a group of *mojados*, they might charge them for being *coyotes*.

A couple of days after we had the lamb at the church, my aunt Rafaela and Don Javier showed up to take me, and then later Gaby, to an open-air clothing market. Our clothes were in bad shape, and we were trying to avoid looking like *mojadas* before our next bus trip. I bought some black pants, a button-up shirt, and a pair of black wedge sandals with thick elastic straps. I was excited that I wouldn't always have to wear my now really worn-out tennis shoes. Besides, the sandals were more comfortable. That time, I did not ask my aunt to buy me any makeup. I had stopped wearing makeup because it made me look older. I had felt that one of the reasons the immigration officials pulled me off the bus the day I was deported was because I had looked like an adult. Though I couldn't deny that in some ways feeling older sometimes gave me more of a sense of security.

After they had taken both of us to get our clothes, my aunt Rafaela gave me another $20 bill to hide in my bra and left us with the group. Christmas was approaching, and I couldn't help but feel homesick when I realized that I wouldn't be able to be with my family for the holidays. I wasn't the only one, as everyone in the group was feeling that regret of not being able to be with their loved ones. I tried to focus on my main goal and find some comfort in repeating a mantra that a good friend from church had given me: "Big goals require big sacrifices."

December 24th arrived, and no one really said anything. Everyone did their best to hide their sorrow, and we all tried to collectively ignore the fact that it was Christmas. On a bright note, we were told that we would be leaving for Veracruz by buses throughout the day. The *Coyota* had us travel in groups of three to avoid suspicion. Gaby left with Dunia and the *Coyota* in the morning.

At around 9 p.m. that night, it was my turn to go. As usual, Noemí and I traveled in the same group. I spent my Christmas on a bus; sitting by myself, and without even my sister, I felt more alone than ever. There were no family gatherings, no *tamales*, no neighbors to visit, and no fireworks. On my way to the bus stop, I heard a few firecrackers in the distance and imagined that it came from a happy family gathering somewhere. Even though it was a difficult Christmas for me, and I would have much preferred to be shooting off fireworks with La Hita and my sister in La Entrada, I was doing what I had to do to reach my goal, and I trusted that God would get me there.

Veracruz was a couple of hours away from Villahermosa. On the bus, I sat away from Doña Roberta. About 30 minutes into the ride, the bus stopped at a police checkpoint and an immigration officer boarded

the bus. I closed my eyes and pretended I was asleep. I prayed to God
to help me go unnoticed and unseen if possible. The officer turned on
his flashlight, quickly scanned the bus, and then miraculously turned
around and got off the bus. We were able to continue on our way, and
the rest of the trip went by without any further incidents. I wanted to
believe that things were starting to look up and that the rest of the trip
would be a little easier than it had been so far.

Just before midnight, we arrived in the coastal city of Veracruz and
made our way to the motel in the dark. Our group spent the next few
days in a motel room with several beds, enough for our slowly shrinking group. At that point, it had been more than a month since we had
left Honduras, and only seven out of the 11 *mojados* remained.

Óscar had decided to stay in Villahermosa because he didn't want
to continue dealing with Doña Roberta. He felt his best bet was to
continue on his own and find another *coyote* to help him. Nancy and
Roxana had remained at Doña Mercedes's, and the young man from
Guatemala had only stayed for a few days. Only Dunia, Rebeca, José
David, Noemí, Daniel, Gaby, and I were left in our group. I never heard
what had become of the other four. I do not know if they ever made it
to the United States or returned home. Wherever they are, I hope that
they found success and happiness in their lives.

On the morning of December 25th, my aunt and her husband, now
also in Veracruz, wanted to give us some time with family at Christmas. They took us to walk on the boardwalk down at the beach. However, we still had to maintain a distance from each other in case the
police or immigration officers showed up. So, my aunt and her husband
walked a few yards ahead of us the whole time. At this point, I was used
to all the precautions we had to take, so being "together" with them,
even if yards away, was still a relief and a source of hope for me.

As we walked along the boardwalk on that cloudy and breezy day,
I could not fully enjoy what a beautiful country I was in. All the time,
I knew in the back of my mind that I was considered a fugitive and an
undesirable for the simple reason that I lacked a specific stamp in my
passport. I was reminded one more time of how vulnerable I was when
a man approached Gaby and me and asked us if we were "available." He
thought we were prostitutes. Once again, I felt God's protection from a
tragedy too common for many teenage *mojada* girls. This time our protection was having Aunt Rafaela and her husband close by. They were
very real angels sent from heaven on Christmas Day.

14

Good Samaritan

After a couple of days in Veracruz, we headed for Poza Rica de Hidalgo. Since Villahermosa, we had been traveling on larger city-to-city buses, and except for one quick checkpoint on Christmas, our luck in avoiding immigration officials was holding out. On my last day in Villahermosa, I saw several *esperanzas,* and they were a sign, a way for God to tell me that we would make it.

In Poza Rica, the *Coyota* took us to a small building that had been converted into a motel. The next morning, I checked to make sure that the $20 bill my aunt had given me in Veracruz was still in my bra, but it wasn't there. I started to panic, but then I thought it had fallen out when I was sleeping. I checked the sheets and blankets and under the bed but didn't find the bill. I double-checked my bra, including the small pockets for the foam pads, but there was nothing. I asked Gaby, but she didn't know anything. I went to ask the others, but no one had seen it.

"Why didn't you tell me you had $20?" asked Doña Roberta in an accusatory tone.

I answered back that I carried some money for an emergency, and I didn't need to explain myself to her. The *Coyota* gave me a quick, sinister grin, then turned and walked away. I could not help feeling that she had found and kept the money. At that point, I understood the reason people had been so surprised that my family had agreed to hire her as our *coyota.* She was a greedy woman, willing to lie, cheat, and steal for an extra dollar. What's worse, Doña Roberta had the gift of persuasion. After she first cheated someone, she would then go back and convince them that the next time would be different, so that she could cheat them out of more money.

As for me, my worst Christmas continued. I felt bad because I had lost the money, but even more so because the money was my emergency fund in case I was deported by the police or abandoned by the *Coyota*. Now I wouldn't be able to pay for a motel, food, or transportation in an emergency.

The following night, I was feeling even more down, and homesick for my friends in Honduras. I decided to head outside and looked for a payphone. I used the last few coins I had in my pockets to call my friend Leticia in La Entrada. The coins were enough to talk for only a few minutes. I told her that I was getting closer to the U.S. border and that if anyone in town asked, she should tell them that I had successfully crossed. I was trying to convince myself of that exact reality: everything would work out and my trip would soon be over.

Two days later, we set off for Tampico—a city in the Mexican state of Tamaulipas. Doña Roberta told us that we would be staying at a house, although when we arrived, it looked more like a hotel than a house. It was a two-story building, and on the second floor, at the top of the stairs, there was a long hallway with several rooms on one side.

The house was owned by two trans women, Doña Elena and Doña Anabel. Given the way Doña Roberta interacted with them, she seemed to have known them for a long time. Our hosts welcomed us warmly with bright smiles and made us feel right at home. They made us feel like the center of attention, even though there were several men staying there in the house as well. Doña Elena offered us food and then gave us a large room where we would stay. It was one of the corner rooms and had a large window with a view of the main street below.

Doña Elena and Doña Anabel treated us like family, and one night they even invited us to watch TV with them. We watched the movie *Amores Perros,* a Mexican drama that was popular at the time. It was the first "normal" night I had had since leaving La Entrada, and I didn't want it to end. I was enjoying the moment so much that I stayed there to watch the whole movie, even though there were several scenes that made me uncomfortable. Later that night, I wished that I'd left and come to the room early like Dunia had done.

New Year's Eve came and went, and we were still there in Tampico, waiting for our next move. I had already resigned myself to another celebration without my family. At that point, I no longer cared about the holidays. I just wanted to get to my family and have this entire journey behind me. I didn't understand why the *Coyota* was keeping us in one place for so long. I wanted to believe she was waiting for the best time to move, but I was finding it hard to give her the benefit of the doubt anymore.

A couple of days later, Doña Roberta informed us after breakfast that we would be leaving that same day. She told us to get our things ready but that we should go quickly and without saying goodbye to anyone. I didn't quite understand why. Doña Elena, Doña Anabel, and many of the men staying there had treated us so well. They opened the doors of their home to us without caring that we were *mojados*. I wanted to thank them somehow for all they had done for us, even if it was just to say thank you. Upstairs in the room where Doña Roberta laid out the full plan of our exit, I finally understood what was happening. The *Coyota* didn't want to pay whatever she had agreed upon for our several days of room and board.

With a deep sigh, and a pang in my chest, I followed her directions, as there wasn't any other option. The plan was for us to head out front in pairs. Doña Roberta would then toss us our bookbags, which we had left in the bedroom, through the front window.

As I was heading out with Gaby, we ran into one of the men who was staying there. He asked us where we were going. I stammered a little, and then I clumsily invented the story that we were going for a walk and would be back soon. Outside, we grabbed our bags and ran away like common thieves.

I felt sad, embarrassed, and angry at the same time. I had been pulled into Doña Roberta's con of this kind group of people. It was unfair what Doña Roberta made us do after receiving so much hospitality and generosity. I never forgot about Doña Elena and Doña Anabel, and I believe that God always rewards people for their goodness and generosity. I will forever be grateful that our paths crossed.

We took another bus, and three hours later, we arrived in Ciudad Victoria, the capital of Tamaulipas. I thought we would head to another motel or a family home, but the *Coyota* shocked all of us when she led us to a Catholic church.

This time, through the help and generosity of the priest and the church members, we would stay in small groups at the homes of several families in the area. Noemí and I would stay together again. My sister Gaby was sent with Dunia to a different house, as Doña Roberta once again had separated the two of us.

The priest introduced us to a woman named Guadalupe, and she told Noemí and me that we were welcome in her home. Before heading off with her, we were reminded not to tell anyone that we were part of a larger group. If we were caught (or turned in), we didn't want to give information that could endanger the rest of the group.

Doña Guadalupe was a woman with a heart of gold. After we left the church, she took us to her mother's house for something to eat. We met her mother, another woman with a beautiful soul. Doña Guadalupe's mother welcomed us with open arms and cooked a traditional Mexican dinner for us. After dinner, we went to Doña Guadalupe's house, and she offered us her daughter's bedroom.

After getting settled, we sat down to talk with Doña Guadalupe in her kitchen. We told her that we were from Honduras and that we were going to the U.S. to be reunited with our families. Doña Guadalupe offered us coffee, which I declined by explaining that it was against my religion. She wanted to know more, and I told her a little about being a member of The Church of Jesus Christ of Latter-day Saints and how we are taught to take care of and value our body because it is our temple. We talked for a while about my beliefs and my church's teachings.

Speaking about my beliefs filled me with pride and passion. Doña Guadalupe enjoyed our conversation so much that she asked me to tell her son about my experiences. She was like an angel from heaven, sent by God to help us. Before going to sleep, I prayed for Doña Guadalupe and her family and thanked God for putting her in my path.

The following day, when we woke up, breakfast was ready for us. Doña Guadalupe had made scrambled eggs and *nopales. Nopal* is a type of cactus native to northern Mexico. The cactus pads are de-spined, chopped into small pieces, and roasted in a pan. Though I had never tried them, and I was nervous about eating a cactus, I didn't want to appear ungrateful, so I cleaned my plate. The truth is that they were pretty good.

Later we went with her to the market, and on the way home, Doña Guadalupe took us by a chapel of the Church of Jesus Christ of Latter-day Saints. She suggested that I talk to the bishop to see if there was any help or support he could provide. The bishop wasn't there, so we spoke with one of his counselors, but, unfortunately, he was unable to help.

I was ashamed and angry about having to ask for charity. My family was paying the *Coyota* to cover my sister's and my expenses, so I should not have been begging for food. We never told the truth to anyone about having a *Coyota* and family members closed by. We were told not to. We returned to Doña Guadalupe's house, and on the way there, I mentioned to her that I was also traveling with my younger sister. Without hesitation, she arranged to have Gaby brought to her house to stay with me. I couldn't have been more grateful.

On January 6, Mexicans celebrate Three Kings' Day, and Doña Guadalupe took us to eat *Rosca de Reyes* at a small local celebration that was being held outside of the neighborhood supermarket. A *Rosca de Reyes* is a sweet bread baked into a long oval shape (like a long and thick doughnut). In the bread, there is normally candied fruit and sweet cream. Also, baked inside the *rosca* are small plastic Baby Jesus figurines that symbolize when Joseph and Mary had to hide Jesus from King Herod. At the festival, we sat at a table to share the large *Rosca*. The tradition in Mexico is that everyone must cut their own piece, and if your piece contains the figurine of the Baby Jesus, then you are supposed to host a party on February 2 and provide all the *tamales* that your guests can eat.

At the table, Gaby cut her piece and found the figurine. We all laughed at the situation, as it was evident that she wouldn't be in Ciudad Victoria in February. It was the first time I had been at a *Rosca de Reyes* celebration, and I found it to be magical. Everything—the music, the decorations, the food, and the laughter—helped me to forget about my worries and our current situation. Gaby, Noemí, and I enjoyed ourselves a while and thanked Doña Guadalupe very much for the experience.

We spent a few more days at Guadalupe's house, and she was always kind and always loving. Her daughter Rosa was equally as kind as her mother. All those nights, she slept in her mother's room so that we could have her room. Rosa's closet was full of so many beautiful clothes. Looking in the closet made me so anxious to start wearing nice clothes again. I even felt the temptation to ask Rosa to give me something from her wardrobe, but I didn't dare. The family had given so much that it would have been extremely rude to ask for anything else.

When we finally left Ciudad Victoria, our next stop would be Matamoros on the Mexico-U.S. border. I was feeling rejuvenated and more hopeful. Despite the hardships and hopelessness that had accompanied a lot of my journey, I had come across amazing people full of love and grace. The past five weeks had been a nonstop rollercoaster of emotions for me. I had experienced loneliness, sorrow, hopelessness, with an almost constant fear; I had also felt the effects of greed—through the *Coyota's* actions. At the same time, I had encountered good people who demonstrated love, hospitality, joy, and hope.

Before saying goodbye to Doña Guadalupe and her family, I wrote down her phone number and email address on a piece of paper and put it in my bra, but I lost it before I arrived in the U.S. Unfortunately,

I wasn't able to keep my promise of staying touch and sending them something from the United States once I arrived. Even today, I remember them when I pray at night. I continue to ask God to protect them and bless them with love wherever they are. I hope that their lives have been blessed for their kindness and for helping us without expecting anything in return.

15

The Train

We took what I hoped would be our last Mexican bus ride to Matamoros at night. I tried to sleep on the bus to try and forget that the immigration authorities could arrest and deport us at any moment, although my concern over that had diminished as the days went by. Increasingly, I felt that my journey was in God's hands, and my confidence grew by the hour. Matamoros neighbors the U.S. city of Brownsville, Texas, and the two cities and countries are divided by the Rio Grande River.

Upon arriving, we took a taxi to a small house on the bank of the Rio Grande where we would spend the rest of the night. From my window, I could see in the distance what seemed to be trees on U.S. territory. After hearing and thinking about the U.S. for so long, I was finally able to see it with my own eyes.

It was the second week of January 2001, and the night was cold. We were as far north as I had ever been. It was the first time in my life that I had been that cold, and I wasn't prepared for it. In my backpack, I had only two sets of clothes. I was wearing my only sweater—which wasn't very thick or warm—and the sandals my aunt had bought me in Villahermosa. After getting the new sandals, I had decided to leave my tennis shoes in Villahermosa. They were beat up and worn and made me look more like a *mojada*. On top of that, we were traveling by bus, so I went with the comfortable and new sandals.

I spent most of that first day staring out the window and lost in my own thoughts. I still couldn't believe I was looking at the U.S. That's where I was heading. I longed with all my heart to be with my family again. I had last seen my aunt Rafaela soon after arriving in Ciudad Victoria. Having that time with my aunt had been helpful in keeping me going. Now, I desperately wanted to get to my aunt Míriam's house and be with La Hita again. It had been so long since I had seen her that

I no longer cared that I didn't get to celebrate my birthday or that I had to spend Christmas and New Year's in a foreign land. Instead, there was just one thought in my head all day and night: cross the border and join my family in the U.S.

The joy and anticipation I felt being this close to my goal was still tainted with some anxiety and fear. Even though we were so close to our goal, we were also at the most difficult part of the journey. I was now worried about being caught by both U.S. and Mexican immigration officers. I didn't know what I would do if I was deported back to Guatemala and had to come all the way back another time. Knowing that my aunt was close by and would meet us in Texas helped me calm my fear.

After that first night, we stayed two additional days and one more night at the house next to the river. Besides staring out across the river, I also took advantage of those days to wash my clothes. I decided that I wanted to do something nice for José David and washed his clothes as well. However, my attempt at kindness blew up in my face, as I ended up staining all his new clothes with fabric softener.

In La Entrada, we didn't use fabric softener when washing clothes by hand. Normally, we would scrub the clothes with bar soap, and then put them in a bucket of water and powdered detergent. After soaking, rinsing, and wringing the clothes, we would hang them out in the sun to "bleach" any remaining stains. In any case, I had little experience in washing clothes because the *muchacha* would normally wash them, so I rarely had to do it.

When José David saw his now stained clothes, he got really upset with me. He had just bought the clothes in his preparation for arriving in the U.S. I tried several times to apologize to José David for damaging his clothes, but each time all I received in response was a complaint about having touched his clothes, a criticism of the job I had done, or both.

José David and I had been growing apart even before the clothes incident. The last time we had kissed was right after our second time crossing the Mexican border, in the house with the tarantula. In some ways, the fight about the clothes might have helped because we both knew that the end of our journey was near, and we would each go our separate ways. We had never talked about any type of relationship, nor had we made any plans for the future. We were just two people in the same experience who needed each other's company. It had felt good to be together in the moment, to have someone for long conversations and the occasional kissing session. However, our shared experience and our relationship were both coming to an end.

Those two days in Matamoros seemed like two years. Anytime I had a chance, I sat there at the window and let my imagination run through all the possibilities and my dreams for the future as I focused on the U.S. side of the border in the distance.

Finally, the night arrived when we would cross into Texas. The *Coyota* announced that we must drop all our belongings and take only what we were wearing. I put on two shirts and my sweater to try to protect myself from the cold. I selected the best pair of pants I had and put on my sandals, as they were the only shoes I had. With the sun setting and the temperature dropping, the cold made my feet start to ache. On top of that, I had lost so much weight during the trip that the little bit of body fat I had left was doing very little to protect me from the cold.

The *Coyota* arranged for someone to pick us up in a car and bring us to the train yard where cargo trains would make a brief stop before crossing the bridge over the Rio Grande into the U.S. The night was quiet and there were very few people on the streets. We got out of the car and headed for a ditch several yards from the train tracks. The ditch gave us a place where we could watch for incoming trains; plus, we could duck into the underbrush to hide if we needed to.

The seven of us were all together this time. There was no longer any need to be in separate groups. José David looked worried and could not stay still. Noemí and Daniel spoke in hushed voices from time to time. Dunia seemed nervous but remained silent. Gaby and I hardly spoke at all. Rebeca was noticeably troubled. It was time for her to leave the soil from the cemetery that she had carried with her from Honduras. She had kept it with her this whole time, but now she would have to leave it. There was no room on the train for anything else, only herself and her dreams.

Waiting in the ditch, we found ourselves with other groups of *mojados* who were also trying to cross the border. Among them was a very tall young man who was smoking marijuana while we waited. It was the first time I had ever seen someone smoking any type of drug. He didn't say anything to me, and I didn't say anything to him except I coughed a few times from the smoke. No one in that ditch seemed interested in conversation that night. Hours went by. It was one o'clock in the morning, and we still didn't know when we were going to go.

As we waited, the knot in my stomach grew tighter with each

passing second. I could not stop thinking about the train ride. I had no idea how we would get on, or how, when, and where we would get off. The *Coyota* warned everyone to be ready to run on her signal. I started to worry about being able to run. My feet were still aching from the cold, and my sandals weren't made for running anywhere, much less on gravel and across train tracks. It was two o'clock in the morning when we heard a train approaching in the distance.

"Be ready; that's our train!" called the *Coyota*.

The enormous machine came to a slow stop, someone in the ditch yelled "*corran*" (run), and we rushed toward a train car, trying to find a place to get on and hide. Attached on the end of the boxcar, down close to the front wheels, there were two hollow metal cylinders. The *Coyota* suggested that we climb into one of those. I quickly looked, and the space was large enough for me to fit in. However, after I thought about it for a second, I felt a sense of terror as I imagined that I could easily fall out and end up being crushed by the train. I didn't want to hide in one of those cylinders, so shaking with panic that the train might leave me behind, I started looking around for a better option.

"This way!" I heard someone whisper. It was the guy I had seen smoking marijuana earlier.

Thinking that anything would be better than riding in that open cylinder, I started running toward where he was pointing with his flashlight. The train was on my right-hand side, and I was running down a parallel set of tracks to reach the indicated train car.

There wasn't a lot of light but enough to see where to step. I could see up ahead the car where people were getting on. Gaby was in front of me and was running much faster. I was behind her and losing ground thanks to my sandals. Just as I had imagined, I was having a lot of trouble running and keeping my balance. Thousands of things were going through my mind at that moment. I was afraid of falling and seriously injuring myself. I was terrified that Gaby and I might be separated by another border if I didn't get on the train. I prayed quickly and fervently in my head and continued to run. "Hurry up, hurry up, hurry up!" everyone shouted. I tried to hurry the best I could, but my feet continued to slide around in the sandals.

My sister got to the train car and was up and inside in a flash. I finally got to the car and saw that we could climb into the car because the door was partially open. Just as it was my turn to climb up, the train started to move again. Thankfully, someone grabbed my hand and lifted me up and through the foot-wide slot in the door. Rebeca was behind me, but she got stuck in the doorway because it was so narrow. Two people worked to pull her all the way into the car.

Inside the train, it was so dark that I could barely see anything. I kept praying and begging God not to let the immigration officers catch us and that Rebeca would finally get in. The train started moving faster, but Rebeca was still stuck. Eventually, she finally made it in, and everyone in the car felt a rush of relief. If she hadn't been able to get into the car, we all would have been at risk of being caught by immigration officers and deported.

Another complication of Rebeca getting stuck was that Noemí and Doña Roberta weren't able to get on the train and had to stay in Mexico. While it was sad to see my friend left behind, I was also grateful that this time my sister and I were together. Once Rebeca was inside the car and we were moving toward the bridge over the river, I sat down on top of a stack of soft bags and started praying to God for help.

"Don't sit on those bags, child!" I heard someone say.

I touched the bags and realized that I had been sitting on top of a load of drugs—marijuana perhaps—although I never knew for sure what it was. It was so dark inside that I couldn't see anyone's face. I could only see a beam of light leaking through the slot where the door was open. I never understood how that guy knew I was sitting on those bags.

The air inside the car was heavy, and it was hard to breathe. All of the sudden, someone ordered us to keep quiet. The train came to a stop, and we saw several flashlight beams shining into the train and then moving on. I assumed they were immigration officers making sure no humans were trying to cross the border. Around eight minutes later, the train came to another slow stop.

"Jump, it's time to get out!" someone whispered loudly.

We all started to jump down one by one. Gaby got out first, and then I jumped down. Rebeca was the last one to get out. We couldn't take the risk of being trapped inside if she got stuck on the way out. Before jumping out, she took off her sweater, which must have been one of the reasons she got stuck when getting in. This time without the sweater, she was able to quickly get through the opening and jump down.

I jumped down from the train, and my feet landed on U.S. soil for the first time. It all happened so fast that I didn't have time to think about it. As soon as we were off the train, we were told to start moving quickly. Instead of an all-out run like when we were getting on the train, we walked quickly in a half-crouch like kids playing hide-and-seek.

We arrived at the back of a neighborhood, and dogs at several houses were barking wildly, trying to make people aware of our presence. We headed for an alley that divided two rows of houses. There were a few dim streetlights, but we moved so fast that I didn't have time to see much of where we were. On top of that, it wasn't the time for sightseeing. All we were supposed to do at that moment was follow instructions, walk as fast as possible, and pray we didn't get caught.

At the end of the alley, there was a car waiting for us. Gaby, José David, and I jumped in. The driver told us to keep our heads down as low as we could. The car started and headed toward our next stop. There in the car, I had a chance to catch my breath, and the reality of where we were started to hit me. I was overcome with a wave of curiosity. I felt the need to see what the U.S. looked like, so I slowly lifted my head to look through the car window.

"Keep your head down; we're going to get caught because of you! Besides, I am the only adult here, and so I am most likely to be deported," José David warned me.

Feeling a bit ashamed, I listened and ducked back down into the footwell behind the driver's seat. Even José David's reprimand couldn't ruin my excitement, though. We had made it across the border. Gaby and I were finally in the same country as La Hita! I closed my eyes and thanked God for taking care of us through the long journey. I knew it would still be a few days before we got to be with La Hita and our family, but at that moment it felt like we had crossed the finish line and our journey was over. At least, that's what I thought.

16

Ransom

We remained crouched in the rear footwells of the car for a few more minutes until it arrived at its destination. The car pulled up in front of a house, and Gaby, José David, and I got out. We were the second group to arrive. Dunia and Rebeca were already there. A few minutes later, Daniel showed up with some other *mojados* who had been on the train with us.

The *Coyota* and Noemí weren't there, but I knew they had missed the train, and I wasn't sure if they would arrive later that night, the next day, or even later. The driver of our car was the owner of the house where we had stayed in Matamoros. There at the house in Brownsville, he seemed to be in charge of everything. Back in Mexico, he had worked together with the *Coyota* on the plan, so I figured he would find a way to get Doña Roberta across the river. I was worried about my friend, but because she was with Doña Roberta, I trusted Noemí would eventually arrive as well.

As soon as we got to the house, we were led out to the backyard. We were taken to what appeared to be a detached room in the back of the house. When I got inside and the light was turned on, I saw that it was a storage room for tools and old boxes. Even though it was a storage room, it was clean and there was a mattress on the floor. It was better than many of the places we had stayed on our journey. It was warm, closed off from bugs outside, and we wouldn't have to sleep on the floor. Although I was tired, we stayed up for a while, trying to mentally go over everything we had just experienced. It had all been so fast, and I could still feel the adrenaline pumping. Besides, I wanted to see if Noemí would arrive that night.

Eventually, my exhaustion and the call of the soft mattress won out, and as soon as my head hit the mattress, I fell asleep. I dreamed that we were in North Carolina with La Hita, my brother, and my aunts. It was the most pleasant dream I'd had in a long time.

111

A few hours later, I woke up from what was basically a long nap, excited and sure that it would be the day we would reunite with our family. The sun was up, and as we walked to the main house, I could see that the houses in the U.S. were very different from houses in Mexico or Central America.

That morning, we met Debora, the owner of the house there in Brownsville. She was a short, light-skinned Latina woman with short gray hair. Her appearance was also very different from that of the people we had met on our journey. Based on the condition of her hair, skin, and clothes, to me she seemed to have a lot of money. Doña Debora told us to use the telephone in the living room to call our families. I picked up the receiver and dialed my aunt Míriam's number in North Carolina and told her that we were in Brownsville, Texas.

"They made it across the border! Keyla and Gaby are both in Texas!" I heard my aunt yell to others in the background.

I could hear the excitement in my aunt's voice. I imagined that she felt a huge sense of relief. She had made her own *mojada* journey, and she knew how hard and dangerous it would be for Gaby and me. I am sure she and the rest of my family had been worrying about us this whole time and were anxious to know that we had made it. It was something to celebrate, although we were still far away.

My aunt Míriam told me that my aunt Rafaela and her husband had gone back home to Miami. She told me that she would let them know we had arrived, and they would arrange to pick us up with Doña Roberta. While I was on the phone, I heard some background noise that was too clear to be simple interference with the connection. I realized that someone was listening to my call from another phone in the same house: it was Doña Debora.

Later, we were taken to a different house. I wasn't sure why, and they didn't tell us. My job was to follow instructions, not to ask questions. We arrived at a small, rundown trailer park that seemed to be in the middle of nowhere. Even though there were several mobile homes there, I didn't see signs of anyone else being there.

We stopped outside one trailer, and we were taken inside. I had never seen a house like this. On the outside, it was long and boxy and reminded me of the metal containers that trucks used in Honduras to transport cargo, except this one had windows and a front door. From the outside, you could tell that it was old, but inside it seemed nice and comfortable to me. There was carpet in all the rooms, which was very different from what I was used to. Our group (minus Noemí) and a few others who had been on the train all stayed there while the driver left with the car.

We were all dirty, and we hadn't been given a place to shower. I wanted to change my clothes at least, but we had left everything in the house in Matamoros except the clothes on our backs. Luckily, inside the trailer there was a large trash bag full of used clothing. We rummaged around in the bag, and I found a sweater three sizes too large, but it was warm and very comfortable, so I put it on. I also found a pair of brown pants and a pair of white tennis shoes. The shoes were used and a little dirty, but they were my size.

I was excited to get a set of clothes for free. In less than 12 hours of being in the United States, I was staying in a carpeted house, sleeping on a mattress, and had a new set of clothes. I was feeling confident that this was what life in the U.S. would be like and that all the sacrifices of the journey were so that I could be in such an amazing country.

We were told that we had to wait for Doña Roberta and Noemí to arrive before heading to Houston. We still had to go through one more checkpoint, and it was one of the most complicated. Like Mexico, the U.S. has immigration checkpoints on major highways several miles inland from the border. There is a checkpoint on the highway between Brownsville and Houston. Just like in Mexico, we would get off the highway and hike around the checkpoint on foot. On the other side, another car would be waiting to take us to Houston, where we were to meet our families.

As we waited there in the house, I had some time to observe more of these new surroundings. That day it was cold, and a thick fog blocked us from seeing much from our windows. We could see that the grass had frozen water on it. Gaby and I were both very curious to know more, but we didn't dare go outside to explore.

Noemí and the *Coyota* arrived at the trailer the next day. They were filthy and looked exhausted from the journey. Doña Roberta announced that in the evening the group would set off for Houston. The plan was to make the hike at night, when the dark would better hide us. Unlike Mexico, in Texas there wasn't a jungle that would hide us as we walked.

Right before the group left, the *Coyota* pulled us aside and told Gaby and me that we wouldn't be going with the group and that we were to stay there in the trailer. Again, I didn't understand what was going on, but I followed instructions. I thought of all the reasons we would stay back: maybe my aunt would pick us up there or maybe we would go another route. We had been split up as a group so often that it didn't seem like anything to worry about at that point. In fact, I thought we were lucky not to have to hike around the checkpoint in the dark and cold.

The next day, Doña Roberta showed up at the trailer and took us to Doña Debora's house. While we were in the house, they talked about the extra money that my aunts would have to pay on our behalf. At some point, they had come up with a plan to extort more money from my family by using Gaby and me as collateral. The *Coyota* had called my aunts and let them know that she wouldn't let us go unless my family paid her an additional $3,000. They had brought us to the house to let me talk to my aunt Míriam on the phone. My family wanted to ensure that we were okay. On the phone, my aunt, all of the excitement from before now gone, instructed me that if at any time I sensed that my life, or my sister's, was in danger, I was to run as fast as I could and find a police officer.

The reality of our situation hit me. My family had no idea where we were in Brownsville, and I had no way of telling them even if given the chance. We were hostages at the mercy of these two greedy and heartless women. They openly discussed in front of us how much more money they could get out of my family. They were like vultures circling a dying animal, anxiously waiting for the first peck.

We were returned to the trailer to await the ransom payment. Sitting there waiting was agony, but at least we were alone. Gaby and I were terrified to be in the same house with the *Coyota* and Doña Debora and hear them brainstorm on how they could use us to get more money. We waited in the trailer for two more days, hoping that at any minute we would hear the news that the ransom had been paid and that we would be set free, but no news came.

On the third day, the *Coyota* returned and told us that we were going back to Doña Debora's house. We didn't have any type of bag and were told to leave everything there. I was wearing the oversized sweater, brown pants, and the white tennis shoes, so I had to leave behind my black platform sandals and the clothes that my aunt Rafaela had bought me in Villahermosa. Gaby left behind a pair of pants in which she had hidden the $20 that my aunt had given her in Mexico. I am sure the *Coyota* later sensed it was there and added it to her pile of money. We got into a car for the quick trip back to Doña Debora's house.

As the car pulled up, I saw a police car on the sidewalk in front of a school several yards away. I turned to my sister and tried transmitting my plan with my eyes. I was sure that if I ran yelling for help, we could reach the police car before we were caught, and they would help us. To me, it was the perfect chance, but we only had a 10-second window if we were going to do it.

My pulse quickened as I got ready to run. At that moment, a thousand thoughts went through my head all at once. First, and most importantly, what if Gaby didn't understand what we *both* had to do? If I ran and she stayed there, I was terrified of what might happen to her. I also thought about what the police would do. Deep down, I didn't want the *Coyota* or Doña Debora to go to jail. I just wanted my sister and I to be able to go with our family. Finally, I thought about what I would do or say when I got the officer's attention. I didn't speak English, and I had no idea if they would speak Spanish.

The moment to run passed, and I stayed there. Whatever happened, I could not risk being separated from my sister. Instead, we walked into the house and sat quietly in the living room to find out what would happen next. A few hours later, we were told to get back in the car. We were being taken to my aunt Rafaela in exchange for the ransom.

We drove to a gas station about five minutes away. I saw my aunt and her husband in their car waiting for us in the corner of the parking lot. Our car pulled up and stopped in front of their car, and we were told to stay put. The *Coyota* got out and walked over to my aunt on the passenger side. My aunt handed over an envelope with the cash, and Doña Roberta signaled to let us out of the car. We ran toward my aunt and Don Javier. As I turned to get in the car, I looked and the *Coyota* was gone. Gaby and I both climbed into the backseat, ready to also leave as quickly as possible.

Once Don Javier pulled out of the parking lot, I felt a huge sense of relief. We were safe, and I thought that finally we were headed to be with the rest of our family. I was so happy to be with my aunt, and I thought that she would be as happy and relieved as I was. My aunt remained looking forward without saying anything. In fact, both she and Don Javier seemed nervous about something. Before I could ask why, my aunt turned around in her seat and told us there was one more thing to do before we could head to North Carolina.

"We have to take you both to Immigration so you can turn yourselves in," my aunt said.

The original agreement with Doña Roberta was that she would take us past the checkpoint, and then my aunt would pick us up in

Houston. We were still in Brownsville, and driving to North Carolina would mean passing through the immigration checkpoint. There, everyone in the car would be required to provide ID or a paper demonstrating they were permitted to be in the country. Aunt Rafaela and Don Javier had U.S. passports, but Gaby and I didn't have anything. If we tried to go through the checkpoint, Aunt Rafaela and Don Javier could be charged with attempting to smuggle us into the country. The choice was either hire another *coyote* to get us around the checkpoint or turn ourselves in to Immigration. After what happened with Doña Roberta, no one was interested in dealing with a *coyote*, so our best bet was to turn ourselves in.

No one spoke the rest of the ride over to the immigration facility. Don Javier drove up to the gate and told the immigration officer that we were his nieces and we had just crossed the border. The officer had us get out of the car and told Don Javier that he should go, as he and my aunt were not permitted inside the building. So, my aunt left with her husband, and my sister and I were once again on our own. I didn't know how long we would be in custody or how much longer until we could finally see our other aunts and our grandmother. My aunt had told us before that if we were arrested by U.S. immigration officers that she could get us out of custody because she was a U.S. citizen, but I wasn't clear on how long that would take.

I thought about the group of *mojados* who became my friends. One day while at Doña Debora's house, we overheard the *Coyota* telling Debora that the rest of our group of *mojados* had all been caught while trying to detour around the checkpoint. Rebeca, José David, and Dunia were deported back to Mexico. Noemí and Daniel were kept in custody because they were minors. Noemí had told me that her parents lived in Houston and were legal residents, so they would be able to pick them up even if caught by Immigration. Months later, I connected with Rebeca when we were both living in Miami. She told me that the group was later able to cross both the border and the checkpoint, and everyone had made it to their destinations in the U.S. I went to visit Dunia at her home years later, after both of us were married. As for the rest, including José David, the night they left to hike around the checkpoint was the last time I saw or heard from them. It is my hope that they are well and that they have been able to realize their version of the American Dream.

17

Immigration

The Immigration building where my aunt dropped us off was a large, multi-story building. We got out of the car and a couple of U.S. immigration officers escorted us into a large room with a few large desks, each facing a couple of stainless steel benches. Behind us, there were two offices with large windows. Inside one of them was a woman sitting alone on a metal chair. I guessed from her appearance that she was from Central America. She appeared to be over 18 years old, and I assumed that she was waiting to be deported back to her country.

Besides the two immigration officers, Gaby and I were the only ones in that large room. We were called up to the desk to give our statements and to be fingerprinted. We sat on the cold bench, and they handed us clipboards with a stack of forms to complete and a pen. We sat there working on completing all the forms for what seemed like hours.

While we worked on the paperwork, the immigration officers asked us about our parents, and we told the truth: our mother died many years ago, and our father hadn't even put his name on either of our birth certificates—that's why we had our mother's last name. One of the officers responded that we were orphans (and made a note in our paperwork). I had never considered myself an orphan, because La Hita and my aunts always looked after us. But in the eyes of the law, yes, we were orphans. Our mother had passed away, legally we didn't have a father, and no one in my family had completed the paperwork to adopt us legally. Now, according to the government of the United States, we were two teenage orphan immigrants. That cold and hard fact resonated in my head.

All of the sudden, I felt the last bit of my energy drain out. It was the middle of the night, and I was tired, hungry, and at my breaking point. I felt so alone that I wanted to curl up in the corner and cry. I just wanted to be back with La Hita. I wanted some adult in my family to be there and take care of my sister and me.

The past few days were catching up to me. While I had spent most of the time in the trailer sleeping as we waited for the ransom, but I was never able to feel rested. Between the fear of what could happen to us and stress of waiting to hear when we would be able to leave, I left the trailer more in need of sleep than when I had arrived.

I tried to lie down on my bench, but I didn't fit. So, I lay down on the tile floor. At that point, I didn't care that it was cold or if it was dirty; I didn't care about the paperwork or answering questions. I just wanted to close my eyes and forget about everything for a little bit. One of the officers told me to get up from the floor. I climbed back onto the bench and sat there with my head in my hands.

"There are still some forms to fill out," another officer called from his desk at the back of the room.

He was a serious-looking man. He didn't smile, but he wasn't rude either. He came over and offered us an apple juice and crackers. Gaby and I were starving because we hadn't eaten for hours and it was getting close to sunrise. We completed our paperwork and then sat on the bench waiting for whatever the next thing would be.

Around 7:00 a.m., an officer took us to another room to pick up some clothes and hygiene products. I was still wearing the oversized sweater and the worn white tennis shoes I had found on the first day in the trailer. A tall, friendly female officer was there in the room and asked us if we had lice. For the past few days, my head had been itching, and I figured it was lice. I nodded in response, and she gave us each a bottle of anti-lice shampoo. She also handed me a blue zip-up jacket, a long-sleeved shirt, gray sweatpants, and a new pair of tennis shoes. Gaby was given the same outfit. The officer then pointed us to a group of benches in the hallway and told us sit and wait for someone to come get us.

In less than 10 minutes, a tall, red-haired woman came over to us. She was not an immigration officer and was dressed in regular clothes. She greeted us and introduced herself. Her name was Diana, and we would be leaving with her in her car. Gaby and I sat in silence the entire ride to Diana's house. Her house was large, with several bedrooms. I went through the front door, and to my left was a dining room with a large table and beyond that, the kitchen. To the right was the living room. Straight ahead was the hallway that led to Diana's room. We were led through the kitchen to the room where my sister and I would sleep.

It was a large bedroom with its own bathroom. Diana told us to shower and change into our new clothes.

I got in the shower and discovered one of the significant differences between La Entrada and the U.S.—hot water. Back in my hometown, we only had cold water, and it was always a painful shock to the system when I poured the first bucket of cold water over my body. This steady stream of warm water felt so good and relaxing. I rubbed in the anti-lice shampoo on my wet hair and waited a few minutes for it to take effect. I rinsed my hair and watched dozens of dead lice rinse out of my hair. I finished my shower and put on the clothes I was given. I felt cleaner than I had been since the morning we left La Entrada. I waited for Gaby to shower and get dressed, and we went out to the living room.

"Wow, you look like two brand new girls!" exclaimed Diana when she saw us. "I almost didn't recognize you!"

That comment got my first response to Diana, a small quiet laugh. The fact was, I didn't feel like talking to anyone. There were two other girls staying in the room with us who were in our same situation, and I didn't want to talk to them at that moment either. I was tired of this entire process. The promise of a better life seemed so distant. We were in the U.S., but I didn't see any sign that this better life would ever arrive. I was tired, stressed out, and frustrated. I started to wonder in my head why La Hita had to come to the U.S., why I had to leave my house and my friends and go through everything that I had gone through up to that point.

We had spent such a long time waiting in strange houses, walking, and riding buses—all while hiding from Mexican and U.S. immigration officers—with the one goal of trying to get to the U.S. so we could be with La Hita and the rest of our family. We had made it to another point that I thought was going to be the end of our journey: first crossing the border, then being freed from the kidnappers, and finally being reunited with my aunt Rafaela. But once again, Gaby and I were left on our own, in the care of adults who were not family and whom we did not know.

I missed La Hita so much it was starting to hurt. At that point, all I wanted was to be able to hug her and feel protected in her arms, but I wasn't even allowed to call her and hear her voice. All of this was too much to process at one time, and so I just shut down while sitting there waiting in the Immigration office.

After a little while at Diana's house, and after my shower, new clothes, breakfast, and a long nap, I began to slowly come back to my reality and even started to respond to Diana and the other girls staying with her. That night, the anxiety and despair returned once the lights were turned off. I started sobbing uncontrollably. I also heard my sister crying from her bed. I cried myself to sleep most of the nights we spent at Diana's house, and I often heard Gaby doing the same thing. I never asked her why she was crying, and she never asked me. It wasn't necessary, because we both knew that we were feeling the same things.

The next day, Diana made us breakfast and drove all four of us to a fenced-in immigration center near her house. At the back of the compound, there was a trailer where we would attend school during the day while we waited to be released. Most of our school time was focused on English lessons. Halfway through the day, we would be taken to a cafeteria in the large building at the front for our lunch, and after lunch we had time for recess outside the trailer. Diana, the teachers, and facility staff were all friendly. They treated us kindly, fed us, and educated us. Overall, we were in a much better place compared to the cold benches of our first night in custody, not to mention the cells of the Mexican immigration lockup. Although, at the time, I could not appreciate those blessings. I was tired and only wanted to be with my family.

At the school, we met other children from Central America, the Caribbean, and South America. There were dozens of children, from elementary age to high school age like me. They were also all staying in different foster homes close by the compound, and those foster parents would drop them off in the morning and pick them up in the afternoon, just like Diana did with us. While we were friendly to each other, no one tried to make friends. We all knew that we were there temporarily, and every day new students arrived, and others left.

In Diana's home, there were a lot of girls coming and going as well. One night, Jasmine—an immigrant from Cuba—came to Diana's house. It was the first time I had heard someone from Cuba speak Spanish, and we had trouble understanding everything she said. In the morning, Jasmine was picked up by her family. I later found out that the immigration system is much easier for Cubans because of the political conflict between the U.S. government and Fidel Castro's regime.

Each day in school, I was learning more new phrases in English. I started to regain my love of the language that I had felt when La Hita bought me that small book of English phrases. Every day we would recite the Pledge of Allegiance, and although the pronunciation was complicated, I memorized the whole pledge, and I still remember it today.

More than anyone else, Diana was always very kind to us. Before and after school hours, she would take us with her on errands to the supermarket and to relax at the park. She bought and cooked delicious food and treated us to ice cream.

Over the days in her house, I developed a habit of eating ice, probably as a way to ease my anxiety. Diana affectionately called me *comehielo* (the ice eater). She pointed out, with a smile, that my habit and nickname would make it easier for her to remember me.

Every morning at school, one of the immigration officials would call the names of those who had to go to the clinic to get their immunizations. Both Gaby and I were called to go several times. We did not have any shot records, so we had to get most of them redone. I was saved from two, though, because I knew that I had already had chickenpox when I was seven, and I had the scar on my arm that showed the doctors that I had already been given a tuberculosis vaccine. Neither Gaby nor I wanted to go to the clinic for shots, but we didn't have records, and we could not call our family to see if we had gotten the vaccines as babies, so there was no escaping the needles.

We finished our first full week at Diana's house, and no one could tell us when we would be leaving. I didn't understand why it was taking so long, and Diana didn't have any answers either. We continued our second week of school all while we impatiently waited to hear any good news.

Later, after picking us up, my aunt Rafaela had explained the delay. After we were dropped off, she was told by Immigration that she had to provide documentation that we were orphans and that she could be our guardian/next of kin. In order to do that, she needed original copies of our birth certificates and my mother's death certificate to be sent from Honduras. It took a little over a week to get the documents shipped to her house in Miami. Once she had all the necessary paperwork, she called the immigration facility in Brownsville to arrange the pickup. Then she and her husband started on the long drive from Miami to come pick us up.

On the afternoon of our ninth day at her house, Diana gave us the news that our aunt Rafaela would be there the next day to pick us up. The following morning, I woke up early. I was ready to get out of there and see my family. I showered and put on clean clothes. I didn't wear any makeup because I didn't have any, but I braided my hair in order to look as nice as I could. Instead of driving us to the compound with the school, Diana took us back to the Immigration building where we had turned ourselves in. My aunt Rafaela was there waiting for us when we arrived. We weren't allowed to leave right away because there was another round of paperwork to be completed. The immigration officials handed my aunt Rafaela a form for each of us. Each one had our photograph and fingerprints, along with our names, height, and weight. These were the documents that we would need to pass through the immigration checkpoint on our way to Houston.

I turned to say goodbye to Diana, hugged her tightly, and thanked her for taking such good care of us. I told her I would call her soon to see if she still remembered me, and she smiled. Diana was an extraordinary woman with a heart of gold. It was clear that she loved taking care of those who were in need. Being placed in Diana's foster care had truly been a blessing in the middle of so many challenges.

As we were leaving, I thought about my experience up to that point with the U.S. immigration system and how it compared to the time when I was deported from Mexico to Guatemala. I remembered the stench of the cells where we were locked up, the face of the officer who invited me to go dancing with him, and the catcalls from the grown men locked in the other cell. In the U.S., things were quite different. While we were officially arrested, no one placed us in a cell. We dealt with a lot of immigration officers: many were nice, others were stern, and even a few were mean, but none of them ever attempted anything inappropriate with me.

I truly felt blessed to be able to start school, learn some English, have three meals a day, and sleep in a comfortable bed. At the same time, I could never shake the feeling that I was a prisoner. It was hard to feel happy or even completely relaxed for those 10 days, because I didn't have or know when I would get what I really wanted: to be reunited with La Hita, and the rest of my family.

As we left the detention center, my aunt Rafaela explained to us the first steps of what would become a two-decade-long interaction with the United States immigration system. Within a week, we were to report to the Immigration and Naturalization Service center, and, in three months, we had a scheduled court appearance in front of a federal immigration judge. During these three months, we were allowed to hire an attorney to prepare for what (I would later learn) was our deportation proceeding in the court.

On top of that, she broke the news that we would have to live with her in Miami, instead of living with La Hita in North Carolina. When the immigration officers released us to her custody, she had to sign a document confirming that she would take care of us and ensure that we would show up for our check-in appointments and court appearances. Those appointments and court dates were scheduled every few weeks in Miami, so that is where we would have to live.

Under normal circumstances, that news would have been devastating, and I would have started an argument with my aunt. However, at this point I was tired of being alone with my sister and would have been willing to live with anyone who was family and who would take care of us. Besides, we were on our way to North Carolina, and I was going to have three days to see La Hita and spend time with the rest of my family. I would worry about the rest later.

18

Family Reunion

My aunt Rafaela walked us to the car where Don Javier was waiting. I was hoping that she would tell us that we were going on a plane to North Carolina. I knew it was a long trip, and I had never been on an airplane. Unfortunately, my aunt told us we would drive because flying would be too expensive.

Don Javier told us it would take more than 24 hours of driving to get to Durham, North Carolina, where La Hita was living with my aunt Míriam. At that point, after everything we had been through in the previous two months, a 24-hour car ride didn't seem that hard to me. We were going to be in the same car the entire time; there would be no constantly changing buses, jumping on and off moving trains, or walking through a jungle. More importantly, we would be making the trip with our family. (Interestingly, I later found out that the trip from Brownsville to Durham was 200 miles further than the trip from La Entrada to Brownsville.)

Once they had received the necessary paperwork from Honduras, my aunt Rafaela and Don Javier rented a small car to drive from Miami to Brownsville, Texas. It had taken them an entire 24 hours, driving almost nonstop to get to us. They picked us up, and we had another full day's worth of driving to get to Durham. They were exhausted, but my aunt Rafaela knew she had to get us to La Hita as soon as possible. It had now been exactly two months since the morning we left La Entrada for Esquipulas. My grandmother was getting sick from her stress and worry about us. We headed north on the highway, for Don Javier and Aunt Rafaela's second full day of driving.

We arrived at the inland immigration checkpoint on the highway north of Brownsville, on the way to Houston. My aunt provided the immigration documents for Gaby and me. The officer at the checkpoint asked a couple of questions and then let us continue on our trip.

Keyla and Gaby the weekend they arrived in North Carolina, January 2001 (family photograph).

We moved through several different states and at first only stopped to buy food, get gas, and use the bathroom. After about 12 hours, Don Javier pulled into a motel. He told us that he had to sleep for a little while. If it had been up to Gaby and me, we wouldn't have stopped anywhere, because we were so anxious to see the rest of the family. Of course, Gaby and I had spent a lot of the trip lying across

the back seat of the car asleep, so continuing our travel was a lot easier for us.

While Don Javier slept, my aunt Rafaela took us to get something
to eat, and I had a chance to look around. The United States was so
different from Honduras, Guatemala, and Mexico. First, the trees and
plants were very different from what I was used to. Also, the buildings and restaurants appeared more modern, cleaner, and more organized. The highways were bigger than the two-lane highway that ran
in front of my old house in La Entrada, and they were in better condition. After Don Javier woke up, we climbed back in the small car
and continued on. As we moved north, the temperature continued to
drop, and we began to really feel what a U.S. winter was. At one point,
we came to a place where it had recently snowed. It was the first time
I had ever seen snow in real life. We stopped for gas, and I jumped
out, excited to touch the snow. It was cold and soft at the same time. I
grabbed some snow from the leaves of a tree, and I put it in my mouth.
I had dreamed of tasting snow since the first time my cousin Fabricio
had told me about it.

More than 24 hours after leaving Brownsville, I saw the "Welcome
to North Carolina" sign as we crossed the state line. My aunt told us
that we had less than two hours until we got to our destination. My
heart started beating extremely fast, and I could no longer sleep. I
stared out the window hoping that the two hours would pass quickly.
I looked out the window into the dark and watched the sky, the road,
and the lights of a few houses that were close to the road. I imagined my
grandmother's smile when she saw us walk in the house.

It was past 10 o'clock at night on January 26, 2001, when we pulled
into the driveway of the white house where my aunt Míriam lived. All
of the lights were on, so I assumed everyone was as anxious as we were.
We got out of the car, and I immediately recognized the house from the
pictures that I had seen in Honduras. My aunt Rafaela rang the door-
bell, and my aunt Míriam opened the door. We hugged tightly, and I
could see tears welling up in her eyes. I hadn't seen her in such a long
time. I immediately asked about La Hita.

"She's in her room; it's over there," answered my aunt Míriam.

She pointed to the door of my grandmother's room and wiped her
tears with her other hand. We knocked on the door and walked in, and
I saw my grandmother praying, sitting on the bed with a rosary in her
hands. Gaby and I ran to hug her, and she grabbed us with a big hug
and started to cry with her head on our shoulders. La Hita was always a

strong woman, and other than when the topic of my mother came up, I had rarely seen her break down and cry, but that day we all cried tears of joy and relief for finally being together again.

"Thank you, God. Thank you, Holy Virgin, for bringing them safe and sound," repeated my grandmother softly, with tears in her eyes.

My aunt Laura arrived with Isaías, whom I hadn't seen for more than six years. He was so different that it was like I was meeting a new cousin for the first time. I had seen several other cousins more recently because they been to La Entrada to visit before. I also got to meet Alberto, my aunt Laura's youngest, whom I had only seen in pictures. My brother Alexander wasn't there yet. At that time, he was living in Florida, but he was on his way and would be there soon.

I couldn't believe I was finally with my whole family. The last time Gaby and I had been with La Hita and all my aunts was at my mother's funeral. That night was such a happier occasion. We talked and laughed for hours. I was sure that my mother was smiling and laughing with us from heaven.

Everyone kept commenting on my height and how tall I had grown. It was late, and we were all tired. My aunt Laura invited me to spend the night in her apartment with her three children. I was excited because my aunt Laura told me that I could sleep on her waterbed. I had seen waterbeds on TV several times and wanted to try one for myself. I was a bit disappointed to find out that sleeping on a waterbed was not as comfortable as it sounded, but it was a new experience, a new adventure I got to try in my new country. Besides, I was with my family, and recently, I had slept in worse places.

The next day we had pancakes for breakfast. I noticed that La Hita looked thinner than when she had been in La Entrada. I am sure she thought Gaby and I looked a little thin, too, though it would have been worse if we hadn't gotten 10 days of Diana's cooking before she saw us. She seemed to be healthy, which I knew was a blessing.

I spent a lot of time that weekend in Durham hanging out and talking with my cousins for hours at a time. After going through so much, I was finally feeling like a regular teenager. It was so nice that at times I thought it might just be a dream, and I would soon wake up in my room in Honduras or on a floor somewhere in Mexico or Guatemala.

After reconnecting with my more immediate family, we went to visit more distant family members who lived in the area. We went to see Eunice. She lived in a mobile home not far from my aunt Míriam.

Her mobile home was so much nicer than the one we had stayed in Brownsville. Her bathroom had an extra-large jacuzzi tub with water jets all over. The trailer was so nice that I had Fabricio take pictures of me there in the bathroom and in other rooms in the house.

It had been a long time since I had seen Eunice. While I will always remember that rainy night when she kicked us out of my great-grandmother's house, I was happy to see her and gave her a hug. One of the things that I picked up from La Hita was to not hold grudges against people, and especially not against family.

There at Eunice's house was my cousin Samuel, Eunice's youngest, who had lived with us years before, when La Hita was taking care of him. Even though it had only been a few years since we had last seen each other, when he saw me, he was shocked.

"Keyla, you are so tall, and so pretty!"

I felt the blood rush to my face. Seeing people's reactions to me showed me how much I had changed in just a few years. My body had changed, and my voice was no longer that of the little girl they used to know in Honduras. The entire weekend, everyone commented on how much I had grown and how different I looked.

The thing that most people mentioned first was my height. When I got to the United States, I was around five feet five inches, which is about average in the United States but is considered very tall for a Honduran woman. The night I arrived, all my aunts stood next to me to see how much taller I was than they were. We all laughed as they told me I had grown, and I told them they had shrunk.

When my brother Alexander arrived from Florida, I ran and hugged him tightly. We could not help but cry. It had been six years since I last saw him. He had grown in that time, but not as much as I had.

"I'm not taller than you anymore, *hermanita* (little sister). You've beaten me!" he commented with a smile.

Another highlight from that weekend was getting new clothes. First, my aunt Míriam gave me a new pair of jeans, a light blue shirt, and a pair of gray tennis shoes. Later on, Fabricio took me to the mall and told me to pick out whatever outfit I wanted. I bought a pair of jeans and a crop-top shirt. I loved my new clothes. It felt good to get away from the baggy clothes found in the trailer and the clothes given to me by Immigration. I had these new outfits that were my size and my style. More than that, the clothes were another reminder that my journey as a *mojada* had ended, and I was starting my new life in the United States.

The three days flew by, and when Monday arrived, it felt like it had only been a couple of hours. My aunt Rafaela and Don Javier had to go back to Miami, so Gaby's and my family reunion had to come to an end. It was time to start the next chapter of my life. We had to start school, and we had four more days before our first immigration check-in in Miami. It was sad to leave after I had just started to reconnect with my family, but I knew that I had to go. I wanted more than anything to stay with La Hita, but I understood all the sacrifices my family had made, and I didn't want my aunt Rafaela to get into trouble. My aunt promised that we would come back again during the summer, at Christmas, and any other time she was able to take us.

The next morning, we woke up before the sun was up to get on the road early. Everyone in the house got up to say goodbye.

"May God be with you and protect you, my child! And may the Virgin Mary guide you well! See you soon," my grandmother said to me as she gave me a hug goodbye.

I said goodbye to my aunts and all my cousins and got into the car with Gaby, Don Javier, and my aunt Rafaela. Our trip to Miami would take us another 12 hours. We arrived late that night, and the city looked just like I had seen it in the movies. The freeway was still filled with cars, and there were lights everywhere. Out of the car window, I stared at the huge skyscrapers that looked like they were made entirely of glass.

As I watched the city, I tried to imagine what this next stage of my life would be like. I was in a different country with a different culture and a new language. It would also be my first time living with my aunt Rafaela and her husband. Finally, I knew that I was different from the person I was when I lived in La Entrada. Those two months as a *mojada* affected who I was and the woman I would become. My experience forced me to grow and mature faster than I would have on my own. I didn't know what my life would be like there in Miami, but I felt that I had the strength and faith to be able to make it.

19

Miami

The morning after we arrived in Miami, we jumped right into our new lives. The first thing we had to do was to enroll in school. My aunt brought us to the school to complete all the paperwork. I was nervous as I walked into this new school, afraid that I wouldn't be able to communicate with anyone. To my surprise, the school principal and everyone in the main office spoke Spanish and helped Gaby and me feel welcome. They told us that we would be put into a special newcomer program for students who had just arrived in the U.S. and had to learn English. As a part of that program, we were assigned an ESL (English as a Second Language) class, though I would be in the 10th-grade ESL class, and Gaby would be in the ESL for ninth-grade students.

The differences in the school calendars always makes it tricky for students coming to the U.S. from Central America. School in Honduras runs from February to November. Right before we left La Entrada, Gaby had finished the eighth grade and I had completed the ninth grade. Schools in Honduras were just getting started in February, but there in Miami, the school year was halfway done. The school had to decide in which grade to place us. They told us it wouldn't make sense to be put in a grade that we had already completed, so I would be enrolled as a sophomore and Gaby as a freshman.

We were handed our schedule of classes, plus the bus stop location and pick-up time, and were told to come back the next day to start school. On my schedule, I had my ESL class along with Driver's Education, Health, P.E., Math, and English and Literature. Gaby had her set of classes, and we realized that we wouldn't see each other much—not even at lunch because we had lunch at different times. On our first day of school, my aunt Rafaela drove us to Miami Senior High School. With over 5,000 students, the school was much larger than my school in Honduras. There were classrooms on all three stories and through the maze of hallways. There was a cluster of trailers out back for classes as well. That first day was a little overwhelming.

Besides the size of the school, there were a lot of other things that I wasn't used to but were nice to have. That first day, I was assigned a locker, and it was just like the ones I had seen on TV shows and movies about American teenagers. I was glad to have the locker, because in each of my classes they assigned me a textbook to bring to class every day. I could take them home if I needed to study or do homework. In Honduras, the teacher was the only person with a textbook. If we needed the information to study, we had to copy it into our notebooks.

In my English and Literature class, the teacher asked me to stand up and introduce myself. While at the immigration center, I had learned to say my name, my age, and give a few basic facts in English. As soon as I got in front of the class, I got very nervous and all I was able to get out was my name. The teacher, trying to help prompt me, asked, "Where are you from?" but I didn't understand the question. I stood there silently looking at the floor.

"*Que, ¿de dónde eres?*" a classmate, Carolina, interpreted the question in Spanish to help me.

I then remembered that book La Hita had given me a few years before, and I remembered the question's meaning and what the correct response should be:

"I am from Honduras!" I answered.

Back in Honduras, learning English was fun and exciting, but now that I was here in the U.S. and had to use it every day, some of that excitement was wearing off. The hardest part was getting over my fear of making a mistake (and being laughed at). In my ESL class, all of us were trying to learn English, and I felt more comfortable trying to say things in English there. In all my other classes, it was a mix of students learning English and those who were raised speaking English. In those classes, I was a lot shyer about speaking English. On top of that, all my teachers spoke Spanish. I could ask and answer questions in Spanish, and if I didn't understand something in English, they would translate it for me.

As I got more comfortable with my new school, I worked on overcoming my fear and tried to use English as much as possible in my classes. I was determined to fulfill my dream of learning English, and I knew that speaking English would help me reach my other goals in this country.

Being in a new country and culture was hard and, being new to the school, sometimes I felt out of place. Luckily for me, I wasn't the only newcomer at the school. There were students from all over Latin America and the Caribbean. Most of my new friends were newcomer students who were in my ESL class. We would spend lunch and recess together on most days. According to the ESL teacher, we were supposed to practice our English with each other, and when we were in class, we tried to speak English. Outside of class, though, we would go back to Spanish.

In my other classes, I made friends with students who were not in the ESL program. The person I spent the most time with was Carolina, the girl who had helped me my first day in class. Carolina was Cuban, and I wasn't used to hearing Spanish in a Cuban accent. I had to ask her to repeat herself a lot in those first few weeks, even though she and I were speaking the same language. Because most of the students and teachers at my school were of Cuban descent, I got used to the accent quickly. I often joke that I had to learn two new languages when I got to Miami—Cuban Spanish and English.

As those first several days went by, I got used to my new school and ended up enjoying it more than I thought I would. Within a few weeks, I had a new group of friends and I was getting more comfortable with the language and the school. I often thought about my friends and classmates back at Plan Escalón in Honduras, but I was feeling more at home here in school.

Adapting to living in my aunt Rafaela's house, on the other hand, was not going as well. My aunt and her family lived in a small apartment that had been created by dividing a traditional-sized house in two and building a permanent wall between the two sides. The apartment had an open area that included a small living room with just enough room for a small sofa. There was a small kitchen, and squeezed in between the living room and kitchen was a four-person round dining table. There were two small bedrooms. Don Javier and my cousin Milton slept in one, and my aunt Rafaela, Gaby, and I shared the other. Overall, the apartment was about a third of the size of my house in La Entrada, but everything was nicer and more modern.

It was difficult to adjust to living with my aunt Rafaela and Don Javier, as I didn't have that type of relationship with them. My aunt Rafaela emigrated to the United States before I was born. We first met when she came back for my mother's funeral. After that, she (and sometimes Don Javier) would come to La Entrada every few years to visit for a couple of weeks. Additionally, they both had very different personalities from La Hita. They were both serious, and I found it diffi-cult to talk to them or build a relationship with them. That along with my semi-rebellious teenage self was not a great combination.

Living in Miami, I began to miss La Hita more and more each day. I couldn't wait until the summer, when we would get to go back to North Carolina. I was enjoying Miami, but I missed the freedom I had in La Entrada. There, I would go and visit my friends whenever I wanted to. After La Hita had left, I didn't even have to ask permission. I just left the house when I wanted to and came back when I felt like it. I never came back that late, as La Entrada shut down around 9:00 every night. Plus, I wasn't interested in doing anything really bad—I just enjoyed my independence.

Confined inside that small space, Gaby and I started to fight a lot. One afternoon, a week or so after moving to Miami, I got very upset with her for some reason that I can't remember. I yelled at her and started to insult her. I was so angry that I didn't know what to do. I ran out of the house, and even though I didn't know the neighborhood, I ran down the street until I was out of breath. I sat down to cry on the grass under a palm tree. I missed my house, my town, my friends, my neighbors. I missed everything about my life in Honduras.

I couldn't stop crying. Sitting at the foot of that palm tree, I began to pray. I asked God to forgive me for insulting my sister. I also asked Him to give me the strength to keep going. I missed going to church. I was scared of straying too far from the path of change and improve-ment I had been on since I started attending my new church.

I sat there and cried for several more minutes until I had gotten everything out; then, I stood up and began to walk back home. A cou-ple minutes later, I saw two young missionaries on bicycles. I could tell by their white shirts and the distinctive black name tag on their shirt pockets that they were from my church. I waved them over and asked if they spoke Spanish.

"Of course we speak Spanish!" replied one of them in Spanish with a strong American accent.

I felt a rush of relief, and I knew they were an answer to my prayers. I introduced myself, told them that I had just arrived from Honduras and belonged to The Church of Jesus Christ of Latter-day Saints, and that I would like to join the local congregation. They told me the church building was close and handed me a business card with the church's address and the schedule of services. I knew that God was with me and was helping me.

I walked back to the house with a smile on my face. I was excited, and I couldn't wait until Sunday, when I could go to church. I apologized to my sister, and we made up.

That Sunday, I woke up early, dressed in a skirt and blouse, and put on my makeup. My aunt Rafaela drove me in her car. Just as the missionaries had told me, the church was only a few minutes away from our house. If I wanted, I could even get there by walking.

I walked in and immediately felt at home. When the main service was over, the missionaries I had met a few days before approached me and introduced me to Aurora. She was the president of the women's youth group there in the congregation. She welcomed me and invited me to join the youth activity night on Tuesday evenings. She even volunteered to pick me up at my aunt Rafaela's house. I was excited to meet new people and be in a place where I didn't feel like an outsider. Going to church services and activities gave me another thing to look forward to each week. It became a refuge for me during this challenging time of transition in my life.

Aurora quickly became an important part of my life. She would take me to church on Sundays and to youth group activities during the week. One day, when I was planning for an upcoming church youth dance, Aurora took me to the mall and bought me a new outfit so I would have something nice to wear. She became like a second mother to me. She was someone I could trust and rely on.

I knew that I could ask for her advice and she would help me when I needed it. Near the end of the school year, Aurora explained that at the start of summer, there would be a weeklong camp for the girls from the church youth groups around the area. The tuition for the camp was $50. I assumed that getting the money from my aunt wouldn't be a problem. But when I asked my aunt in front of Aurora, she told me that she would like to help, but she didn't have the money.

It was on that occasion that I learned that life in the United States wasn't the way I had always imagined it. Each time someone came from the U.S. to visit us in Honduras, they always arrived loaded with extra clothes and gifts. When living in La Entrada, I assumed that it was easy to earn money in the U.S.

I realized that the reality for most people, and especially for immigrants, was very different. Earning money came only from hard work over long hours. My aunt Rafaela, for example, worked the night shift and earned about six dollars an hour, which was the minimum wage in Florida at the time. Many weeks she would work over 40 hours so that she could pay for the basics for her young son, Milton, and for Gaby and me.

The rest of my aunts were in a similar situation. Everyone in my family worked hard to make ends meet. When I found out how much my aunt Rafaela made, I did the math on how much she had needed to work in order to send $100 each month to La Hita back in Honduras. The result broke my heart. The financial support my grandmother received from her daughters represented a large sacrifice on their part. When I was in Honduras, dreaming of a life in the United States, no one had explained how difficult it was for an immigrant to achieve their dreams. My aunt couldn't afford to give me $50 for camp, because she didn't have that much extra money lying around. Fifty dollars was more than a full day's pay for her.

I realized that I should be more grateful for all the sacrifices my aunts had made over the years to support my sister and me even though they each had their own children and responsibilities. Without their support, it would have been impossible for La Hita to work and take care of us after my mother passed away. I felt very blessed to have my family. I knew that I had to continue studying and learning English so that I could achieve my dreams and make my whole family proud.

In the end, an anonymous donor from the church donated $50 for me, and another for Gaby, and we were both able to attend the camp. It was another confirmation that my church family cared about me and accepted me as one of their own.

Three months after arriving in Miami, we had our first court date in immigration court. We had contracted a lawyer, Mr. Brown, whom my aunt found with the help of a legal-aid service. Because we were considered a low-income family, he charged only a small fee. At the hearing, Mr. Brown spoke for us while Gaby and I sat at the table next to him. The hearing was conducted in English, and even though I had an interpreter, I didn't follow what was going on. The truth is I didn't really try to understand. Mr. Brown met with my aunt before the hearing to discuss the case. I trusted my aunt to know what to do because she had lived here for so long, and I trusted Mr. Brown because he was a lawyer. Gaby's and my roles were to show up at the hearing and sit with the attorney.

After each court hearing, we were required to go to the U.S. Immigration and Naturalization Service (INS) to have our fingerprints taken and to attest that we were still living at the same address with my aunt

Rafaela. We were given another hearing in three months and headed home.

We had no concrete answers. I had no idea how many more times we would have to appear in court or if we could be deported on one of those appointments. The lawyer didn't have any answers, nor did he seem to care much about our case. We only saw him the days we had a hearing, and he would meet for a few minutes with my aunt right before we would go into the courtroom. I wondered if he would do more if we were paying him more, but unfortunately, it was all my aunt could afford.

20

Teenage Challenges

When I lived in Honduras, I was always very skinny. I wanted to gain weight, but I never succeeded. When I got to the U.S., that all changed. In Honduras, we had enough food to eat all three meals, but we had only the basics: rice, beans, tortillas, and occasionally meat or chicken. La Hita didn't keep snacks at the house, and we only had desserts on special occasions like birthdays. At my aunt's house we had snacks, and for the very first time, I could eat ice cream at home. It was all new to me. Every morning, I woke up, and while waiting for the bus to pick me up for school, I would have a big glass of ice cream for breakfast. It was so good. Even though my aunt had a lot of different snacks and treats, ice cream was my favorite.

At school, we ate food two times a day, and the food was delicious. For breakfast, we had sliced fruit, bagels with cream cheese—my favorite—and orange juice every morning. For lunch, we had the choice of a typical Cuban dish—like *arroz con pollo* (chicken with rice)—pizzas, or hamburgers. We also had a choice of a side dish like *congrí* (rice and beans) or fried plantains. Also, because we were in what was considered a low-income household, Gaby and I received free breakfasts and lunches at school. Many of the Cuban and Cuban American students complained about the food, but to me, it was always delicious.

In Plan Escalón back in Honduras, we didn't have lunch. La Hita would give me 10 lempiras to buy a breakfast. That was enough to buy a Coca-Cola and a *baleada*, a famous Honduran dish made of refried beans, cheese, and cream folded in a large flour tortilla. School would get out at 1:00 p.m., so I would eat lunch when I got home from school.

In Miami, I started to gain weight. At first, I was just recuperating all the weight I lost on my journey as a *mojada*. But I didn't stop gaining, and in a few months, I weighed 20 pounds more than I had weighed before leaving La Entrada. It was the heaviest I had ever been.

Besides the extra food, I didn't exercise as much in Miami as when I was in my hometown. In La Entrada, I walked everywhere that I went. In Miami, we used the car to go everywhere. Every morning, the bus would pick me up at my house and drop me off in front of the school. In the afternoons and weekends, Don Javier drove us to the beach or the park. Anytime we went shopping for groceries or to run an errand, even if it was around the corner, we would go in a car.

Everyone in my family noticed that I had gained some weight, and at first, they told me that living in the U.S. had been good for me. As I gained more weight, they started to call me *gordita* (chubby). In La Entrada, the curvy women with thick legs were considered the best looking. When I lived there, all I wanted to do was gain weight. Back then, I never thought I'd be upset to have the nickname *gordita*.

The desire to gain weight didn't last long for me in Miami. I was no longer excited to have the extra pounds. Being called *gordita* started to bother me and made me focus on my extra weight. Plus, now I was in the United States, in a city, at a time when all of the TV shows, movies, and advertisements told women to do whatever they could to be as skinny as possible.

Every day I would put on makeup and do my hair to go to school, but I didn't feel pretty. I tried to feel attractive, but I always felt inferior, and, in some cases, I was made to feel inferior. Most of the Cuban and Cuban American students looked down on those from Central America and called us *indios* (Indians). I was called *india* not just because I was a newcomer or from Honduras. I knew that it was also because my skin color was darker than most of the Cubans and Cuban Americans.

At my high school, there was very distinct separation of students. The newcomer students would sit together at recess and lunch and talk to each other in Spanish. We shared the language and a common experience, and we felt more comfortable with each other.

The Cuban American students hung out together and normally spoke English. Most of them were light skinned and some could pass for white. Almost all of them were bilingual, but they often looked down on non–English speakers, even more so if they were Central Americans. They were normally the first to laugh when someone made a mistake while trying to speak English.

The African American students would also sit together, and they would always speak English. The Afro-Cuban and Afro-Dominican students who were new to the country and were still learning English would normally join us newcomers.

There was another important dividing factor with the girls in the school. There were the popular and pretty girls—and everyone else. The pretty girls would usually wear short shorts or skirts and low-cut shirts. They seemed to have high self-esteem, were the most popular, and all had boyfriends.

The boys in school seemed very immature in my opinion. To me it appeared they only wanted a girlfriend for two reasons: to be able to brag about having one and to have someone to mess around with under one of the school's stairwells (the popular spot for hooking up when I was there). I didn't get a lot of attention from the boys; they mostly preferred the light-skinned girls. Truthfully, I wasn't interested in being anyone's girlfriend, but it would have been nice to know that a boy was attracted to me.

The biggest difference between Miami Senior High and Plan Escalón to me was what students wore to school. We had uniforms at my Honduran school, and girls could not wear makeup or paint their nails. If we wore a uniform skirt above the knee, we would be taken to the principal's office and ordered to unstitch the hem of the skirt to make it longer.

There in the U.S., I could wear whatever I wanted. I could put on makeup and do my nails, too. I didn't have a lot of clothes, so I had to get creative. I only had two pairs of jeans. I tried to switch up my outfits slightly so that people wouldn't know that I was wearing the same clothes several times a week.

After a few months, my new life didn't seem so exciting. I was tired of my new school. Everything felt so different. I was friendly with many of the other girls from my classes, but I never felt a deep connection with them. Life in Honduras was so much easier. I missed being surrounded by humble and honest people who loved me as a friend.

On top of that, I felt helpless to change things. I was tired of hearing the message that I was less valuable because my skin was darker and I didn't speak English. I was tired of being called *gordita*. What made it worse was that I started to believe those things about myself. First, I didn't feel pretty. Then, with the extra pounds I had gained, I didn't feel attractive. I didn't know how to feel better or what I could do to lose those extra pounds, and that's how my eating disorder started.

At home, I would go to the bathroom after meals to throw up everything I had eaten. I would do the same thing at school. Each day after breakfast and lunch, I would head to the bathroom and then rejoin my friends as quickly as possible so no one would get suspicious. I felt free to eat as much as I wanted, because I knew I was going to vomit right after. Also, I realized that after I threw up, I was still going to feel full and not want to eat anything else.

Once in the girls' bathroom, another student heard me throwing up. When I came out of the stall, she asked me if I was okay and if I was doing it intentionally. I was afraid that she was going to tell someone or try and take me to the school counselors. I lied and told her that the food had made me sick

"Well, take care of yourself," she replied and left the restroom.

I'm sure she didn't believe me. Maybe she knew what I was going through and had experience with bulimia herself.

This went on for several months. I lost all the extra weight and even a little more. My family no longer commented on how fat I was, but that I was too skinny. In May, my aunt Míriam came to visit us in Miami. I overheard her ask my sister if I was eating enough. I had been able to hide my eating disorder from my sister, so she didn't have anything to tell my aunt. No one in my family knew what I was going through.

As the school year was winding down, Aurora pulled me aside several times to talk with me about treating our bodies with respect. At first her lectures were about the midriff shirts that I was wearing to school. She didn't want me to feel pressured to wear revealing clothing to fit in with the popular girls or get more attention from boys. I don't know if she suspected anything about my rapid weight loss, but she never mentioned it. Instead, she challenged me to set a goal to work on my self-esteem. I looked through a booklet given to young women in the youth program at church. I found a list of strategies that I could use to help improve my self-esteem.

First, I had to accept that no matter my physical appearance, there would be people around me who would criticize me regardless. I had to learn to love myself and not worry about what others thought or said. I started with the goal of being able to stand in front of the mirror and say out loud one nice thing about me. I did this every morning for several weeks. At first it was hard, and a couple of times I had to repeat some of the compliments. Eventually, it got easier to compliment myself. I got to a point where I would randomly look in the mirror and tell myself how pretty I was, because I felt that way.

I started to feel better, and I lost the desire to purge after eating. I also learned about eating healthily and not eating too many calories. I stopped eating ice cream every morning, and I stopped eating tortillas with every meal.

Things were starting to improve. I was able to walk away from the dangerous cycle of bulimia. The school year was ending, and I would be heading up to North Carolina to see La Hita and the rest of my family soon.

21

Changes

The end of the school year arrived. Gaby and I were able to attend the weeklong girls' youth camp right after, and then we headed up to North Carolina to be with La Hita. My aunt Rafaela drove us to my aunt Míriam's house in Durham but had to head back to Miami the next day to work.

During those summer months, I spent a lot of quality time with my cousins, my aunts, and my grandmother. I spent most of my time hanging out at the house, dancing, and listening to music with my cousins during the day. Every night after my aunt Míriam and aunt Laura finished work, we would all meet at my aunt Míriam's house for a large family dinner. My cousins and I would talk until late at night and sleep in each morning. It was amazing to have my family so close. The days went by so quickly, and before I knew it, the summer was over, and it was time to return to Miami.

My aunt Míriam drove us down to Miami at the end of August before the start of the school year. It was a sad morning saying good-bye to everyone, because we had no idea when we would be back. Trips from Miami to North Carolina cost money and time away from work, and it was becoming too expensive for my family. Gaby's and my journey as *mojadas* was an enormous expense. My family had paid a lot of money to the *Coyota* to bring us, plus all the money that my aunt Rafaela and her husband spent staying in Mexico with us. On top of that, they also had to pay the ransom money to free Gaby and me. Those debts had to be paid, and I felt bad asking my family to spend more money to take us back and forth to North Carolina all the time.

We returned to Miami Senior High School to start the school year, and I was given terrible news. I was going to be placed into the ninth grade for the 2002–2003 school year. The office tried to explain that it had to do with having only attended the school for a semester and

142

with my bad grades both at Miami Senior High and at Plan Escalón. I didn't completely understand the reasoning, nor did I know what or whom to ask for more information. I sat there and did the quick math in my head—I wouldn't graduate until May 2005, when I would be 20 years old. I was disappointed and felt sad for losing a year and a half of school. Regardless, I knew I had to keep going and finish school no matter how long it would take. "God has a plan, and He knows what He is doing," I repeated over in my head.

As classes started, I stayed focused on doing well and working toward graduation, no matter how far away it seemed. Even though I was pushed back to the ninth grade, I kept a positive attitude. Surprisingly, I felt very comfortable at school.

I had now been in the U.S. for seven months. My English was getting better, and I could understand the content I was reading a lot better. I was also seeing an improvement in my pronunciation, and I could understand most people when they spoke to me in English. My grades improved significantly until I was getting A's and B's in all my classes.

At the start of that school year, I was experiencing the birth of a new Keyla. Back in Honduras, I never considered myself to be a good student. Outside of my cousin Fabricio helping me learn to read when I was young, no one had encouraged me to get A's or told me that I could do well in school. I did just enough to keep from failing and came to believe that not failing was the best I could do. I did not consider myself smart or capable of doing more.

That year, things were different. I felt driven to study and learn as much as possible. I paid attention in class. I participated, I asked questions, I took the risk of trying to speak in English, even if I knew the teacher spoke Spanish. I made a lot of mistakes, especially in English, but I was determined to learn from them. My teachers noticed my progress and encouraged me to keep going.

Of all my teachers that year, my ESL teacher, Mr. Edwards, was the best. Mr. Edwards was white and didn't speak Spanish, so he couldn't translate what we didn't understand. We (both he and the students) were forced to repeat ourselves in English over and over until we understood one another. His class was the most challenging, but it was still my favorite, and I learned a lot from him.

Thanks to his ESL classes, I was also able to improve in my other classes. After the first semester, I got an A in my English and Literature class, even though it was the subject where students learning English normally had their lowest grade. I was really proud and a little surprised. My English and Literature class was a regular class, not a special one just for students learning English.

Mr. Pérez was my English and Literature teacher. Even though his parents were immigrants from Cuba, he always denied knowing Spanish and would only use English in class. I always suspected that he spoke Spanish and tried several times to talk to him in Spanish. Each time, he told me he didn't understand and asked me to repeat myself in English. Finally, at the end of the year, when we were saying goodbye, he spoke to me in perfect Spanish. Seeing my reaction, he told me (with a huge smile) that he always hid that he spoke Spanish to help force students like me to practice and improve our English. I couldn't be mad at him, and I admit that he was right: I wouldn't have made as much progress in English if it hadn't been for his little trick. I was lucky to have great teachers like Mr. Pérez and Mr. Edwards.

In December, I turned 17 years old. Aurora offered to take me to a restaurant and told me I could bring my sister and my friends. I didn't have any close friends, so it was just Aurora, Gaby, and me. Still, that birthday dinner made me feel loved. It was such a change from my birthday the year before in Guatemala.

Aurora had always cared about making me feel special. She was always there to listen and give me advice when I needed it. I was so grateful for her caring and friendship. Even though she would lecture me sometimes when I needed it, I never felt like she was judging me or condemning me for my typical teenager mistakes.

For Christmas, we had two weeks off from school. We were able to go stay with my aunt Míriam in North Carolina to spend a few days with her and La Hita. When we got to Durham, it was all covered in snow. I felt like I was in a fairy tale. My aunt Rafaela had lent me her camera, and I spent those days taking pictures of the snow and my family.

In addition, my brother Alexander came to visit while we were there. I hadn't seen him for almost a year. He had moved to another city in North Carolina right after we arrived from Texas. I missed living with him, and I wished we could see him more often. Having my older brother around this visit made Christmas with my family much more special.

Just like with my birthday, Christmas was very different that year compared to the previous year's. Instead of sitting alone on a bus, I was there in my aunt's house with La Hita, my cousins, my aunts, my brother, and my sister. We ate *tamales* and danced, and I gave everyone a huge hug at midnight when I was able to tell each of them *"Feliz Navidad"* in person. I felt like this was going to be a much better year.

Back in Miami, I returned to what had become my normal life. I had officially been in the country for an entire year, and I had adapted to my new reality. I felt comfortable at school. I missed my friends in Honduras much less, and I had found another church family there in Miami.

At home, I was able to exercise a little more freedom. Gaby and I were able to occasionally walk to a Burger King that was around the corner from my aunt's house. We would share a hamburger combo meal that we were able to buy with money that my cousin Fabricio had given to us for Christmas. In addition, next to the Burger King there was a store where I could get my pictures developed. The camera that my aunt Rafaela let me use was a traditional film camera, and anytime someone gave me some money, I would go to the store to develop my pictures and buy a new roll of film.

Unfortunately, there was one part of my life that was not getting better: living with my aunt Rafaela and her family. My relationship with my aunt wasn't always the best. I always felt uncomfortable about the fact that I had to ask her permission for everything. I never felt like it was my home, and I felt like a long-term visitor. It was very different from living with La Hita. I missed La Hita, and I couldn't stop comparing her with my aunt Rafaela. That friction ended up causing a lot of fights between my aunt and I.

The thing we fought about the most was my going to church. That year, I had started attending a gospel study program called "seminary" sponsored by my church. Seminary classes were held at the chapel early in the morning on school days. My aunt didn't understand why I had to go to church all the time, and each time it was brought up, we ended up in an argument. I couldn't understand what she wanted from me or why she was so upset that I wanted to strengthen my faith and improve myself.

The seminary classes were canceled after a semester due to a lack of participation, so I was then only going to church on Sundays and activity nights on Tuesdays. The fights, however, still continued.

One weekend, I had volunteered to help Aurora decorate the chapel for her daughter's baptism ceremony. That same weekend, my aunt Rafaela and her husband had planned a weekend camping trip. Even though I told her that I wanted to go to church and that I was supposed to help Aurora, she made me go camping with Don Javier,

Milton, and Gaby. I felt bad for canceling on Aurora and for not being able to go to church on Sunday, and I couldn't hide my feelings. I didn't want to be there. Things started to get worse after that trip.

I was also having problems with Don Javier and my aunt Rafaela's son, my cousin Milton. Really, the only thing that we agreed on was that I was a visitor there. Milton didn't like us to touch or use any of his things.

Someone had given me a CD of the Mexican pop singer Fey. Gaby and I wanted to listen to the CD, but we didn't have a CD player. We used Milton's but didn't ask his permission. He saw that we were using his CD player and went to his dad to tell on us. Don Javier turned off the music and asked us not to use his son's belongings ever again. I was angry but didn't say anything. However, when they weren't at home, I would still use the CD player. One day, I had forgotten to take my CD out of the stereo when I was done. I came home from school the next day, and my CD scratched so badly that it was ruined. I complained to my aunt and her husband, but they told me it was all my fault for using Milton's belongings.

I was so upset and felt so alone. I didn't have a mother or father who would stand up for me in a moment like that. I had La Hita, who had raised me and who I felt like understood me, but she was almost a thousand miles away. I didn't know what to do, so I started to look for any excuse to be at church and away from my aunt Rafaela's house.

By early spring 2002, I felt like something had to change. Living at my aunt Rafaela's house was increasingly uncomfortable. I felt like my aunt and her husband no longer wanted Gaby and me living there. Honestly, I couldn't blame them. I know that we were a significant expense for them. Also, it was a small apartment and adding two more people made it uncomfortable for everyone.

One night, I prayed and asked God for clarity and help in making the right decision. I decided to call my aunt Míriam to tell her that I wanted to move to North Carolina. She spoke with my aunt Rafaela, and they decided that we would move to Durham with my aunt Míriam.

I always appreciated all the effort and sacrifice my aunt Rafaela and her husband had made for Gaby and me. There were some good moments. My aunt Rafaela bought me a porcelain doll for my 17th birthday, and I still have and treasure it to this day. A few weeks after the CD player incident, my aunt bought a CD player for Gaby and me so we wouldn't fight with Milton anymore. Still, the fights between my aunt and me continued, and I knew that a change would help us all.

I felt sad to leave my school and my classmates, and especially to be away from Aurora. But I knew deep in my heart that it was for the best. The only remaining concern was our appointments with Immigration. My aunt Míriam had agreed only on the condition that we would return to Miami to attend our court hearings.

Because we had successfully showed up to our previous hearings, our court dates would now be scheduled six months apart instead of three. While that made it easier to move to North Carolina, it didn't mean that our case was progressing. Every time we showed up for court, it was the same routine. A quick meeting with the lawyer in the hallway, sitting silently in the hearing for 10–15 minutes, and then heading over to the INS building so that they could take our fingerprints. The good news though was that, at least for another six months, Gaby and I wouldn't be deported.

During spring break, my aunt Míriam came to Miami to pick us up. Gaby was as excited as I was about moving to North Carolina and living with La Hita again. Before the break, I said goodbye to my teachers and friends at school. The most difficult goodbye was with Aurora. She was sad when I told her that I had decided to move to North Carolina, but she understood that it was the best for me.

"May God bless you and always guide your path!" she told me as she hugged me tightly. She had been like a second mother to me during my time in Miami. She did and always will hold a special place in my heart.

Don Javier wasn't at home when we left in my aunt Míriam's car, and so I was never able to say goodbye to him. My aunt Rafaela told me later that he was upset because we hadn't said goodbye, and that he considered us ungrateful and rude. Perhaps he was correct. By that time, I felt so overwhelmed and exhausted in that house that all I could think about was getting in the car and leaving. There were a lot of factors that played into the breakdown of my relationship with my aunt and her family. (I admit that me being a teenager was one of them.) However, none of that changes the gratitude that I still feel for both my aunt and Don Javier after so many years. I will never forget how they flew to Guatemala to meet me when I felt so lost and alone. I will always be grateful that they were willing to follow and protect us through our journey in Mexico. I am thankful for them picking us up, for driving us around the U.S., and for all the time that they welcomed us into their home.

The first thing I did when I moved to Durham was to look for a local congregation because I wanted to keep attending church. I looked up the address and phone number in the phone book, and I called to find out the schedule of meetings. I was still embarrassed to speak English on the phone, so my cousin Fabricio helped me.

That first Sunday, I went to church and realized that this was going to be a big shift for me. Up to that point, all of my experience with The Church of Jesus Christ of Latter-day Saints had been in Spanish. This congregation was almost all Americans, and the meetings and classes would all be in English.

I met the leaders of the young women's youth group, and none of them spoke any Spanish. They were very friendly and always did their best to understand me and make me feel welcome. The leaders helped to arrange rides for me to and from church. Unlike Miami, the chapel was miles away from my aunt Míriam's house and walking was not an option.

Most of the girls in the youth group only spoke English. It was a little intimidating at first, but I had some help. There was a small group of Spanish-speaking members of the congregation who were there to welcome me and help me out. One family from Venezuela, the Lara family, had two daughters in the young women's group, and they translated for me in the beginning until I was more comfortable and my English improved.

Additionally, in the main worship service, the church had someone providing live Spanish interpretation through a headset that I could wear. I continued to use it even after my English improved. I always felt more connected to God when I sang and prayed in my native language.

My aunt Míriam enrolled us at the local high school, Southern Durham High School, to finish the school year. The school was much smaller than the one in Miami: there were about a thousand students, and the building was much smaller and easier to navigate. Also, the school population was different. The large majority of the students were African American. There was a small but significant group of Latino students, mainly from Mexico. There was also a group of white students about the same size as the Latino population.

Southern High was also different because it was easier to make friends there. Durham was a small city compared to Miami, and the people in general were much friendlier. Neighbors and even strangers would wave to me when I walked by their house. The same was true in the school, although I noticed that this time the boys were more interested in meeting me than the girls.

One day at lunchtime, I was sitting alone at a table, and a boy named Felipe came over and invited me to sit with him and his friends. I knew that some of the attention was because I was the new girl in school, and also, I was 17 by then and looked more like a woman than a girl. I could tell that Felipe was attracted to me, but I only saw him as a friend. In fact, I became friends with all the boys in his group, and we sat together at lunch every day.

I started to make friends in my classes as well, and one day a classmate came over to my house to work with me on a school project. The whole time I was in Miami, I never had any friends to visit me at my aunt Rafaela's house.

I was also able to get out of the house more there in Durham. My aunts were a lot more social and would take me to visit their friends and attend parties at their houses. Overall, I felt I was a better fit for that city and at that school.

22

High School Senior

I started the summer of 2002 with a brand-new experience. My ESL teacher suggested that I apply for a special course on simultaneous interpretation offered to bilingual students. I had to take an English entrance exam to qualify for the course. I didn't think that my English would be good enough to be accepted, and I thought about not applying. My English had improved a lot in the last year and a half, and especially since coming to North Carolina, and my ESL teacher encouraged me to try the exam and see what might happen. Much to my surprise, I passed the admission test and was admitted to the course.

The weeklong course was held at Duke University. In the course, we would participate in exercises to help us develop the ability to simultaneously listen and speak. During my court hearings and in some of my church meetings, I had benefited from a live interpreter, but I had never realized how difficult it was to listen in one language, translate what they heard, and then speak in another language all at the same time.

After the course, I wasn't ready to become a professional interpreter, but I did take away some valuable lessons. I improved my English, and I learned a few strategies that I could use to help me better understand my classes and even help other newcomer students in school and church. Also, I finished the class more determined to improve my English in any way that I could.

In the summer of 2001, my favorite singer, Shakira, had released her first album in English. I had memorized all her Spanish songs up to that point, and I decided to use her songs in English to help me improve my English. I purchased the album and played it over and over while following along with the lyrics in the booklet included with the CD. I quickly learned each of them by heart and sang along, even though I didn't understand everything that I was singing. It helped me enormously with my pronunciation. I would also look up in the dictionary any words or phrases I didn't know and then compare them to the Spanish lyrics. There was no better way to learn a language than doing it with Shakira's music, which I loved. I thought about how I could convince my ESL teacher to only use Shakira's lyrics for our class in the coming year.

Fall arrived and I got ready to start the new school year. I was so excited to start the school year because it would be my last year in high school. At the end of the previous school year, my ESL teacher Ms. Harris had pulled me aside and notified me that I would be promoted to the 12th grade the coming fall. My teacher and my counselor had been impressed with my performance and progress those last couple of months at Southern. So, my counselor had taken another look at my transcripts from Miami and Honduras and determined that I should have gotten more credits for courses than they had given me at my school in Miami. So instead of being a sophomore, I started my senior year in August of 2002.

I was told that to qualify for graduation with the class of 2003, I would have to take all academic classes. Southern's schedule was different from Miami's because we took eight classes total, four in the first semester and four in the second semester. I was really looking forward to using the extra two slots in my schedule to take art and music classes, but I was more interested in finishing the year with my high school diploma.

That first semester, I took Geometry, ESL, Chemistry, and Biology. Taking all those classes at the same time was very challenging for me, especially Geometry and Biology. The geometry teacher assigned a never-ending pile of homework. My Biology teacher was very strict and required every assignment to be formatted and completed in a very specific way. If I wrote my name on the wrong side of the paper, or if I didn't write the date or class period, he would throw it away regardless of whether the answers were correct or not.

On top of that, right in the middle of the semester, we had to travel to Miami for an immigration court hearing. It was nice to be back in the warm weather, and we even got to go to the beach while we were there. I also had the chance to visit Aurora. We ended up being in Miami for seven days, and because there was no scheduled school break, I missed a whole week of my classes.

I worked hard to get caught up on my classes before the end of the semester. It was hard to do so with Geometry because of the amount of work I had missed, but I was able to get a passing grade. Unfortunately, I was not able to make up missed work in Biology and ended up failing the class. I met with my counselor, and she told me that I would have one more chance to pass Biology in the spring semester, but if I failed it again, or if I failed any of my other classes, I would not be able to graduate that year. I begged her to at least switch me to another teacher's class for my second attempt at Biology. She agreed and assigned me another teacher.

I was feeling positive about still being able to graduate in the spring. Ms. Harris kept me after ESL one day near the end of the semester and told me that I was going to be transferred out of the ESL program and into the traditional program for my last semester. This would mean that I would have to take a regular English class (in North Carolina my ESL class counted as my English Language Arts credit as long as I was in the ESL program). It also meant that I would have to take and pass the North Carolina End-of-Course Tests in English, Math, and Biology.

I couldn't understand why Ms. Harris was doing this to me for my last semester at school. I had only been in the country for two years, and there were students still in the ESL program who had been in the U.S. for over four years. I didn't feel prepared to take the same state tests as the native English–speaking students. I begged her to keep me in the program, but she was convinced that I was ready for this next step. I was glad to hear that she thought I was ready, but I knew my path to graduation had just gotten a lot harder.

I started the new semester ready to do whatever I needed to do to accomplish my goal. It was up to me if I wanted to graduate or repeat my senior year, and I decided that failing wasn't an option. I stayed after school and even sometimes during lunch to get help when I needed it.

That semester, I had Algebra II, which was easier than Geometry because my new teacher didn't assign so much homework. Also, the Algebra teacher was very kind and motivated me to keep learning. She knew that it was difficult for me to explain the solution in English on the board. She saw that I could get the answers correct on my paper if I thought it out in Spanish. That was what made math my favorite subject in the U.S. Numbers are the same in both languages, and I didn't have to think in English to multiply, divide, or solve equations.

During one of my first Civics classes, I knew that I was going to get through the class. That day, the teacher asked if anyone knew the Pledge of Allegiance. I had memorized it when I was in the Immigration detention center in Texas. I cautiously raised my hand, and the teacher, a little surprised, called on me. I stood up and recited:

"I pledge allegiance to the flag of the United States of America, and to the Republic for which it stands, one nation under God, indivisible, with liberty and justice for all."

As soon as I sat down, all of my classmates looked at each other and then, all of the sudden, they all started laughing. My face was all red because I did not understand what I had done wrong. Maybe my pronunciation wasn't the best, but I thought I had done a good job. They all noticed that I was about to break down, and the teacher explained that they weren't laughing at me: they were laughing because none of the students, including those born in the U.S., could recite the pledge from memory. The teacher congratulated me, and I felt a lot more confident that I could pass the class.

I was most concerned with my Biology class that semester. When I met my new teacher, Mr. Moore, an older African American man who had been teaching for more than 30 years, I knew that this semester would be different. Mr. Moore was a very kind and encouraging teacher. He stayed after school every day to help students and told me that I could get extra credit for staying after and getting extra help. A few weeks into the class, I met with him, and we set for me the goal of getting a B+ by the end of the semester.

I studied and read the biology textbook. Up to that point, it was the most difficult book I had ever tried to read in English. As I went through the semester, I was understanding more than I thought I would. The same was happening with my other classes. My English was improving so quickly that at times I would surprise myself with what I was understanding or able to say in class. I still made mistakes, but I didn't feel embarrassed for making them. I was able to have conversations with my teachers and classmates on what we were studying in class.

My teachers continued to work with me through the semester, and I was able to pass all of the state end-of-course tests. I passed the Biology exam with a B! Mr. Moore congratulated me on my achievement and on all the hard work I had put in to get there.

That school year, I felt that I had made a complete turnaround from how I was in Honduras. There, I wasn't interested in studying or putting in extra effort to get a better grade. When I arrived in the U.S., I saw that my chance to build my future and accomplish my dreams was tied to learning English and doing well in school. I also had several teachers who pushed me to take on challenges and to set and accomplish big goals. As I look back, I wish that I had been able to come to the U.S. earlier and have all four years of high school to work, study, and to improve myself. I didn't get discouraged, and I did my best to take advantage of the time I still had left in school.

That year at Southern High School, I once again felt like I was part of the school community. It was similar to how I felt in my years at Plan Escalón. I wasn't one of the most popular girls, but I had a good group of friends. Like the previous year, most of the time I hung out with Felipe and the group of boys, as there always seemed to be way less drama with the boys.

That year, I also found a best friend, a girl named Lizeth who had just arrived at the beginning of the school year. Lizeth was also from Honduras and had arrived with her mother. They had decided to leave Honduras after a robbery at Lizeth's mother's store. During the robbery, Lizeth had been shot in the arm. Her mother was afraid for their safety and decided to move to the United States.

Lizeth's journey was a little different than mine. She came to the U.S. on a plane because she already had a visa to travel to the U.S., and she was already bilingual because she had attended a bilingual private school in Tegucigalpa. We started to sit together more at lunch, and we both went over to each other's houses. What was even better was that Felipe stopped chasing me, because he had a crush on Lizeth. That was great for me because I really wanted to be Felipe's friend the whole time anyway.

That year, I decided that I wanted to have a more typical American high school experience. For the Spirit Week pep rally, Gaby, Lizeth, and I all dressed up in red and white (the school colors), and we spray painted our hair red and white as well. I was going to join in on "Senior Skip Day," but I realized I preferred to be at school more than at my house.

The other typical American school tradition that I was excited to try was prom. I had seen proms many times in the movies while still living in Honduras, and never imagined I would ever be able to attend one myself. Felipe and his friend Juan invited Lizeth and me to go with them, and they paid for the tickets and for a package of pictures.

On the day of the prom, Felipe arrived at my house with Juan. Felipe was driving a nice car that he had borrowed from his father. Lizeth had come over to my house earlier to get ready with me. My cousin

Fabricio did my hair and makeup for the dance. I had never been so dressed up. I was wearing a long, red formal gown, and Lizeth had a formal black gown. Felipe and Juan were wearing tuxedos with vests and bowties to match the colors of our dresses. It was a magical night. First, we went to dinner and then headed to the party. The school had rented a ballroom in a local hotel and had decorated it just like I had seen in the movies. There were ice sculptures, lights, and loud music. We danced, took pictures, and talked and laughed with our friends. It was amazing, and I didn't want the night to end.

After prom and exams, the only thing left was preparing for graduation. As a part of the senior experience, the school hired a photography company for our senior photo shoot. The session included pictures of us in our cap and gowns, and one in our regular clothes. Since I was a little girl, I have always loved photography, and these professional photo shoots were amazing. I wanted to buy the all the pictures they took of me, but it was far too expensive. I was afraid of not being able to get anything, but my cousin Samuel gave me money as a graduation gift, and I was able to purchase the cap and gown photos. I was so happy to have professional pictures and to graduate, that I gave one photo to each member of my family and to all my friends.

My graduation was on May 25, 2003. I hadn't felt that excited for years—or possibly ever. I dressed in high heels, a black skirt, and a nice blouse that my aunt Laura lent me. I put on makeup, curled my hair, and then I put on my red cap and gown. As I looked at myself in the mirror, I couldn't stop smiling.

Gaby, Fabricio, Lizeth, and my aunt Míriam all came to watch the ceremony. La Hita couldn't attend because she was sick, but before I left the house, she hugged me and told me how proud she was of me. When they called my name, I walked across the stage to collect my diploma. I saw my aunt Míriam crying in the audience. I knew that she was happy and proud of me. I imagined that my mother was there, too, watching proudly as I accomplished one of my dreams.

After the end of the ceremony, we went home. Some of my classmates were going to elaborate graduation parties. I didn't need any other type of celebration. Having graduated from high school was enough for me. Sitting there with my diploma, I felt so blessed. God had given me such an excellent opportunity in letting me come to the United States and finish high school. Even though for most of my life I had thought I was not intelligent, I had seen that through hard work and dedication I could accomplish any goal. I was confident that I would never give up on anything, and I was prepared to overcome any obstacle.

Southern High School had a significant impact on my life. The people I met there, especially my teachers, supported me greatly. I graduated with my head held high, knowing that I had done my best. I was so proud of myself. I would tell everyone I saw that I had just graduated from high school. I don't know how many times I repeated it or how many people I said it to. This achievement didn't mean much to some, but it was the most important thing I had accomplished since I had arrived from Honduras. All the effort that I put into learning a new language and studying day and night had been worth it. I felt so thankful for the immense sacrifice my family made in bringing my sister and me from Honduras to the U.S.

23

Undocumented Immigrant

Success in high school helped me to re-evaluate who I was and how far I could go. When I was told that I would be a senior, I started to think about what would come after my high school graduation. I discovered a new Keyla, eager to learn and grow, and I wanted to continue studying after high school.

My first attempt was to apply for a scholarship. One day in school, one of the counselors told us seniors about a scholarship that would help pay for college. I decided to apply, but as I was filling out the application, I noticed one of the boxes asked for a Social Security number. Another asked to check whether I was a U.S. citizen or permanent resident. I didn't have a Social Security number or permanent residency, so I left those questions blank, completed the rest of the application, and sent it in. I was hopeful that the significant improvement in my grades would help me and perhaps allow the sponsoring organization to look past my immigration status.

I also investigated the local community college. I knew that my family didn't have money, and paying for a large university would be impossible. I knew that there were a lot of students at Southern who were in a similar financial situation, and I had heard teachers talk about the advantage and low cost of community college.

In my research, I found out that the community colleges in North Carolina had two tuition categories. The cheaper option was in-state tuition for students who lived in North Carolina. According to the state laws back then, if a person was not a U.S. citizen or permanent resident, they would have to pay the much higher out-of-state tuition. When I saw the difference in the cost my heart sank. Out-of-state tuition for a community college would end up costing more than that of the large state universities.

Around that same time, I received the response from my

scholarship application, and as I was expecting, my application had been denied. My dreams of being able to study after high school were crashing all around me.

In defense of my naivety, I knew that I had come to the U.S. as a *mojada*, and I knew before I left Honduras that it would be a very difficult journey. What I didn't understand was how arriving as a *mojada* would continue to affect me and limit my opportunities years later. In all the discussions with my family and the immigration lawyer, no one had ever explained the system to me. I was learning this very difficult lesson at a time when continuous reminders were all around.

At church, as spring was starting, the common question that adults would ask members of the youth group was where we would be going to college the next year. Most of them answered Brigham Young University (a prestigious private university run by our church), and others would name a local university or the community college. I would keep my eyes on the floor and hope that they wouldn't notice that I didn't have an answer.

At school, I would run into similar questions from teachers, though not as often. As a senior, I would attend various meetings with groups and organizations regarding our plans after high school. At one of those, a motivational speaker and recruiter from the U.S. Air Force spoke to us. The recruiter told us about the duties and responsibilities of those in the Air Force. He also discussed the benefits and experiences gained from serving. It was all very exciting, and for a little while I allowed myself to dream about that being a possibility for me. But I quickly remembered that doors like that were closed for me. I excused myself to the bathroom, trying to hold back the tears until I was out of the room.

I was not the only one at my school dealing with concerns about the future. In fact, I had a better outlook than many students because I was able to graduate high school. Juan Carlos was a friend of mine from school who had also come as a *mojado* from Honduras. We were both seniors together. At the end of the spring semester, he told me that he had failed a class that he needed to graduate. He was already 20 years old and decided not to keep trying to graduate. He knew he couldn't go to college and would end up working in construction anyway. He told me that in his situation he didn't see the point of getting a high school diploma.

After graduation, I couldn't go to college. If I wanted to continue studying, if I wanted to fulfill my dreams, I had to find a way to finalize my immigration process. Just when I had finally discovered my passion for learning and pursuing my education, my immigration status prevented me from doing so.

All the while I was working to graduate and plan for my future, I still held out hope that my case in the immigration courts would work out, though my family and I were losing faith in that dream.

When it was time for us to go for our court hearing in the fall of 2002, none of my family members were able to take us all the way to Miami, so Gaby and I had to travel by Greyhound bus. In a car, Miami was a 12-hour drive, but in a bus, it was over 18 hours to get to my aunt Rafaela's house.

Going to the courthouse always gave me a feeling of anxiety. The building was very large, with small courtrooms spread out over several floors. Spread throughout the building, in foyers and hallways, were people sitting and waiting (many for several hours) for their scheduled hearings. Almost all of them had looks of fear, anxiety, or despair. They, like me, knew that every court appearance could end in a deportation.

At our hearing, I was expecting the usual quick back-and-forth with the judge, and that we would head back to my aunt Rafaela's house afterwards. That day, however, the judge asked our lawyer a lot more questions than usual. I didn't really understand what was going on, even with the help of the interpreter. The questions came quickly, as the judge appeared impatient with our lawyer. Plus, they were using a lot of terms that I didn't understand in English or Spanish. I guessed that the judge was expecting something from the lawyer to move our case along, but he had not done it. I never found out because after the hearing, the lawyer left before explaining what was happening or what we should do.

After returning to Durham with no progress except another court date, my aunt Míriam told Gaby and me that it was no longer possible to continue with the case. The lawyer wasn't accomplishing anything, and it didn't make sense to keep paying him. Plus, the trip from Durham to Miami was costing so much in time and money that they could no longer afford to send us two times a year.

At that moment, I felt my heart sink. It was true that we weren't making progress in court, but as long as we had our case in front of the judge, something could happen. If we stopped showing up, there would be no hope of resolving my immigration status and being able to study after high school.

Months later, after I had missed my court date, I talked to one of my youth leaders about my frustration over abandoning my court case. She spoke to several members of the congregation, and they joined together to help Gaby and me. First, someone found a new lawyer and negotiated the fee structure to take our case. One of the local church leaders came to my house to meet with my aunt Míriam and explain how the church members wanted to help.

The agreement was that the members would pay the initial fee to hire the lawyer and that they would help me with the travel expenses if my aunt could not. They had collected money from several families. Also, a few families had offered to pay me to clean their house and babysit in order for me to earn money to pay for some of the expenses myself.

The new lawyer, Ms. Garcia, was able to get us a new court date in the summer of 2003. My aunt Míriam, with some financial support from the congregation, took us to Miami so we could continue with our case.

We met with Ms. Garcia in her office the day before the new court date. She explained the strategy of our case in a mixture of Spanish and English. Even with all the legal terms, I was pretty sure that I understood the basic plan. She would submit an application for asylum for my sister and me. Because Gaby and I were two teenage orphan girls without any family in Honduras, we were in danger of kidnapping, rape, or murder if we returned there. And, with Honduras's political situation, the government there was unable to prevent or prosecute those types of crimes against unaccompanied young women.

As we walked into court the next day, I asked God to allow me to obtain legal status to continue my studies and work. The lawyer introduced herself to the judge and explained the legal reasoning for our new petition. The judge asked Ms. Garcia a lot of questions about us and our situation in Honduras. They both started to talk using complicated legal phrases that I couldn't follow, but I did hear the lawyer mention "political asylum." After a few minutes of that discussion, the judge excused us from the room so she could speak with the lawyer in private.

Sitting there in the hall, I was nervous. I knew that we could be in trouble for missing the last court date, but Ms. Garcia seemed to know what she was doing, so I tried to stay optimistic. The lawyer joined us in the hallway and gave us the good news that the judge had agreed with her initial argument. Ms. Garcia told us that she would submit the formal application with evidence before our next court appearance.

Gaby, my aunts, and I were excited with the news. The lawyer seemed very optimistic that the application would be approved. Gaby and I would have permission to live, work, and study here in the U.S.

I was excited to get back to the church in Durham and tell everyone the good news. Just as in La Entrada and in Miami, I had found a second family within the congregation of the church. I had youth leaders who looked out for me, and I had made several friends in the youth program. Those girls would often invite me over to their houses for dinner, and their families would welcome me into their home.

Shortly after graduation, during one of those visits, my friend's parents asked me about the progress of my immigration case and my plans for after high school. It was hard for me to explain everything in English, and they didn't speak a word of Spanish, but I managed to explain my issue of not being able to afford community college nor being able to work.

Following the dinner, they contacted a family friend in Utah who was willing to help me find a solution to my situation. The family friend offered to hire me as a live-in housekeeper and nanny there in Utah. The plan was that I would work during the day so that I could afford to attend a community college near their house part time.

The father of the family in Utah was in the area for business, and I had the chance to meet with him, as we were both trying to see if the plan would work for both of us. In our conversation, he asked me if I had a Tax ID number. He told me that he was willing to pay me, but that I would need to have a Tax ID so he could report my wages.

This was the first time I had heard of the Tax ID (officially called the Employer Identification Number by the IRS), and I didn't know if I had one or not (it turns out that I did). A Tax ID is a number that is assigned to a business and is used to file federal taxes. Undocumented immigrants in the U.S. can apply for a Tax ID number from the IRS as well. They cannot be used by an immigrant to get a traditional job with a company, as they are only for tax purposes. Basically, undocumented immigrants, who don't have the right to work in the U.S., are expected to pay taxes on the money they are not supposed to be earning. Also, those people who pay undocumented workers can deduct those wages from their taxes by reporting them using the immigrant worker's Tax ID number.

In the end, I was not able to go to Utah to work and study. After my immigration hearing, I was hopeful that my situation would be resolved quickly. Plus, we had a court date coming up, and traveling from Utah to Miami would be much more expensive. I stayed at home in Durham, which brought its own set of challenges.

When my aunts bought a house the summer before my senior year, it brought all of us who were in Durham together to live in the same place. The house was only about 15 minutes away from my aunt Míriam's house, but it was in a more rural area. On the property was a larger house at the front, with a smaller detached apartment behind. Initially, my aunt Laura and her children, La Hita, and my aunt Míriam and her son slept in the front house. Ritza, Fabricio, Gaby, and I slept in the apartment in back.

Having this many people in a house was not typical in the U.S., and one of the students who rode the bus with Gaby and me started laughing and making fun of us one morning when he saw all the people who were living there in one place. He asked me loudly how many people could fit in one house. I glared at him but didn't respond. He didn't know the story behind the family's sacrifices, and I realized he wouldn't understand even if I explained it to him.

On one hand, we were used to a lot of people living in the same house from our time living in La Entrada. Besides, my family was willing to make this sacrifice so that we could help each other out. This worked out well in some ways. There were more people to help pay the mortgage and other bills, and to help with cooking and cleaning. It was also nice because my aunt Laura and I were the same size and she let me borrow her clothes, which expanded my wardrobe options significantly.

However, there were times when having that many people in the same house became difficult and even traumatizing. Sometimes things got tense between my aunt Laura and me. She has always been a very neat person, and it is difficult to keep the house spotless with so many people living there. She was also very particular about cooking food. I didn't have a lot of experience, but I wanted to learn, and I wanted to help out. There were times that I would be sent from the kitchen for cutting chicken the wrong way or for some other minor offense. When that would happen, it was usually followed by some version of "*No sirves para nada*" (literally translated as "You are good for nothing").

I was aware of and grateful for all the sacrifices my family made to take us in and take care of us. I admired my aunt Laura and everything she did and sacrificed to raise three children as a single mother. I already felt useless for not being able to help with bills and rent, and hearing that same message ("You are good for nothing") repeated only reinforced how I felt.

As the year continued, the number of people living in our house grew. My brother Alexander moved in shortly after we moved there. Later, my cousin Mario also moved in to the house for a little while. Since my abuse when I was a little girl, I had managed to repress a lot of the specific details of the event; plus, it had been years since I had seen Mario.

One afternoon, Mario and Alexander were at home, and I came into the room. The two of them were joking around, and they started to make comments about my physical appearance now that I had developed the body of a woman. They called me *La Tetanic* (a Latin American actress and TV personality known for her overly large breasts). It was hurtful and traumatic. I left the room and went to my room sobbing. I wanted to be anywhere but there. At that point however, there was no other place for me to go. Plus, I was terrified of making a big deal out of it, because I was afraid that people would find out about the abuse. At that time, I still felt guilty and thought that the abuse was my fault.

In those times when life at home was overwhelming, I found refuge in the church and with my church family. They had been so supportive and were willing to accept me for who I was, rather than judging me for how I looked or what I could or couldn't do in the kitchen.

After graduation, I was able to get out of the house more often. As had been promised, I had been hired to clean the house of one of the senior citizen brothers from the church. Also, a few days a week, I babysat for a friend of my aunt's. I would watch two girls, aged one and a half and four years old. Sometimes I would also take care of the eldest daughter, who was 10 years old. I was earning $25 a day. It wasn't much, but I managed to save enough to pay for the additional lawyer's expenses. I was also able to cover some of my costs to go to court in Miami.

I was eager to be an adult, to be able to work, earn my own money, and be independent. I no longer wanted to be a burden to my aunts. Without the documents that allowed me to work, my options for a full-time job were limited. I could find someone to pay me all in cash or buy a forged work permit, but the latter option terrified me. My immigration court case had a chance, but if I got caught using forged documents, I knew that I could be arrested and lose my case.

Also, to help with household expenses, I started working in the evenings that summer as a fill-in for my aunt Míriam. She had taken a cleaning job in the evenings because her day job didn't pay enough. It wasn't a job where all the workers would show up at the same location and clock in and out. My aunt Míriam and my cousin Ritza were assigned to be the cleaning crew for a specific floor of an office building.

Once school was out, my aunt offered that I could take her place, and I accepted. I brought along my cousin Isaías, who was in middle school, and between the three of us, we were able to finish cleaning the offices and be home by 10 o'clock. It was hard work, and I wasn't able to get my part done without help. I was happy that I was able to help with rent, food, and bills.

Unfortunately, the job didn't last long. The cleaning crews' coordinator showed up one evening and demanded to see my Social Security card. Without considering the consequences, and for the sake of being honest, I told him I didn't have one. He then fired me/my aunt Míriam and my cousin Ritza. Although she did have a work permit, he fired Ritza for being a part of the whole thing.

As summer was ending and I was still looking for a way to continue my studies, I came across a flyer advertising a new nursing assistant (CNA) class for bilingual students. I was very interested because it would allow me to utilize my bilingual skills. In addition, getting into the field of nursing sounded interesting. One of my youth leaders at church had suggested that I try it because they thought I would be a good fit. Plus, recently La Hita had been very sick, and I had been helping take care of her while she was bedridden.

The program was at Durham Technical Community College. When I called to get more information, I was told that it was aimed at Latina women who spoke both languages. As I had finished high school, my English was much better than before. I could read, write, and hold conversations in both languages.

Because it was a specialized vocational course, I only had to pay the course fee, which was around $300, and there was no additional out-of-state tuition charge for those who were not permanent residents. The program lasted three months, plus a one-month clinical internship. I would be able to obtain a nursing assistant license by December of that year.

I was excited about the opportunity of continuing school and starting a new career. I was able to pay the registration and for books with the money I had made babysitting. My brother, Alexander, bought my stethoscope and other medical tools that were needed for the class.

Alexander and my cousin Samuel also helped me with other expenses throughout the course. The biggest help was with getting to school and back home. It was a community college, so there were no school buses, and we lived very far from the closest city bus route. At first, I would get rides from my aunts, but the classes were in the evenings, and it was a lot to ask of my aunts after long days of work and taking care of their own young children.

Finally, my brother offered to lend me his car to drive. I only had a learner's permit, but I had learned how to drive when I was 14, back in La Entrada. With a learner's permit, I was supposed to have a licensed driver in the car with me, but I was willing to risk it in order to complete my classes.

I enjoyed this new experience of learning after high school. There were a lot of new terms and concepts, and the course required a higher level of English than the interpreting course I had taken the previous summer. My classmates were all friendly, and we all helped each other when someone didn't understand something about the class, and translated it if necessary.

I completed my clinical internship at the Durham VA Hospital. The training was quite different from just studying terms in a book. I was given a set number of patients, and I had to bathe them, change their sheets, and measure how much they were eating and drinking. I had to keep their charts updated with the abbreviations that we had learned. It was hard work, but I found out that I found joy in helping the patients and talking to them.

I finished the course with good grades; however, I was not able to take the state exam to get my license. On the exam registration form, there was the box asking me for a Social Security number that I did not have. I had the knowledge and enjoyed the work, but I was not able to take the exam like the rest of my classmates. They all had the correct documents, a green card or work permit, to get their licenses and work. Some of them decided to work at the hospital, and others chose private clinics or home health care. I stayed at home, hoping for the day when I would have the correct documents so that I could join my classmates in this American Dream.

24

Love and Pain

The summer of 2003 had seen major events in my life. In October of 2003, a random encounter would end up changing my life completely.

Twice a year, our church held a regional conference for all of the local congregations in the area. I borrowed my brother's car and invited my cousin Fabricio to go with me to the conference about 30 minutes away in Chapel Hill.

My brother was fixing up the car at the time, and there was usually something that didn't work, but it wasn't always the same thing. One day, when driving to my CNA class, the rain started pouring down. Unfortunately for me, that was the week that the windshield wipers stopped working. That Sunday in October, there was a problem with the battery, and the car didn't always start when it was supposed to. One of the reasons I asked Fabricio to come was so I wouldn't end up stranded by myself.

We made it to the conference, and when it was over, the car would not start. As we were standing there with the hood up, some of the members from my congregation came over to see if they could help. The missionaries also came by to see how we were.

We were there several minutes, but we couldn't do anything because no one had jumper cables. Then, a tall white man in a suit walked up to us. He started talking with the missionaries who were helping me, and he offered us a set of jumper cables. We were able to get the car started, and he and the missionaries stayed there talking while they waited to make sure the car didn't die again.

The guy was clearly not Latino, but he spoke Spanish with the missionaries. He told them that he had been a missionary in San Fernando, California, a couple years before. There in California, he had learned to speak Spanish while working with the Latino community. He had learned Spanish from them. Other than a quick greeting, he didn't

166

try to talk much to me. I had the feeling that he didn't want to talk to me because he thought Fabricio was my husband or boyfriend, and he didn't want to flirt with a married woman.

The tall guy left, I thanked everyone who helped us, and Fabricio and I drove back home. On the way, I told Fabricio that the young man who had just helped us seemed like a good match for my cousin Ritza. We both laughed, and I kept driving.

"We found you a handsome guy; he's about 26 years old and speaks Spanish!" I told Ritza when we got home. We all burst out laughing.

Even though I thought the tall guy was good looking, I immediately thought of connecting him with my cousin because I wasn't really looking to date anyone new. The truth was that there was a young man whom I liked who had recently returned to Utah. His name was Brad, and he had been a missionary in Durham. While nothing romantic happened between us, we had become friends, and I wanted to see if it could be something more.

At that point, I still was trying to find a way to go out to Utah and work as a nanny/housekeeper and continue my studies. I figured that it would give me the opportunity to see if we could work as a couple. In high school, I had avoided dating a lot of the guys because they seemed immature to me. Also, many of them wanted a lot more than kissing. When I was still a young girl in La Entrada, I decided that I wanted to save myself for the man I was going to marry. All through school, I kept that same desire. I knew God had a special someone waiting for me.

My grandmother supported my choice but had her own opinion of whom I should end up with. After I was done with high school, she told me several times that she wanted me to get married to a friend of my brother who was also from Copán, Honduras. Even though he was handsome, I never accepted his invitations to go out on a date. For one, he drank too much, and to me that was a warning sign that he wasn't the right man for me.

In addition, I was more and more interested in marrying someone who had been raised in the American culture. At church, I always noticed how well most of the American men treated their wives. One night, during a dinner at the house of a family from church, the husband got up to change the baby's diaper while his wife was cooking dinner. They were a great team, and I thought to myself that I wanted the same thing.

The culture in which I was raised is a *machista* (macho) society. I had never seen a father change a diaper in La Entrada. It was considered a woman's job. Growing up in that environment, it was engraved in my mind that I needed to marry a man who would be my teammate and would not try to be my master. On top of that, I had dreamed of getting married in a Mormon temple, and I wanted to marry a worthy man who could take me there.

Two weeks after the car-breakdown incident, I attended a multiday church conference for young single adults. This time, I brought my cousin Ritza. The event was a combination of a social and spiritual networking activity for young adults from the north-central section of North Carolina. There were talks, a service project, a special church service, and a dance to help people meet and socialize. The first night was the dance, and surprisingly, the first person I saw when I entered the venue was the tall guy who helped us with my brother's car.

"Hi, how are you? Do you remember me?" I asked.

He stood there looking at me with his mouth half-open, looking confused. He started to say something but stopped.

"You helped my cousin and me a few days ago with our car when it wouldn't start," I tried to remind him.

He took another moment to respond, "Of course, I remember you! Nice to meet you. My name is Mark."

I wasn't sure that he did remember me, but I was dressed differently. When he first met me, I was wearing a long jean skirt and a sweater, and my hair had loose curls. That night, I had on flared-leg jeans and a brightly decorated shirt, and my hair looked very different. I had taken out my braids that afternoon and so my hair was very wavy.

I introduced him to Ritza, and apparently there wasn't much of a connection between them, because their conversation was over in less than two minutes. He and I hit it off right away. We danced together several times that night and spent the majority of the conference together. He told me he was born in Germany on an American military base and how he had moved around as a kid because his dad was in the Army. We talked about the time he spent in California as a missionary and the semester he studied in Mexico City.

He clowned around most of the time, and although he seemed a bit immature to me, we had a lot in common, and I had a lot of fun with him. The conference lasted from Friday to Sunday. I saw him every day, and he was always in a good mood and took every opportunity to joke around with me, and we spent most of the time laughing. On the last day, I decided to pay him back.

"You are such a flirt!" he told me as a joke.

I immediately turned away, and I acted like I was upset. Mark saw and got nervous.

"I didn't mean to offend you. I'm so sorry!" he added, now sounding concerned.

"I'll tell you what, give me your number so I can take you out for dinner and salsa dancing to make it up to you," he continued.

I loved to go dancing salsa, but I tried to stay in character and didn't respond. *A gringo who likes to dance salsa?* I thought to myself and started to smile.

"Of course, I would like to hang out with you," I finally let him see my smile.

A week later, Mark finally called me, and we set up a time to go dancing that weekend. I liked the idea of going out dancing with him, although I still wasn't sure if I would like him enough to date him.

We went dancing at a local club, famous in the area for salsa dancing. I wore black pants with flared legs, a long-sleeved button-up blouse, and platform heels. Mark wore gray slacks, a black button-down shirt, and dress shoes, and looked very handsome. He spoke Spanish very well, almost better than me, and danced salsa as if he had grown up in a Latin American country. He was full of surprises. We had an amazing evening and left the club a little after midnight. Mark didn't want to have me out too late on our first date, so my family wouldn't think he was trying to take advantage of me.

When we arrived at my house, he walked me to the side door, just off the kitchen. As we were saying goodbye, I heard my brother yelling loudly in the house. He had been drinking and was fighting with his girlfriend. The yelling got louder and louder until everyone in the house woke up. They tried to calm my brother down, but he was so angry and drunk that it was impossible. He ended up in the kitchen, throwing appliances around and screaming threats to anyone who tried to calm him down. My grandmother appeared in her nightgown after the noise woke her up and shouted to Mark:

"Alexander has gone crazy. Grab him!"

Mark grabbed my brother, pulled him out of the door and into the carport, and pinned him to the ground. Alexander yelled and tried to break free, but Mark was much taller and stronger than my brother.

"Let go of me, you gringo son of a bitch! Don't you dare come anywhere near my sister again!" Alexander swore at Mark.

I was so embarrassed. My date with Mark had gone so well, and now all this family drama was ruining everything. Needless to say, there was no kiss at the end of the date. There never was going to be one, even without the unexpected end to the date. By that time, I had a no kiss on a first date rule. On top of that, I still liked Brad and wanted to give that relationship a chance. I thought of Mark more as a friend.

Thankfully, my brother's threats didn't scare Mark away, and we hung out the next week, but as friends—at least, that was what I told myself. The next week, he invited me to a park to play basketball. I had always enjoyed playing basketball in Honduras because I was so much taller than everyone else. In the coming weeks, we spent more time together, but I was still trying to convince myself we were just friends. I had even asked him to try and find good deals on plane tickets to Utah for me on his computer. He knew it was to see Brad, so I don't think he tried very hard.

Early in November, I got sick with a bad cold. I talked to Mark on the phone and told him about my cold and how there was no medicine in the house. I didn't have money to buy any. The next night, the phone rang. My cousin Ritza answered because I was on another call with Brad. She ran into the room and whispered to me that the *gringo* was on the phone. I jumped out of my chair and grabbed the phone.

"Hi Keyla, can you walk out to the front of your house just for a second?"

I opened the door and saw the lights of a car, and it was him. I couldn't believe it. I wasn't expecting him. I was in pajamas and my hair was a mess, but for a moment, I didn't care. Mark handed me a paper bag with cough medicine, cough drops, and a box of Theraflu.

"I was in the neighborhood and thinking of you, and I knew you were sick. I thought you could use some of this," he said as he handed me the bag.

At that point, I knew that Mark was not playing games, but that he cared about me enough to make the long trip to my house. My aunt's house was a 45-minute drive from Mark's apartment in Chapel Hill. It was just the sign I needed to open my heart to him.

On my 19th birthday the following month, our church sponsored a dance for the single young adults, and I met Mark there. We danced together most of the night, and before going home, Mark told me how much he liked me and wanted me to be his girlfriend. I didn't know what to say to him because I was still trying to figure out my own feelings toward him and toward Brad. I went home without giving him an answer, and he tried to mask feeling completely rejected.

The next day, he invited me to go to the movies. When the film started, I couldn't focus; I was still feeling confused about my feelings, and it was making me nervous. Mark reached out in an attempt to put his arm around me. I turned toward him, and somehow our faces ended up inches from each other. I could feel his breath on my lips and couldn't resist anymore. A month after our first date, we kissed for the first time.

We were together a lot the rest of the month of December. We would go out a couple times a week, and I would spend most Sundays after church at his apartment. I enjoyed the time I shared with him.

When Christmas arrived, we ended up on opposite ends of the country. Mark went to California to visit friends, and I went to Miami to visit friends and family. I still didn't know whether or not I wanted to be his girlfriend. Some of my friends and family still didn't know him very well and found him somewhat immature. It was true that he would constantly make jokes, but that was just the way he was. He had a good sense of humor and always succeeded in making me smile even in the worst of times. But I was still afraid to trust him. I was scared of falling for someone, feeling the taste of real love, and then being abandoned. I didn't want to get hurt, but I didn't want to lose him either.

Most of 2003 was very tough for La Hita and her health, especially in the fall. She suffered another heart attack and was in the hospital for several days. After her recovery, she was still up and down. She would spend several days in bed, and then would be up and about for a while before ending up back in bed.

My CNA classes were in the evening, and I didn't have a full-time job, so I took care of La Hita during the day, when everyone else was at school or at work. We watched soap operas together and took occasional walks around the property when she was feeling strong enough. My aunts had bought her chickens and built an outdoor stove to help her feel more at home. La Hita had always preferred to be outside when she could.

I was also put in charge of preparing healthy meals for her. The doctor had ordered her to not eat any salt. She would get upset because she hated to eat bland food.

"This doesn't taste good if you don't add salt, Keyla!" she constantly complained.

Luckily, she didn't need as much care as my patients at the VA hospital. She was able to go to the bathroom and bathe by herself. However, she always needed someone around in case she fell and to monitor her for another heart problem.

In those days, the missionaries would visit us at home from time to time, and my grandmother talked with them a lot. At one of these visits, La Hita told them that she was happy that I was baptized in their church, because she had seen how much I had changed (for the better) since then. This came as a shock to me because I still remembered when she pleaded with me, through tears, to remain a Catholic because those were my mother's wishes. Hearing that she was happy with the results of my decision and proud of who I had become made me extremely happy. I always knew that I had made the correct decision getting baptized. Building a closer relationship with God had helped me overcome so many obstacles during the last few years. La Hita's words echoed in my heart for months and years later.

La Hita's constant health problems had also prevented her from doing what she really wanted, which was to return to La Entrada. For more than a year, she had been telling my aunts that she wanted to go back to Honduras.

Since she first arrived in the U.S., La Hita had been back to our hometown one other time to visit, but that was when her health was a lot better. Now, it was too risky to travel.

La Hita wasn't happy in the United States and never had been. She enjoyed being around her family, but she never felt at home in Durham, no matter what was tried. Through my conversations with La Hita, I knew that she wasn't looking to just visit Honduras and then return. She wanted to go back home permanently. I was an adult, and Gaby would graduate from high school shortly. We had family around us in the U.S.

When La Hita talked about returning to Honduras, my aunts reminded her that she had what a lot of people didn't, a green card, and she should take advantage of it by traveling back and forth. Her response was always that she didn't want or need the green card, and that it would be better if they gave it to someone else who would use it.

By the middle of November, La Hita was doing better and had finally convinced my aunts to buy her a ticket home. The night before she left, she asked me to sit on the couch to talk with her.

"Always be a good girl, Keyla. Don't play around with your life," she advised me.

"I'm going to be all right, Hita. Don't worry so much about me; I'm going to be fine," I replied.

I was about to leave for a church activity, so I grabbed my things and left the house. For a moment, I had a feeling that she was saying a final goodbye to me. But then I thought it was all in my head and dropped the idea. That same night, she also pulled aside all my cousins to give them advice before she left.

On December 25, Gaby, Ritza, and I were at my aunt Rafaela's house in Miami. We heard my aunt answer the phone and then we heard her yell, "My mother has just passed away!"

Even though I heard it clearly, it took a long time for me to comprehend what my aunt had just said. I looked around the room. Everything seemed to be in slow motion. My aunt and Ritza were in tears. Gaby sat there motionless, speechless.

After my brain finally caught up, I understood what was happening: La Hita was gone. The woman who had played the role of my mother for most of my life was no longer there, and I wasn't by her side to say goodbye. I was overcome by a wave of grief. If I had known that when she pulled me aside that night that it would be the last time I would see her, I would have hugged her tighter. I would have stayed there with her for the whole night.

My heart dropped as the next thought hit me—I couldn't go to Honduras for her funeral. I felt so powerless at that moment! My entire soul was screaming to go and see her. At that moment, I felt capable of anything—including heading back to Honduras the same way I had come—to be able to say goodbye. At the same time, I knew that La Hita would have never wanted me to do that. I couldn't throw away all the money spent and the sacrifices she and all my aunts had made for me to be in the U.S.

In the end, only my aunt Rafaela was able to go to Honduras for the funeral. Everyone contributed to pay for the funeral expenses, and my aunt traveled on behalf of everyone. Like me, most of the family didn't have the immigration status to leave the country and be able to return. The idea of going to see La Hita was just a fantasy to most. I tried to comfort myself with the knowledge that she would rest in the cemetery next to my mother. I had faith that she was able to find some peace after finally being reunited with the daughter she had lost so many years before.

La Hita had many friends in La Entrada, and everyone loved and respected her. Some days, it was difficult to accept that La Hita was gone. Oftentimes it felt like she had gone on a trip and would soon be back.

I struggled to understand and accept that the woman I had admired most in my life was no longer around to mentor me. I felt so grateful for all of the sacrifices she made for me over so many years. All her care, attention, and even her nagging, had been worth it. I was blessed to have had the support and love of a true fighter like her. All the good I have done in this world and everything I've become is thanks to her. I will forever be grateful for her love.

25

Marriage

I first thought of telling Mark about my grandmother's death. All I wanted was to be with someone who would hold me and tell me that everything was going to be okay, but Mark wasn't anywhere near. Mark was on the opposite side of the country; I cried all alone and hugged my pillow. Days later, I was able to see him, and he expressed great empathy and compassion toward me.

On New Year's Eve of 2003, almost at midnight, we were dancing to a song, and Mark handed me a flower and a card in which he had written: "Will you be my girlfriend?" I took the card, smiled, hugged him, and said, "Yes, yes, I want to be your girlfriend!" It was official: we were together.

One of the first things we did as an official couple was to go to Fayetteville, North Carolina, and meet his parents. I was a little nervous about it: his parents didn't speak Spanish, and I was afraid of making a mistake in front of his family. Mark and I mostly spoke Spanish when we were together. He spoke Spanish as well as a native speaker and understood almost all of the slang and all the swear words. It was one of the things that helped me feel so comfortable around him.

Mark's mom was the first to greet me. She expressed her condolences for the loss of my grandmother and offered me a hug. Mark's dad was more serious but welcomed me in the little Spanish he knew. Mark has five sisters, but not all of them were there. I already knew Olivia because she went to the same church as us. It made the night a little less stressful to already know another person in his family.

We sat around the table and prayed before having dinner. I could feel the love and harmony that existed in that home. Everyone was very kind to me, and the evening felt like a success. I was happy to have met my boyfriend's family.

About a month after becoming a couple, we were in Mark's

Keyla and Mark's wedding invitation picture, spring 2004 (family photograph).

apartment for what had become our Sunday routine. Mark had cooked dinner, and we were sitting on the couch talking, trying to extend the time until we had to drive 45 minutes back to my house. Mark looked me right in the eyes and I heard him say, "I love you!" I wasn't expecting it, and it caught me a little off guard. It was so sweet and sincere.

As I looked back into his eyes, I felt the same thing for him. "I love you too!" I answered back. We stared into each other's eyes, and we both smiled. Right then, we knew it was time to plan our future together.

Having expressed our love for each other, Mark and I both took the bold step to bring up the subject of marriage. In some ways it felt crazy to talk about marriage that quickly, but at the same time, in my heart it felt right. Looking into his eyes, I knew I wanted to be with him for the rest of my life. If we loved each other and wanted to spend the rest of our lives together, it seemed obvious to discuss getting married. Why not sooner rather than later?

Over the following weeks, we had moved past the topic of getting married, and started discussing life as a married couple. Mark was in his last semester of college and was preparing for a yearlong master's degree program in teaching. During the master's program, he would have to complete a full-time student-teaching internship and would be limited in how much he could work. He knew about my immigration status and how I couldn't work in anything more than what I was doing, babysitting a few days a week. Mark was confident that we would be able to make it work, one way or another. He even told me that, if necessary, he would postpone his master's program and get a full-time job. I told him that option seemed too extreme. I knew how important it was for him to finish his studies. We were crazy in love, but we still needed to be rational before making big decisions.

Mark was studying to be a Spanish teacher and wanted to teach at a high school.

"Even after I graduate, I think we will still be poor. I won't make much money as a high school teacher," he said to me one day.

I didn't think it could be true; how could an American with a college degree be poor? Perhaps his concept of poverty differed from mine. To me, poor was my family, who were undocumented workers and didn't even know English. Coming from a different social background, he and his family seemed almost rich to me. I hugged him tight and said: "We are not, nor will we be poor!"

Our discussions and plans continued, but we kept them to ourselves. Before sharing with our families and friends, we both wanted to pray and ask God about our decision. I wanted to marry Mark with all my heart, but I wouldn't do it if God said no. Mark felt the same way. Mark received his answer within a few days; after several weeks, I was still not sure. Mark waited patiently for me because we both had agreed that the answers should be individual. A month later, during a time of fasting, I finally got my answer. From my early teen years, I had dreamed of finding a man who would respect me and love me unconditionally. God had heard my prayers, and I truly felt like He had put Mark Sanders in my path.

In March, we announced our plans to our families. Mark had always tried to respect my family and our traditions. My father wasn't around, so we went to speak individually to both my aunt Míriam and my older brother Alexander to let them know of our plans to get married. My aunt Míriam cried with emotion and told us that she agreed that we should go ahead if it felt correct in our hearts and our spirits. Alexander was also on board with our plan. Everyone in my family had noticed Mark's love for me, and they were growing attached to him, jokes and all.

Everyone in my family was happy for us, though they had a few questions and concerns, including how soon we would get married. The biggest obstacle was explaining that we would be married in the temple, and they would not be able to attend the actual marriage ceremony.

One of the central beliefs of the Church of Jesus Christ of Latter-day Saints is that if a man and woman are married inside one of the temples, they will be married for eternity. Ever since the missionaries had taught me this doctrine, I had dreamed of being married in a temple. Because the temple is considered a sacred building, it is only open to members of our church who have completed specific entry requirements. Therefore, my family (and some of our friends) wouldn't be able to enter the temple.

My aunt Míriam didn't understand and suggested that I should get married in her church. I tried to explain why it was so important to me to be married in the temple, and that it had been a goal of mine since I was 15, but I could not make her understand.

I asked Mark to meet with my aunts and explain it to them. I was so impressed with how he handled the whole situation and was able to talk with my family, understanding our language and culture. I was more convinced than ever that I had found the right man. Although my family was disappointed that they would miss the wedding, they understood that a temple marriage was what we wanted, and they respected our decision.

In early April, I called Ms. Garcia, my lawyer, because I hadn't heard anything about my immigration case or my application for political asylum. To my surprise, my sister and I had been approved to work in the U.S., and we were able to apply for a work permit while the asylum case was still in process.

We could have gotten our work permits as soon as the lawyer had submitted the official asylum application months before, but she had never told us. I took it as another sign that God had plans for me and my future husband. I knew that had Ms. Garcia told me sooner, I would have taken the opportunity to go out to Utah.

I was so excited to tell Mark about the permit. It meant that I could finally take the state exam and become a certified nurse's assistant. Finally, I could get a job working in a hospital or a clinic. It seemed like one of our major concerns—how we would live while Mark finished school—had been answered.

I still couldn't get a job until I received the work permit card. In order to get the physical card (officially called the Employment Authorization Document), we would need to go through the same process as about every immigration application—go to a U.S. Citizenship and Immigration Services (USCIS[1]) center to have our fingerprints taken, get passport-style photos, pay the lawyer to complete the application, and wait 30–90 days for a response.

I was able to pay for the lawyer's fee from the money I had earned from babysitting. The closest USCIS center was in Charlotte, North Carolina, about three hours away. Mark volunteered to drive Gaby and me because my brother could not. I accepted Mark's offer, although I was worried that he would lose a day of work at his job.

Mark was still in school and had a scholarship to pay for tuition. He had to work part time to pay for living expenses. He was very careful with his money. He didn't have much, and his parents didn't pay any of his expenses. He was able to live on this income because he managed his money well and didn't spend more than he should. I felt bad that he would miss a day's pay, yet I knew he was willing to help me because he loved me.

After the asylum application was in, the next step was our court date in March in Miami. Mark volunteered to drive me to Miami, too, and even though I felt terrible accepting this huge favor, I couldn't say no. Otherwise, I didn't know how I would get there. My aunts were not able to keep paying my immigration expenses. I was an adult and out of high school, so I was responsible for paying the lawyer and figuring out the trip as well.

As the date got closer, I was worried about being able to pay for it all. My babysitting job was very unpredictable: some weeks I would work three days, and sometimes I wouldn't work any. In the end, I managed to work just enough to cover the lawyer and some expenses for the trip. Mark wanted to pay for gas, but I didn't let him. It was my trip, and he was going because of me. Mark's sister Olivia came with us so we would have three drivers and not have to stop at a hotel. In Miami, we stayed at Aurora's house, which also helped us save money.

The night before our court appearance, Mark and I were sitting and talking with Aurora's husband, Don Alvaro, about life and our upcoming wedding. Mark and I were still undecided about when we would get married, how we would support ourselves, and how much we would need to prepare before the wedding. As we discussed our concerns with Don Alvaro, he smiled and told us:

"Just pick a date for your wedding! Our Father in Heaven will provide everything you need; you only need to have faith. Everything will be fine."

That same night, Mark and I picked a date for that August for our wedding and trusted that God would help us make it happen. Now that we were planning a life together, my potential deportation was a reality that we had to always keep in mind. I wanted to be with Mark for the rest of my life, and the thought of being separated from him terrified me.

The next day, my sister and I went to our court hearing, and Mark went with us. As we exited the elevator, I saw a woman crying uncontrollably with her children. Her husband was being detained in that same courthouse and would be deported. I felt deeply sorry for her, and I was immediately overcome with a feeling of uncontrollable fear. I could soon be in the same situation as that woman's husband, or it could be Gaby.

During our appearance in court, our lawyer, Ms. Garcia, explained to the judge that I would soon be getting married. After some discussion with the judge and the attorney for the government, it was recommended that I drop my case for political asylum once I was officially married. After the hearing, Ms. Garcia explained to us that I had a better chance resolving my immigration status through my marriage to Mark. She also pointed out that because I entered the country at the age of 16, I had less chance of being granted asylum than my sister, who arrived at 14. Ms. Garcia explained that by separating our petitions, Gaby was almost guaranteed to have her asylum petition approved.

Before leaving Miami, we got additional good news. First, the court appointments were rescheduled to once a year. We had been present at our last couple of hearings, and the judge knew that we were no longer living in Miami. That would help save a lot on travel and lawyer's fees. Also, both my sister's and my work permit applications had been approved, and we would receive the cards soon. The entire trip was a huge blessing for us both.

Upon arriving back in North Carolina, Mark surprised me with the engagement ring we had been shopping for since we decided to get married. Mark knelt and handed me the ring, a card, and a rose.

"Keyla, will you marry me?" he asked me nervously.

Giant tears filled my eyes, and I covered my mouth with my hands to muffle my scream. I said yes, and we hugged and kissed through the tears. We had a date and a ring. Now I was only four months away from being with the man of my dreams forever.

Before getting married, Mark and I talked about all his previous relationships. He said he didn't want us to have any secrets and recounted everything about his past that he thought I should know. He wanted me to be sure if he was good enough for me before getting married. He told me that he would understand if I decided to leave him after our talk, but there was nothing that would make me leave him. He was a good man who was human and made some mistakes in his life.

That night, I decided that I should also share with him things from my past. I didn't want to hide anything from him, no matter how embarrassing or hard to discuss. I told him about the abuse I suffered as a child and the things I used to do with my friends when I was still very young. Mark was the first person I had ever talked to about my childhood abuse. Deep down, it was something I wished I would never have to talk about, but I found the confidence to tell him about it. Up to that point, I had always believed that it was my fault for everything that was done to me and that it did make me a sinner. I felt dirty. I wanted my future husband to know about it so that he could be sure he wanted to marry me. As I finished my story, Mark was very supportive in his response:

"Keyla, that was sexual abuse; you didn't do anything wrong."

I told Mark that there hadn't been any penetration and so it couldn't be sexual abuse. Before then, I had always thought that sexual abuse had to include rape of some kind. He told me that it was considered sexual abuse if someone touched me without my consent. For the very first time in my life, I understood that I wasn't at fault and that I had nothing to be ashamed of. We both ended that evening more sure that we wanted to be married to each other.

Right at the start of our wedding preparations, Mark once asked me who was going to pay for the wedding. At first, I didn't understand why he was asking the question. In my culture, the groom pays for everything, including the dress, the shoes, and the honeymoon. That was the first time Mark had heard of that. At the same time, I never knew that in the U.S. it was customary to have the bride's family pay for everything in the wedding. At the end of this cultural exchange, Mark asked me again:

"So, who's going to pay for our wedding?"

"I don't know," I replied.

We both spoke with our families, and they both agreed to help us with the wedding. My aunt Míriam volunteered to buy the fabric for my dress, and Eunice volunteered to sew it because she was an expert in dressmaking. My aunt Rafaela bought a *tres leches* cake, and my aunt Laura helped cook some of the food. My mother-in-law helped with the decorations and invitations and sewed the bridesmaids' dresses. Mark's eldest sister helped us with our short honeymoon in Myrtle Beach. With the help of both families, we had everything we needed to have a simple and beautiful wedding.

We were to be married on August 7, 2004, in the temple of The Church of Jesus Christ of Latter-day Saints located in Apex, North Carolina. Right after the wedding, we had arranged for a ring exchange ceremony in the church building next to the temple so my family could be there and see us exchange wedding rings. Later that evening, we would have a reception at the church building in Chapel Hill where we attended church.

As I began to consider my guest list, I didn't know where to start. There were so many people whom I wanted to be a part of that special day for me. Along with my friends from Durham and in Miami, I invited Elder Keyser, the missionary who baptized me, and Aurora and her family. I also sent an invitation to my best friend Leticia in Honduras. I knew she wouldn't be able to come, but I wanted her to know that I wished with all my heart that she could attend my wedding. Had it not been for her, I would never have been baptized in the church, and I might never have met Mark.

On the day of the wedding, my cousin Fabricio paid for me to get my nails and hair done. My sister-in-law Olivia spent the entire morning with me while I got ready so I wouldn't have to be alone. Once inside the temple, I put on my ball gown–style white dress and looked at myself in the mirror. I thought that I looked just like a princess from a fairy tale. I walked into the celestial room where Mark was waiting for me before we would go into the sealing room together. I walked toward him and showed my dress with a twirl and asked him how I looked.

"You look gorgeous!" His eyes were shining with tears.

The room where we were married was not very large and only allowed about 30 guests. There was special seating usually reserved for the mothers of the bride and groom. Aurora was there, and I asked her to sit in that seat because I felt as if she was there to represent my mom. That day especially, I missed both my mother as well as La Hita. Even though I couldn't see them, I knew they were there with me. I could feel their presence and their love, and I knew that they were crying the same tears rolling down Aurora's cheeks.

Mark and I left the temple as husband and wife. I felt I was living my very own fairy tale. Everyone told me how beautiful I looked and how gorgeous my dress was. Eunice had done an amazing job, and I will be forever grateful to her for making my dress. Unfortunately, three days before my wedding, she received the news that the love of her life had died of a heart attack in Honduras. She decided not to go to the funeral because she didn't want to leave my dress unfinished.

The ring ceremony was beautiful, and my family and our friends who could not join the temple ceremony enjoyed watching Mark and

Mark and Keyla on their wedding day, August 7, 2004 (K. Stewart).

Keyla and Mark on their wedding day, August 7, 2004 (K. Stewart).

me exchange rings. Then, Mark and I drove over to the reception in his little red Toyota Echo with the word "Newlyweds" written on the back window.

At the reception, we were joined by an even larger group of family and friends. We danced to Latin music, and everyone enjoyed the food my aunts had helped make. For our first dance, Mark chose a very romantic song in Spanish called *"Por Amarte"* by Enrique Iglesias. I knew that marrying him was the best decision I had ever made in my life. I could feel how happy he was as we danced close together and he put his lips on my cheek. I couldn't believe we were now husband and wife forever.

At the end of the night, and as I began to say goodbye to my family, I realized that I would no longer be living with them but with my new husband in our new apartment. Saying goodbye to Gaby was one of the hardest things I had done up to that point. When I hugged her, she hugged me back, and we both started crying uncontrollably. As we cried, everyone around us began to cry too.

Gaby and I had always been together. In Honduras, after our cousins and brother moved away and our household kept shrinking, Gaby and I were the last ones left. Since being on our own in La Entrada, and then through our journey as *mojadas* and our entry into the immigration system, we had gone through things together. As we moved from Honduras to Miami to Durham, we were always there for each other. Neither she nor I had realized it until that moment, but when I left with Mark that night, our lives would be moving in two different directions.

26

Working Woman

At the beginning of the summer of 2004, my work permit card arrived in the mail, and I was finally able to work in more permanent jobs. The father of the girls that I took care of was a manager at the fast-food restaurant Bojangles. When he found out that I had a work permit, he offered me a job at his restaurant. Finding that job was a huge blessing at a time when I needed it the most. I earned a little more than minimum wage (about six dollars an hour) and was assigned part-time hours only during the times when the restaurant was the busiest. I was happy with that because the job helped me to contribute to our wedding budget as well as save some for upcoming lawyer expenses.

I started out as a "packer." It was my job to pack the bags of food based on the order that was posted on a screen in the back. After two weeks as a food packer, I was promoted to cashier. After I received my promotion, some of the other female employees weren't happy at all. At that time, all of the packers were Latina women who spoke little to no English. All of the cashiers were African American women. When I was moved to the cashier position, the other packers started a rumor that I was having an affair with the manager and that's why I was promoted so quickly.

Despite what others thought, I was promoted because I was able to speak both English and Spanish. Besides that, I would always try to stay busy even if there were no customers. I would grab the broom and sweep, or I would take the rag to wipe down the tables so the restaurant would look clean. I was so excited to have the job and eager to work that I couldn't just sit around wasting time. Once, the shift manager didn't see me at the cash register and asked for me. I imagine that he thought I was hiding somewhere to take an unscheduled break. When he found me, I was sweeping the carpet at the entry door, and his expression changed from anger to contentment in a heartbeat.

A couple weeks before the wedding, I told the manager that I wouldn't return after my honeymoon because I was going to get a job as a nurse's assistant in one of the local hospitals. Although he was reluctant to lose me as an employee, he congratulated me because he knew it was the best for my personal and professional growth. He also asked me if I knew any hardworking, bilingual people like me, but I told him I didn't have anyone in mind at the time. In reality, I didn't know if someone bilingual would agree to work for six dollars an hour. Working at Bojangles gave me experience, and although not all of it was positive, it made me appreciate my new job at the hospital.

Another benefit of having my work permit was that I could finally take the North Carolina state assessment for my Certified Nursing Assistant (CNA) license. I scheduled the exam and had to look through my class readings and notes because it had been several months since I had been in class. I did well on the exam, and in a few weeks, I received confirmation that I had passed and a copy of my CNA license.

I applied for a job at Durham Regional Hospital, where La Hita had been a patient several times when she was sick. I applied for a full-time position in the cardiac ward, where they treated my grandmother, because it brought back memories of her. However, there wasn't an available position on that floor. I was offered a part-time position as a roaming CNA, which meant that I would be assigned to the floor where I was needed that day.

I was able to choose the hours and days I wanted to work. I decided on the weekday shifts, even though night and weekend shifts paid more, so I could spend more time with Mark. There was always a need for CNAs at the hospital. And even though it was a classified as a part-time job, I was able to work 36 to 48 hours a week.

At the hospital, I had to learn a lot of things quickly, including how to use the computer and the other machines and equipment I would need. However, I rotated through all the floors, so I had to be trained several times on some things because sometimes different floors had different procedures. Every day I was assigned eight to 10 patients to look after. Mainly, I was assigned to routinely take their blood pressure, respiration rate, and pulse. At the start of the shift, I changed their bedding, measured their urine, checked their catheter, and helped them get dressed and bathed. For those patients who were immobile, I had to change their diapers or bedpans and clean them up after. Even though most people didn't want to do this task, I didn't mind it. I enjoyed being able to take care of patients, even if it included changing a diaper.

For most of my days, I was assigned to the intensive care or emergency units. I was dying to work on the maternity floor with women who had recently given birth. They were patients who didn't need so much care, and I could see the newborn babies. Only on very few occasions was I able to work in that section.

Mark was studying for his master's degree and was completing his student-teaching internship. I worked 12-hour shifts whenever I could. That way, I was able to work over 40 hours in a week, and the overtime would really help with household expenses. My income was enough for rent, food, electricity, water, cell phones, and eating out from time to time, but on a minimal budget. Plus, I liked working long shifts because I could work only four days and then enjoy a long weekend. During winter, the days were shorter; I would start work very early, before the sun came up, and by the time I finished, it was dark again.

My family didn't like the fact that I was the only one working while Mark was studying. They thought Mark was taking advantage of me, because I was the only one working. Although they didn't say it to my face, I knew that's what they thought, as the rumors would always make it back to me. I was confident that I had just married the man of my dreams and my small sacrifice would help us be in a better position next year. After he was finished with school, Mark would work full-time as a teacher, and I could start college like I had always dreamed.

We didn't have much during that first year of marriage, but it was an incredible time. Our apartment wasn't luxurious. Almost all of the furniture was used hand-me-downs. We had received a new bed, a 20-inch television (this was before the era of flat-screen televisions), and several kitchen appliances as wedding presents, and they were a great blessing to us. It was a great year, and we succeeded in making that apartment a home full of peace, tranquility, and love.

Mark treated me very well and pampered me a lot. I would always find love letters all over the house and roses when I least expected it. He would help with the housework, and when I would come home late from work, dinner would be ready. That was why I was so inclined to marry someone raised in the American culture. I have never been a supporter of machismo and the idea that women should be doing all of the housework and taking care of the children. Mark wasn't raised that way, and so we worked as a team in the house.

While much of my new adult life was falling into place, I also began to suffer from my first bout of depression as an adult. I had never suffered from it in my childhood or adolescence. Of course, I did have long, sad days, but it was never to the extent that my mental state compromised my quality of life. I began to feel down most days of the week. At times, I didn't want to get out of bed and struggled to find the strength to go to work.

Looking back, it was a lot to come to terms with in such a short time in my life—losing La Hita, getting married, moving to a new house, and starting a new job. I am convinced that starting my relationship with Mark when I lost my grandmother was the best thing that could have ever happened to me. Because of his company and the time required to plan the wedding, I didn't have the time to sink into despair following the loss of the woman who raised me. In addition, the chance to establish my own home gave me a break from so much, including the negative comments from my family members about me and my religious beliefs. Having a shoulder to lean on and having someone who shared my faith, listened to me, and didn't judge me was what I needed to be able to find some peace and rest at home finally.

I struggled to get through my depression, even though at that time, I didn't understand everything that was happening to me. At the same time, I at least found some comfort because with Mark, I no longer had to pretend to be strong. I could be myself, and I could cry openly as much as I needed to. At the time, I was confident that my husband would never judge me or criticize me for it.

After nearly a year into marriage, Mark received his master's degree in education from the University of North Carolina and began his new job as a Spanish teacher. Mark was very passionate about working with teenagers, and he wanted to work in a school with a high population of Latinos and African Americans. That was where he knew there was the greatest need for education. He was not interested in teaching at private schools or those schools in very affluent areas. So, I suggested to him that perhaps he might apply to work at the same school where I had studied and where Gaby was about to graduate. That's how Mark applied and got his first job as a teacher at my alma mater, Southern High School.

With Mark's new job, we decided to move from Chapel Hill to a nicer apartment in Durham. Up to that point, we had lived with one car, a 2000 Toyota Echo that Mark had purchased used from his parents. On days that I needed the car for work, Mark would take the bus or ride his bike to school. Because we would both be working in different parts of the city, we decided to buy a second car.

Additionally, my sister Gaby moved in with us. During our first year of marriage, I would pick her up most Fridays after school, and she would spend the weekend at our house. Gaby had graduated that summer as well, and so she moved in with us permanently. A third benefit provided by the work permit was that I could pay in-state tuition for classes at the community college. The fall of 2005, I began my studies at Durham Technical Community College. I took two classes each of those first two semesters and passed all of them with As. The classes were basic English and math courses and weren't too difficult, but I studied hard because I wanted to have a high GPA. My plans were to continue with nursing and become a Registered Nurse (RN). There were two different options to become an RN, a two-year program at the community college or a four-year program if I transferred to another university. I wanted to have both options open, and I knew that I needed to have good grades to do so.

While I was studying, I continued to work part time at the hospital. Despite having a part-time job and my husband working as a full-time teacher, it was tough to cover all of our expenses. Mark earned slightly better as a teacher because of his master's degree. However, for him to finish the degree, he had needed to get student loans. Because of his scholarship, he was able to finish his undergraduate degree without any debt, but the scholarship did not cover any graduate school. However, his teacher's salary wasn't enough to cover all our general expenses and the student loan payment. So, I had to keep working part time.

One expense that we couldn't cover was health insurance for me. I wasn't able to get health insurance through the hospital because I was designated part time, and even though I would work up to 48 hours in a week, they were not required to offer benefits to part-time employees. The hospital was very aware of the laws and would limit my hours every so often so that I wouldn't automatically be reclassified as full time. In that way they were able to avoid offering me insurance. In addition, the cost to add me to my husband's work insurance was too high. We couldn't afford food or rent if I was added, so we sacrificed and hoped I wouldn't get sick.

It was then that I understood what Mark had tried to explain to me sometime before we got married. He told me that teachers didn't make enough money to support a family of two, let alone if we wanted to have children. I couldn't understand how an American with a bachelor's and master's degree could have a job that paid so little. I never imagined that his salary would be so much less than what most of the men in my family were earning working in construction. My eyes were being opened to the economic realities of the world, and it made no sense.

It wouldn't be easy to improve our quality of life relying on Mark's salary alone. I knew everything would work out eventually, although it would take years of patience and hard work. I knew that God had a plan for my family, even if I didn't have all the answers right then. My husband was dedicated to being a teacher and helping young people. Although I disagreed with the injustice of how poorly teachers were paid, I knew that he was doing what made him happy. The only thing I could do was to continue with my part-time classes so that I could one day get a better job in the future.

I started my second year of classes at Durham Tech in the fall of 2006. I was done with the introductory classes, so I was taking more challenging classes. I took English, Psychology, and Biology that semester. Several of my classmates advised me that those classes were too hard to take at the same time, but I didn't listen and wouldn't realize my mistake until later in the semester.

I continued my work at the hospital, but I was enjoying it less and less. First of all, I had a hard time making friends there because I rotated between all the floors based on who was out or where they needed help that day. Everyone on the regular floor staff saw me as an outsider, and we never really got to know each other.

One of the results of not having friends was that I became the target of some of the regular floor RNs. One day I was reported to the CNA manager because, allegedly, I didn't know how to measure vital signs. The nurse supervisor then made me measure the vital signs of a patient to show her I knew how to do it.

The RNs would often give the CNAs lists of things to do for the patients. Some of the RNs were polite when giving orders, but many would make sure to demonstrate that they were more important by the way they talked to us. One day, one of the nurses went way too far. She raised her voice at me in front of everyone there at the nurses' station. She rudely ordered me around as if she were my mother and I was a child who had misbehaved. One of the other CNAs advised me to report the nurse. I did so, but no one followed up with me. I knew that nothing would happen because I was the CNA, and she was the RN.

I was getting tired of the work environment at the hospital and began to doubt whether nursing was for me. I loved caring for the patients, and on many occasions they expressed how grateful they were for my help. In the end, I decided that along with the other important changes in my life, I needed to find a new place to work, so I left the hospital.

In August of 2006, as Mark and I celebrated two years of marriage, I felt that something was missing in our home. So, we started talking about the possibility of growing our family by having a baby. We had talked about kids before we got married, and he and I agreed that we wanted to have three children. We knew that if we had a baby, we would have more expenses, but we were willing to make the sacrifice.

Just one month after we started trying, I got pregnant with my first baby. One morning when I was off work, I took a pregnancy test and saw that it was positive. I was overcome with excitement. I was going to be able to fulfill my dream of becoming a mother. When Mark came home from work, I told him the news and he couldn't believe it. He thought I was playing a prank on him. After I showed him the test, he laughed and hugged me. Neither of us could stop smiling the rest of the day.

When we broke the news to our families and friends, everyone was as excited as we were. Some of our family had been asking for a while when we were going to have children, because we had been married for a while and still showed no signs of wanting to be parents.

I didn't know what to expect with pregnancy and hadn't imagined the extent of the physical challenge it would be to create a new life. My first trimester was especially hard. I was unable to concentrate on anything. I kept forgetting things and I was exhausted all the time. The first change I had to make was to drop the classes I was taking. Perhaps if I had listened to my classmates' advice and not taken the three challenging classes that semester, I could have done it. However, the subjects required a lot of time and concentration—both things I was lacking at that moment.

During my first weeks of pregnancy, I switched jobs to a private health clinic in the area. I liked the new job and the increased responsibilities. I was responsible for seeing all the patients, measuring their vital signs, and collecting important information from them before they saw the doctor. My memory was failing me, and as I was learning the job, I had to write everything down in a notepad and review it several times.

I was enjoying the job and being a part of a team. However, as I spent more time there, I noticed a disturbing trend. The main doctor, who was also the owner of the clinic, treated the patients very differently depending on who they were. If the patient was an American (whether white or Black) who was a native English speaker, the doctor treated them as quickly as possible, smiled all the time, and gave them as much time as needed for their appointments. If the patient was Latino, and especially if they spoke no English, the doctor made them wait longer, and in the exam room the doctor spent as little time as possible with them. On top of that, the doctor (in Spanish) talked down to these patients and demonstrated through tone and attitude that the patients were a lower class.

The clinic was a private clinic that provided services to those without health insurance. Most of the patients were from lower-income households. Because most of the staff was bilingual and it was extremely difficult for undocumented immigrants to get insurance, most of our clients were immigrants from Latin America.

The patients could sense the mistreatment, but they didn't say anything because they were in need. The clinic was close by, and they could explain their medical situation to the doctor in their native language—and if they were there in the clinic, they had a genuine medical need (almost none of the patients came to the clinic for check-ups or preventative care). I could never understand how the doctor could treat people that way. First, she was from Latin America, so at some point she had been an immigrant to the country as well. Second, most of the patients were Spanish-speaking immigrants, and the clinic would not have had enough patients to survive without them.

The more I saw the doctor's exchanges with the patients, the more I felt helpless. I was a simple CNA and couldn't tell a doctor and the owner of the clinic what to do. Plus, I was pregnant, and my (growing) family needed my paycheck.

It was getting harder to work with that doctor. (The clinic had two other staff doctors who treated all their patients with the same respect and professionalism.) The injustice and racism toward people who were like me made me angry. I had come to the country as a *mojada,* and I didn't have insurance either. At that time, because I had a work permit, I was being seen for my pregnancy appointments at the public health clinic. At the public clinic, I had never experienced that kind of disrespect from the staff. All of the doctors and nurses were courteous, professional, and supportive.

At the same time, I had experienced racism in this country, and I knew firsthand how the patients at the clinic felt. One day when I was still working at Bojangles, a man made fun of my English. He laughed and imitated what I had said with an overexaggerated accent. I felt awful and ran to the bathroom to cry. It wasn't the first time it had happened to me. But that particular situation made me feel sad and frustrated that someone was making fun of my efforts.

When I was working at the hospital, there were times when my patients' family members asked for another CNA. I knew I hadn't done anything wrong because my supervisor would have said something to me if it was my mistake. I realized that they didn't want a Latina to be the one helping their loved ones.

Once I moved here to the U.S., it didn't take me long to realize when people had something against me. They didn't always have to say it out loud, but I could feel their discontent with and hatred toward me. Knowing when someone is a racist is a skill you develop when you are a person of color. You don't need someone to say something to your face to know the prejudices they carry inside.

I continued to work in the clinic, though being there was contributing to my already growing mental health concerns. I took a couple of days off when I had a fairly severe attack of depression. I found it impossible to get out of bed in the mornings, and I would cry over anything. When I returned to the clinic, in a moment when I was distracted, I ended up sticking myself with a used needle. When I went to talk to the doctor, I tried to explain my current situation and my pregnancy, but she was very dismissive and insulting to me, and she ended up firing me. I later found out that she was upset that I hadn't told her I was pregnant when she hired me, and she listed my firing as "for cause" because I had lied to her about being pregnant.

I was worried about not having a job, and yet I knew that my mental state would not allow me to get another one right then. However, after the initial shock was over, I was relieved to be away from the clinic, and I could now focus my energy on improving my mental health and getting ready for my baby boy.

27

Decision Making

Through the wedding, working, going to school, and everything else in life, my case with immigration continued and was always in the back of my mind. The day after our first anniversary, I had my next hearing in court. Ms. Garcia's plan was to officially separate Gaby's and my cases and for me to withdraw my petition for political asylum. Mark and I were both a little nervous because my stay in the U.S. was based on my petition for asylum. If I rescinded that petition, I wouldn't have a pending motion with the court, and I could be subject to deportation.

During the hearing, the two cases were officially separated, and the lawyer informed the judge that I was officially withdrawing my asylum petition. Ms. Garcia also informed the judge that Mark and I were now legally married and that we had submitted our I-130 application. The judge noted that my case would essentially be put on hold to allow for me to adjust my immigration status based on my marriage to a U.S. citizen. Gaby was given a new court date, and I was sent home to continue the visa application process with the USCIS.

A few weeks after the wedding, Mark submitted the application used to establish our relationship as a legally married couple, officially called the I-130. It is the first step in applying for an immigrant visa for your family member. After submitting the application, we would be given an appointment for an in-person interview. The purpose of the interview was to assess if the marriage was genuine or if it was an attempt to defraud the government and get a green card.

The official posted timetable for I-130 processing was six months. However, we knew that waiting times for applications with the U.S. immigration system could stretch into years, so when we passed our first anniversary without a response on the I-130, it wasn't a major concern. As we passed our second anniversary without any word from USCIS, we started to worry. Mark called the customer service line several times, but the only response we got was that the application was still in process and that a letter with the interview appointment would be sent in the mail once they processed the application.

Around that time, Mark talked to his grandmother and told her of the frustrating situation. She lived in Washington, D.C., and was friends with a member of Congress. She told Mark that she would ask her friend to see if he could get any answers. With one call from a staff member in his office, we had our answer on the delay.

It turned out that Ms. Garcia had not correctly filed the paperwork on the withdrawal of my asylum petition, and USCIS would not process the application until the pending court case showed that it had been resolved. Luckily, I had kept all of my immigration paperwork, and we were able to resolve the issue by submitting a copy of the court order. A few weeks later, we had our scheduled appointment for the I-130 interview. When I think back to this time, I wonder how long we would have waited if we didn't have a connection to a member of Congress.

Our interview was scheduled in early 2007. I was around four months pregnant and definitely showing the day we attended our interview. As we drove the USCIS facility, I was growing more and more nervous. I had talked to a couple of people who had been through the process, and I had heard many nightmare stories from others. I knew that they could separate us into different rooms and ask us random questions about each other. Plus, we had heard that Mark or I could be arrested there in the facility if the interviewer felt we were lying. Mark and I were in love, and our relationship and marriage were based on that love. But I was still nervous. We put together a binder of evidence based on the instructions for the interview. We included pictures from when we were dating, pictures from our wedding, a copy of our marriage certificate, a copy of our wedding DVD, and a letter from the pastor of our church.

Our interview started together in a small office. The USCIS agent began by asking basic information: name, date of birth, and where we lived. We were both expecting to be separated after these initial questions. The agent then asked me about our wedding and how I had met Mark. We handed over the binder of photographs. The interviewer randomly selected a photo of us and some friends, pointed at someone in the picture, and asked us who that person was. We both answered simultaneously that he was our friend Alejandro.

"Who is Alejandro?" the interviewer asked.

"He's a friend from church who is also in one of our wedding photos," Mark replied, pointing out that he was also in one of the pictures taken on our wedding day.

The interviewer asked if we had children, and I told him I was pregnant.

"How far along are you?"

"Four months!" we both answered at the same time.

"Where did you get married?" asked the interviewer.

"In the temple of the Church of Jesus Christ of the Latter-day Saints in Raleigh," I replied.

He then closed the binder and handed us back the wedding DVD without playing it. He ended the interview and approved our application. I had been so nervous and the interview ended so quickly that I sat there for an extra few seconds, not knowing what was happening. Mark must have felt the same way because he stayed in his chair as well. We had been waiting for over two years and had spent the last month worrying about and preparing for a long and intense interview, and the whole thing was done in about 10 minutes.

As we walked back to the car, I felt relieved and happy all at the same time. Of course, there was never any doubt in our minds that our marriage was real. We had been married for almost two and a half years, we had gone through all the steps necessary to be married in the temple, and I was pregnant with our baby. I honestly had never thought of marrying someone for a green card. I know people who have taken that route, and I don't judge them. I have no way of knowing their situation or what led them to that decision. I feel blessed that I met and fell in love with someone from the U.S. who loved me and wasn't worried about my immigration status.

With that step of the immigration process behind us, I could focus on preparing for my baby boy. When I was a teenager still in Honduras, I once dreamed of a white, blue-eyed boy riding a bicycle in the backyard of my house in La Entrada. From that day on, I always knew that my first child would be a boy. When the doctor confirmed through an ultrasound that it would be a boy, I wasn't even surprised, just really excited to meet him.

Due to my job dismissal and being pregnant, Mark started to work in an afterschool program at the school and signed up to work at a college prep program at UNC over the summer. That helped us a little bit with expenses, but paying for the upcoming hospital bill was a big concern for us. Because I didn't have health insurance before I got pregnant, there was no way to get covered and we would have to pay the

entire hospital bill. To help cut costs, I went for my pre-natal visits at
the public clinic, and we didn't have to pay for anything. As for the
birth, we prayed that it would be uncomplicated and trusted God to
help us find a way.

A week after my original due date, we drove to Duke Hospital on
June 23, 2007, so that staff could induce my labor. After I had been more
than 30 hours in labor and endured three hours of pushing, the doctor,
worried about the baby and my health, advised me that the best course
of action would be to get the baby out via Cesarean section. In all the
planning and preparation, having a C-section had never crossed my
mind. I was so physically and mentally exhausted that I was hit with
an immediate wave of anxiety. I felt sick and vomited all the water and
Gatorade (the only thing I had ingested in those 30 hours) in my stomach. The medical team immediately set me up for the C-section, and I
was in the operating room in about 10 minutes. Mark joined me shortly
after, and a few minutes later, I could hear my son screaming. Mark
brought him, all wrapped up like a burrito, over so I could see him.
I felt like a train had run me over, but the happiness I felt when I met
my beautiful baby boy, Isaac, couldn't compare to anything else in the
world. He was a healthy, beautiful baby.

After the C-section, Mark stayed by my side, caring for me in the
recovery room and never leaving me alone. The nurses took Isaac for a
bath, and we could hear him crying in the other room. I felt completely
out of energy; there were times during the surgery that I had literally
felt close to death. I wanted to sleep, but my mouth was completely dry
from the medicine they had given me to prevent me from vomiting.
I felt as if I had walked for hours in a desert with no water. I finally
passed out/fell asleep, and after sleeping for a couple hours, I was able
to hold Isaac in my arms.

I ended up having to spend several more days in the hospital
because Isaac would rather sleep than eat, and because of that, he had
lost too much weight. Mark stayed with me in the hospital for the first
couple days, but on the third day, he had to complete a few last items
with his summer job so that he could be paid. I didn't want to be alone
at the hospital, but I understood. After Mark left, a new daytime nurse
came to the room.

"Where are you from?" the nurse asked me.

I replied I was from Honduras, and her face changed immediately.
"You will have to change your son's diaper!" she replied rudely.

I was surprised by her change of attitude. She knew I could barely move but refused to help me. All of the other nurses had been so helpful and supportive up to that point, when Mark was still around.

I felt awful after the way she treated me. I was so emotional, and I couldn't stop crying. What I thought would be a short time away from Mark turned into hours. When Mark came back, the nurse changed her attitude and treated me better, just because my husband was white.

Upon leaving the hospital, we filled out a questionnaire, and I described my awful experience. No one from the Duke Hospital ever called me to apologize or tell me they would act on the matter. Perhaps they thought my survey wasn't critical because I wasn't an insured patient, or just because I was Latina.

Once we were home from the hospital, we were both at a loss as to how we would pay the medical bills. After a five-day hospital stay and a C-section, the bill totaled close to $30,000, which was almost my husband's annual income. We had talked to a social worker at the hospital and she helped us fill out an application for charity care, which was medical-bill relief provided by the hospital. A few weeks later, we received the good news that almost all of the medical bills had been taken care of through care credit, and we only had to pay a couple thousand dollars, which we were able to do through monthly installments over the next couple of years.

Having a new baby at home was a brand-new world for both of us. Being a parent was a unique experience, full of excitement and challenges. I was so excited to have this brand-new baby. Luckily, Mark was home for the summer and helped by changing most of Isaac's diapers and feeding him at night so that I could sleep better.

A few weeks into my new role as a mother, things started to get more difficult. My depression worsened, and at that time, it was more substantial than before. I was tired all the time, and I struggled to get out of bed. On top of that, I felt angry all the time, especially with Mark. On some days, it seemed like everything he did just made me more and more upset. When he was around, we fought more and more, and when I was alone, I couldn't stop crying. It got so bad that I wasn't sure that our relationship was going to make it. It was like all the feelings of love I had for Mark had suddenly turned into anger, and there wasn't anything that had happened that could explain why.

Near the end of the summer, when Mark was heading back to work, one of the older women from church came by the house to visit me and see how I was doing. When we sat down and started talking, everything came up all at once. I told her how I was feeling, how I felt angry, sad, and depressed all the time. She told me that it sounded like symptoms of postpartum depression—she knew because, decades earlier, she had been through the same thing after having her own children. She later provided me with some books on postpartum depression and helped connect me to some community resources.

That visit was directed from heaven, as it was exactly what I needed in the moment. As I read about postpartum depression, I knew that it was exactly what I had. Going through the list of symptoms was like reading a checklist of exactly what I was going through. I felt a huge sense of relief as I finally was able to figure out what was happening to me. The symptoms continued, but knowing what I was dealing with helped me to find solutions to work through the problem.

Through one of the community resources, I was able to get connected with a social worker who would come visit me at the apartment once a week. We would talk about how I felt and put together action steps that I could work on throughout the coming week. Slowly, I started to feel more hope and optimism in my life. Over the next few months, I felt better able to take care of my son, and the initial excitement I felt in having a baby started to return.

At the same time, my relationship with Mark started to improve as well. Knowing what I was going through helped him to be able to understand and support me. In all, it was a long journey through postpartum depression, but I eventually was able to get through it and feel like myself again.

By March 2008, we decided to hire a new lawyer. We could no longer count on Ms. Garcia. After the I-130 was approved, every time we talked to her about options for moving forward with my case, she maintained the opinion that we should wait and that eventually the president or Congress would change the law. Starting in 2006, the topic of immigration reform had become a major political talking point. There were proposals from the House of Representatives, the Senate, and the White House. With all three groups proposing some type of immigration reform by 2007, it appeared certain that there would be some type of law passed that would help me to gain my green card.

Without a change in the law, I had limited options. Once I had rescinded my petition for asylum, I was basically left without any legal status. Without the asylum petition, I was not able to renew my work permit, which meant that I could not continue to work as a CNA and I couldn't take classes at the community college and still pay in-state tuition. On top of that, the state of North Carolina had revamped its laws for immigrants, and I was no longer able to renew my driver's license. Once my license expired, I wouldn't be able to legally drive a car or get car insurance.

Most people assumed that because I had married a U.S. citizen, I would automatically be given a green card. Unfortunately, the legislation had changed for those who entered the country "without inspection" (the official designation for those who cross the border without going through an U.S. immigration checkpoint). The new requirement was that I would have to leave the U.S. in order for my immigrant visa to be processed. Ironically, after dropping my asylum petition and going through the immigration process as the spouse of a U.S. citizen, I had fewer opportunities and was moving into the "shadows" of being a *mojada*.

The main reason for deciding to switch lawyers was the last conversation we had with Ms. Garcia. My husband and I were both concerned about me losing my license. With the recent official cooperation between North Carolina law enforcement and ICE (Bureau of Immigration and Customs Enforcement—the immigration police), there was a real concern that being stopped by the police could lead to me being handed over to ICE for deportation. Ms. Garcia downplayed the idea and told us that she would be able to get me out of custody. She told us that I should not leave the country and that she would find ways to delay long enough for the immigration reform to pass.

Around that time, we were having dinner with our friend Alejandro and his new wife. Alejandro had also come to the U.S. as a *mojado*. After going through the I-130 process, he returned to Mexico to process his immigrant visa and came back to North Carolina with his permanent residency. He recommended that we talk with the lawyer he had used for that process. The next day, we called to set up a phone consultation with a new immigration lawyer, Ms. Smith.

During the consultation, Ms. Smith was professional and, more importantly, very honest with us. She told us that she would not give legal advice on what may happen in Congress, only what our options were at that moment. She explained to us that the only way to obtain my permanent residency was to return to Honduras and apply for an official pardon.

The law applied a 10-year penalty on individuals who entered the country without inspection and had stayed in the country for more than six months. In my case, because I had married a U.S. citizen, I had a right to an immigrant visa/permanent residency, but I had to serve a

10-year penalty living outside the U.S. before they would give me the visa. Ms. Smith explained that I could apply for a waiver of that 10-year penalty, but I had to do it while living in Honduras. She told us that the approval rate for Central Americans' waiver applications was about 50 percent. Ms. Smith told us that our case appeared more favorable and that she would help us to build the strongest application packet as possible. She finished by saying that she could not tell us what we should do; we would have to make the decision as to whether or not I should leave the U.S.

When we finished the call, both Mark and I were more than a little disheartened, but we were relieved to finally have a straight answer on exactly what our options were. Like many immigrants, I had heard rumors, stories, and "legal advice" from friends and relatives who were going through their own immigration processes. Now that we had the two options—stay and wait for the law to change, or go back to Honduras and risk it being for 10 years—we had to decide what our next step would be.

I couldn't stop thinking about the possibility of having to stay in Honduras for 10 years. Mark and I talked about it and thought the risk of leaving was too much. My life and family were in the U.S. We could always choose to leave later, but once I left, there was no way to take it back. However, before we made our final decision, we decided to pray and ask God. Prayer had always been a help in difficult situations, and Mark and I had made it a habit in our family before making big decisions, and this was the biggest decision so far. The moment we finished our prayer, I felt a deep restlessness in my heart; Mark felt the same. We stared at each other and knew what it was. The choice of staying in the United States wasn't the right one. We both felt and knew that it was God's will for us to go to Honduras. Understanding His decision made my whole being feel at peace. I knew we had to go.

"So, we're going to Honduras!" Mark said with tears in his eyes.

I was sure that everything would be all right if I followed what God told me. We were afraid: we didn't know when to leave, where we would live, or how we would make a living. We only knew it was the right decision to leave, and we had faith that everything else would work out.

We informed our families of our decision to go to Honduras. They were not convinced that leaving was the right choice, and no one was happy about it. But they respected our decision and our faith. The news quickly spread among our friends. Everyone was speechless; they couldn't believe that Mark and I would be going to live in Honduras, a dangerous country, with our toddler son.

We decided to leave in August of that same year, before the school year started. At that time, Mark had started teaching virtual classes to help get more income. He asked if the company could give him more classes so that he could teach virtually full time the coming school year. Based on that, we decided that living in a city would be best because the internet would be faster and more reliable than in La Entrada. San Pedro Sula didn't seem appropriate for us to live in because the crime rate was very high, and it was very hot and humid year round. We decided that we would move to the capital city, Tegucigalpa. Being up in the mountains, it had a much nicer climate, and we guessed that it couldn't be more dangerous than San Pedro Sula.

I felt a mixture of excitement and fear about returning to Honduras. I knew things had changed, because I stayed connected with some friends still living there. My biggest concern was that Mark and Isaac were going to be with me. I knew that Hondurans usually treated Americans well, but I also knew that there was a lot of crime, and it was common for locals to believe that Americans were loaded with money. At least in my town you always heard that. Kidnapping people who had money was a common crime in Honduras. Mark and I even briefly considered implanting a locator chip in Isaac before we left.

My life was about to change in a way I couldn't even imagine. It had been nearly eight years since I left Honduras. My life, my friends, and most of my family were in the United States. My biggest comfort was that I wasn't going to be alone. I had a loving husband who would be by my side the whole way.

Gaby got married that summer, and a couple weeks after her wedding, we packed up our belongings, went around to say goodbye to family and friends, and drove to Fayetteville. My mother-in-law had offered to let us store most of our things in their garage. We packed six large suitcases with clothes, diapers, and other baby items we thought we would need for a long stay in Honduras and stored furniture, dishes, and everything else.

The day before we flew out, we were at a large family farewell dinner at Mark's parents' house. Right before dinner started, my friend Leticia called me to tell me that an American had been robbed and killed and that things were very dangerous for foreigners over there. I told Mark about it, and he tried to remain calm, but I could tell he was worried. Then, holding back tears, he told me that everything was going to be all right. When Mark's family heard, they all started crying with us.

Mark's parents tried their best to make the dinner one we could all enjoy, but it was hard to ignore what was coming for us. I was so overwhelmed, that I couldn't really talk. Mark's family all cried as we hugged and said goodbye. They all told us that they hoped we would be back to the U.S. soon.

Our flight gave us a long layover in Miami. My friend Luisa came by to see me and meet Isaac. As I got ready to board the airplane in Miami, I knew that once the plane took off for Honduras, there was no turning back. I lifted my head and walked onto the plane, trusting God's will.

After eight years, I was heading back to my country and my hometown. I thought about how much I had changed since that November morning back in 2000. I felt like a different person and that in some ways I was returning to a new and different country.

28

Back to My Roots

The flight from Miami to Honduras lasted a little over two hours. As the plane crossed over the Honduran coastline, I took a moment to admire my country from the clouds. Everything was so green. Off to the right I could see the mountains to the west. I knew that I was born somewhere in those green lands, and yet I was afraid to go back.

My brother Alexander had returned to Honduras the year before, and he came to the airport to pick us up. My cousin Ritza was arriving on another flight later that afternoon. She had agreed to come along to visit Honduras and help us take care of Isaac for a few days while we looked for an apartment in Tegucigalpa.

The San Pedro Sula airport was very different from what I remembered. When I had gone there to say goodbye to my cousin Fabricio, it all had looked nicer. There was no air conditioning in most of the terminal, and the heat made me feel exhausted. Mark was feeling the same thing. He told me how beautiful my country was, but not until after he had found a bathroom to change his pants for shorts.

We found one part of the airport with AC, but it was not as strong or as cold as those in the U.S. As we waited for Ritza's flight to arrive, I walked with Isaac all over the terminal to keep him busy. I was worried about him getting sick because he was touching everything with his hands and then sucking his thumb.

My cousin Ritza finally arrived after four long hours. We walked out to the parking lot and loaded all of our luggage into the vehicle. It was an extended-cab truck—a small-bed model that was not sold in the U.S. The truck belonged to Fausto, my cousin Ana's husband, who had sent it with one of his employees, Julian, and my brother to pick us up. Julian drove, Mark was in the passenger seat, and my brother, my cousin, Isaac, and I were in the back.

After leaving the airport, Julian took a wrong turn and ended up lost in downtown San Pedro Sula. My brother got out of the truck to ask for directions and shouted back to Julian:

"Hey, watch out that no one jumps in the back to steal the luggage!"

At that moment, the reality of being back in Honduras hit me. I was back in a place where I had to worry about someone running up and grabbing a suitcase from the bed of the truck. On top of that, Julian reacted like what Alexander had just said was completely normal.

After about 45 minutes, we were able to find our way out of the city and onto the highway headed toward La Entrada. On the edge of the city, the police stopped us and noticed that we were carrying several suitcases in the back of the truck. It was clear from the luggage and my husband's white face and blue eyes that we had just come from the U.S. After a brief conversation about the headlight, it was clear that they wanted money. They threatened to take Julian's license and make him pay a large fine. The officer asked for 50 American dollars. I took a 500-lempira bill (about 25 dollars) out of my purse and paid the police bribe. Just hours after arriving in my country, it was yet another reminder not to forget where I was.

The officer accepted the bribe and let us continue on our trip. I looked at Mark, who was sitting in silence in the front seat.

"Where have you taken him, Keyla?" I kept asking myself.

The road to La Entrada was longer than I remembered. The streets weren't like the highways I had become used to in the United States. These were curvy mountain roads without streetlights and with potholes everywhere in the road. Luckily, Julian knew how to avoid most of them.

Mark fell asleep up front, and Isaac fell asleep on my lap. I was able to close my eyes for a short nap as well. We had been up since three in the morning to make our flight, and we were all exhausted.

A couple hours later, when we arrived at La Entrada, I opened my eyes to see how much the town had changed. It wasn't easy to see much because it was dark and raining. I could see that there were more buildings and businesses than before. I could also point out same major landmarks. I could see the metal sheet roofing of the stalls in the market. As we came down the large hill, I could see the Texaco, and my godparents' hotel and pharmacy. Some places looked the same, but a lot had changed.

We arrived at my cousin Ana's house in the Las Brisas neighborhood behind the bus terminal. They all welcomed us with smiles, hugs, and food. My cousin offered us beans, fried plantains, cheese, cream, and handmade tortillas for dinner. I missed the Honduran food, and when I sat down to eat, it brought back many memories of my grandmother's cooking.

Unfortunately, we couldn't take a shower that night because there was no water service. I could see that some things still hadn't changed. The water shortages were still as bad and unpredictable as before, and the electricity was still constantly failing. Luckily, that night the electricity was working, and my cousin kindly offered to let us sleep in her air-conditioned bedroom.

Although I was exhausted that night, I had a hard time falling asleep. I couldn't stop crying. There was no turning back. I was back in Honduras and couldn't return to the United States, even if I wanted to. Mark tried to comfort me, but that night seemed to be the longest of my life. I finally cried myself out and fell asleep.

A short while later, Isaac started crying in the middle of the night. We checked his temperature; he had a very high fever and diarrhea, which was precisely what I was worried about. His sudden exposure to new germs, food, and water was affecting him. We had no medicine with us that would help lower his fever; we didn't know where or if there was a pharmacy open at that time. Plus, we didn't know if there was a hospital nearby or how we would even call for an ambulance.

We did what we could with damp towels, and he was able to sleep for 30–45 minutes at a time. We finally gave up and got up around six in the morning. We thought that giving him a bath might help. There was no water in the kitchen or the bathroom. The only place I could bathe him was outside in the *pila*. The water was so cold. Mark was new to using a *pila*, so I showed him how.

I could tell the water service had been out for a while because the *pila* was less than half-full and the water looked like it had been stagnating in there for a while. It had a film on top, and I could see some mosquito larvae swimming back and forth. I had no choice because it was the only water available. I grabbed *a pana* (medium-sized plastic bowl used to scoop water out of the *pila*) and moved the water around to try and disperse the film and larvae. I scooped up some water, and as soon as I poured it over Isaac, he immediately stiffened and I heard him lose his breath for a moment. When I poured the second *pana* of water on him, he had caught his breath and let out a scream that reminded me of his first cries as a baby, but much louder. I worked as quickly as possible to wash him with soap and rinse him off so that I could wrap him in the towel. In less than two minutes, he was washed and in a clean diaper and clothes.

Once we were all dressed (Mark and I didn't bathe in the *pila*), we headed out to find a doctor because Isaac was still running a fever. We first went to the office of Dr. Diaz, the doctor who always took care of my grandmother. The office was closed up, and there was no sign indicating when it would open.

Across the street was a small market where my friend Leticia's mother had a small booth. I knew that Leticia would often run the booth, so I walked over to see her and see if she could tell me when Dr. Diaz's office would open. Leticia recommended a new doctor who she had met at church. She closed the store and went with us up the hill to the doctor's clinic.

The clinic was quite humble. As I walked in, I couldn't stop making comparisons with the United States. Now that I had lived in the U.S. for so long, I could not help noticing the gap between the facilities in the two countries. The doctor attended us right away and was very kind. He told us that Isaac had an ear infection and gave us a list of medicines to buy from the pharmacy. The list of medicines he gave us was a literal handwritten list on a small piece of blank note paper. In Honduras, and especially in small towns like La Entrada, you didn't need a doctor's prescription to buy medication. He told us to come back in the afternoon so he could check up on Isaac. Once we got the medicine for Isaac, he started to look better, and I was able to start to relax.

Later that day, after all of us had a nap, I took my small family on two important visits that I had been waiting to take for a long time. Back during our first year of marriage, Mark had asked me what I would do first if we went to La Entrada. I answered almost immediately, "Go see my old house and go visit my mother's and grandmother's graves."

We first went to see my house in the El Triángulo neighborhood. The neighborhood had changed quite a bit since I had left. The biggest change was that my great-grandmother's house, where I had lived during my early childhood and where my mother had passed away, was gone. The entire row of houses had been torn down, and a large two-story mini mall had been built. I had known the house was gone, but it was a shock to see the changes in person.

I walked around the corner to my old house where I had lived with La Hita and Gaby. I walked into the yard and my mouth dropped open. An old family friend had been renting the house for the past few years, and she had not taken care of the house. The backyard was filled with old tires, car parts, and trash. All of the fruit trees had been cut down. My grandmother's outdoor kitchen had been ruined.

Inside the house, the former renter had left a bunch of junk. The walls were cracked, and the floors were covered in dirt. The house seemed so dirty compared to how clean La Hita had always kept it. I was so excited to show my husband my house, but I barely recognized this place.

As we walked around and through the house, I felt a mix of nostalgia and sense of being homesick. I went into La Hita's old bedroom; it was also the one where she had passed away. The house had never felt so empty.

Ever since I arrived in the U.S., I have had a recurring dream of being there in my old house. The scenes have changed through the years, and as Mark and Isaac entered my life, they would also make appearances there in my house. One scene that always was a part of the dream was that La Hita was there in her outdoor kitchen or our nice, clean yard. Being back at the house was a fresh reminder that La Hita was gone. I walked around the neighborhood to see some of my old neighbors. Some of the neighbors were gone, as they also emigrated to the United States after I left. The ones who were still there had grown up, some married with children. My husband went with me everywhere as I showed him around the neighborhood. Everyone wanted to talk to him and was surprised that he spoke Spanish so well. He wasn't like the usual Americans who always come to Copán Ruinas.

After living in the U.S. for so long, I had forgotten how friendly people were back in my country. Everyone whom we visited invited us in and offered us food or at least a cold glass of Coke. My husband and I had gotten out of the habit of drinking soda, and we would ask for ice water. Everyone would look at us strangely when we told them we preferred water. In La Entrada, people always wanted to give their guests the best, and soda was always considered the best option for guests. There were times when someone would send a child or a *muchacha* out to the *pulpería* (small corner store) to buy a three-liter bottle of Coke if they didn't have any in the house.

That afternoon, we took Isaac to the doctor's office again, and he seemed like a new person. He was back to his typical easygoing and curious self. The doctor advised us to make sure he didn't suck his thumb, which we told the doctor was next to impossible. He then told us to at least wash his hands frequently. The doctor was quite friendly and told us that he had lived and worked as a doctor in the United States for a few years. He hadn't billed us for that morning's visit, and I was a little shocked when he told us we could pay for it later in the afternoon.

Being used to the sky-high prices and the medical system in the U.S., I left the clinic in awe. I had been able to have my son evaluated by a doctor two times and gotten medicine for him in the pharmacy all in one day. In fact, the entire process took less than one hour total. All of this for less than $50. As I thought about the cost in lempiras, I knew that most locals would find 1,000 lempiras to be too expensive. After we left the office, I needed to go to the bank to exchange some dollars for lempiras. Mark walked into the bank, and when he came out, he told me that the teller was trying to flirt with him. We laughed together because it was predictable. Mark looked so different from everyone who lived in La Entrada. I didn't get upset. I have never been a jealous woman, and besides, I knew the kind of man I had married, and I trusted him.

After the bank, we went to the cemetery. I entered through the main gate of the cemetery and made my way to our small family mausoleum. Even after all those years, I remembered exactly where it was. The cemetery was full of scattered graves and above-ground tombs, and it was hard not to step on some of them to get to where my family was. The "path" was very narrow, and the cemetery was situated on a steep hill.

I got to the mausoleum and opened the gate. My grandmother had contracted to have it built shortly after my mother had died. The last time I had been there most of the nine spaces were empty. I looked and in the three-by-three grid of crypts, all but one was now occupied. La Hita was in the upper-right space, and my mom was in the lower left. My grandmother's grave had no name. My mom's had only a black metal cross with her birth and death dates handwritten in white paint.

As I stood there, I got a lump in my throat. I was hit with a small feeling of grief and loss, but I also felt grateful to have the chance to visit La Hita's grave and once again see my mother's. My husband stood silently holding Isaac while I quietly grieved for my two maternal figures. I talked to both of them and told them about my life, my sorrows, and my joys. I introduced them to my husband and my son, Isaac. I told them that I was happy and that I was a very blessed woman. I could feel that they were both there, listening to me and comforting me.

Now that I was a mom, I could understand my mother's suffering better. I could finally empathize with what she felt that afternoon when she left us alone in this world, not knowing what would happen to us.

I could also better understand my grandmother's distress and suffering for the child she had to bury. La Hita had cried many times over the death of her daughter.

La Hita also spent many nights crying and worrying over Gaby and me. I knew that she was concerned that I wouldn't make good choices in my life, especially in my early adolescence when I was so rebellious. She also spent nights worried when she didn't have money to buy us clothes or shoes. As Mark and I were worried about how we would live in Honduras, I better understood that pain. I felt blessed to be there in front of their graves, telling them about the woman I was now and letting them know that their efforts had been worth it.

The sudden move to Honduras and not knowing when I could return to the U.S. was still a concern, but I was happy to be back in my country and to reconnect with my roots. In those first days in La Entrada, things still felt foreign to me. The sky and clouds somehow looked very different from those back in North Carolina. In addition, there were distant mountains that I hadn't noticed before. Perhaps because I was so used to them when I was living there before, I hadn't been able appreciate how beautiful they were. The biggest impact on me was the poverty. Little by little, I understood why God told me to return to my hometown. But, on the other hand, I was afraid because the circumstances weren't so easy. If I couldn't return to the U.S., life would be very hard in Honduras. I was so used to the American comforts that I found it challenging to adapt to the hardships of my land.

I had forgotten how poor my country was; everywhere I looked, there were people in need. There were dozens of small children selling food and chewing gum in the bus terminal, wearing dusty brown clothes and no shoes. Women walked up and down the stopped buses, selling saran-wrapped styrofoam plates of fried chicken and *tajadas* (sliced pieces of fried green banana). Some were dressed in old and humble dresses, and others were wearing jeans, high heels, and makeup. On all the women, it was easy to see the sun damage and the nutritional deficiencies in their skin and hair. It broke my heart to see such need, let alone to imagine my son having to do that kind of work and being exposed to the evil of the world on the streets.

I was once again reminded of all the blessings I had been given in my life. I was starting to realize that God's purpose for me returning to Honduras was more than just fixing my immigration status. As we prepared to head over to Tegucigalpa, I questioned what else was in store for me and my family.

29

Tegucigalpa

On the morning of our third day in Honduras, Mark, Isaac, my cousin Ritza, and I set off for Tegucigalpa to search for a place to live. Fausto drove us to Copán Ruinas so we could take a higher-end bus line to Tegucigalpa. There were several buses that left from the bus terminal in La Entrada, but they stopped at every small town along the way. On top of that, the higher-end bus line was considered a safer option for cross-country travel.

The total trip lasted about eight hours. Isaac behaved wonderfully. In fact, Isaac never gave us much trouble the entire time we traveled around Honduras. He was easily entertained with a few toys, slept a lot, and hardly cried at all.

Before heading to Honduras, Mark and I, through our church, had contacted a family living in Tegucigalpa—the Trujillo family. They had agreed to help us and even offered to let us stay at their house while we searched for an apartment. Mark was reluctant to accept because we didn't know them, and he didn't want to be a burden. My mother-in-law advised that he should be more willing to accept help from others. We didn't know a single person in the city, and I didn't even know the city or how to get around. The last time I had visited Tegucigalpa, years before, I was only there for one day, when my grandmother came to apply for her U.S. visa.

When our bus finally arrived in the Honduran capital, Don and Doña Trujillo were there waiting for us at the bus stop. We had to get a taxi because all of the suitcases didn't fit in the Trujillos' car. Doña Trujillo explained to the taxi driver where the house was located and helped negotiate a fair price. The Trujillo family lived in a large house in an area known as El Hatillo near the top of the mountain El Picacho located on the northern edge of Tegucigalpa. As I would later learn, Tegucigalpa was two different cities, Tegucigalpa and Comayagüela.

The two were located in a compact valley and had merged into one compact urban area. The valley was surrounded by mountains on all sides.

The next day, Mark and I took a taxi back down the mountain to look for our new home. We had contacted an agency to help us find an apartment. We spent the day visiting apartments, but we didn't find anything we liked. The search was difficult because we were used to certain things being standard with apartments. We quickly realized that we had to ask if the apartment included basic appliances like an oven or a refrigerator. On top of that, we came to Honduras thinking that it would be much cheaper to live there than in the U.S. In La Entrada, I knew that I could rent an entire house for 3,000 lempiras (about $150) a month. In Tegucigalpa, the prices were much higher, and many of the apartments we visited listed their price in U.S. dollars.

By the afternoon, we were getting desperate, and we found an apartment that we thought could work. The real estate agents helping us took us to an internet café so we could complete the application and email a bank statement to the landlord. Once the landlord saw that the statement was from a bank in the U.S., he called back and told us that the rent he had quoted the agents had just gone up.

Mark and I decided to keep looking, and Mark stepped out of the internet café to call an ad for an apartment we had seen in the paper. Carlos, one of the realtors, came out and told Mark he shouldn't use his cell phone on the sidewalk.

"Motorcycle assaults are really common here. They will drive up, snatch your cell phone, and drive off. I think it would be safer if you put it away," Carlos advised Mark.

We didn't have the latest model or very expensive cell phones, so neither of us had worried about getting our phones stolen. It was another lesson that we were having to learn to adapt to our new reality. Back in the U.S., we could use our cell phones wherever we wanted, but we couldn't do that in this city and most of Honduras.

The day ended, and we went back to the Trujillo house feeling tired and dejected. The stress of everything was starting to overcome us both. We said a quick prayer while still outside and then headed in for dinner, hoping that we would soon find a way forward.

We didn't have to wait long, as we met the Trujillos' adult daughter Valeria, who had just arrived back from a trip that evening. She told us that she would take us the next day in her car, and she was sure that together we would find something. She was so kind and optimistic that after dinner I felt a surge of her energy. I was confident we would have more success in the morning.

The next day, Mark and I let Valeria speak on our behalf because it seemed like people everywhere were looking to rip us off. People knew we weren't from there. It was evident that Mark was American, but I also no longer spoke Spanish like a native Honduran. I had been in the United States so long that my accent had changed, and people kept asking me where I was from. Valeria would let us know if the price was right for the apartment and the area. She also helped us to know if the neighborhoods were safe or not.

After lunch, a friend of Valeria's called about a furnished apartment that was about to be available again. We went to see the apartment, and it was perfect. It was located in a nice neighborhood within walking distance of a mall with a supermarket. The apartment had two bedrooms, was fully furnished, had an air conditioner in the master bedroom, and even had a washer and dryer. The building's parking lot had a tall electric gate and seemed very safe. In fact, the owner's son lived in the apartment above with his wife and baby.

Mark particularly loved the front of the apartment. The living room had two large sliding glass doors that opened up to a large balcony. Besides the doors letting in a lot of light, the apartment had an amazing view of the city and the mountains in the distance. The price was very reasonable, and we signed the contract with the owner that afternoon. We wanted to move in as soon as possible, but the apartment wouldn't be ready for a couple weeks.

We went back to La Entrada for a few days while we waited for the apartment. I made the most of the days in my hometown. I was able to visit and catch up with more friends and visit with my godparents. We also went to visit the Mayan ruins around La Entrada and the large archeological park of Mayan ruins in Copán Ruinas.

Mark loved exploring the ruins and museums and getting to know my country. I was excited to get reacquainted with Honduran food. The Honduran food in the U.S. never tasted as good as it did in Honduras, no matter who cooked it. The whole time we were in La Entrada, Fausto and Ana took care of us and made us feel at home. Their love and attention really helped us not feel as overwhelmed with all the change.

At the end of the two weeks, we headed back to Tegucigalpa to get settled in our new life. We had shipped a box of things we thought we would need for the apartment, and we were able to buy everything else from the stores at the Cascadas Mall, down the street from our new apartment. I was again surprised at how expensive things were in Tegucigalpa. Even though we were paying in lempiras, things for the house cost as much as and sometimes more than they cost in the U.S. The one advantage to being in the city was that we could use our credit cards most places. When we were in La Entrada, we had to pay for everything in cash, which meant we had to make several trips to the bank in a week or carry large amounts of cash on hand.

We arranged for home internet service so Mark could work teaching classes in the virtual school, and we had purchased a Skype phone with a North Carolina phone number. That way, our families could call us in Honduras, and it wouldn't charge them as an international call. We got the fastest internet package available. It was less than half the speed we had in North Carolina, and it cost over $100 a month. It was clear that having internet at home was a luxury that most Hondurans could not afford.

With our apartment put together and Mark working, life started to get back on track. But living in a new city was hard for both of us because we didn't know anyone. We began to attend a local congregation of our church, and I started to make some friends there, but it took some time.

Several weeks after arriving in Tegucigalpa, I fell back into my depression. I missed my friends and family in the U.S. I felt very alone there in Tegucigalpa. Mark worked from home all day while I took care of Isaac. Luckily, the school had assigned Mark enough classes that we would not have to worry about money. Some days, I would take Isaac for a walk in the mall. We would go to the indoor playground and then buy an ice cream cone.

We didn't have a car, and I felt trapped in that small little area between our apartment and the mall. When I was feeling especially lonely, homesick, or trapped (or all three), I would take Isaac to visit La Entrada for a couple days. I felt better in a place where I knew people and had some family. However, it was over eight hours by bus each way, so I couldn't do it every weekend.

One day, when meeting with the pastor of the congregation (called a "bishop" in The Church of Latter-day Saints), I told him how I was feeling, and he recommended that I see a psychologist. I started seeing Dr. Augusto, who was just what I needed. In our sessions, I began to talk about everything that had happened to me during my childhood. It was difficult to begin, but once I started down that path, I started to feel better as I shared with a mental health professional all of the trauma that I had been through. The doctor diagnosed me with moderate clinical depression and mild anxiety. He prescribed an antidepressant and gave me some things that I could work on to help improve my day-to-day life.

First, Dr. Augusto recommended that I get on a regular schedule, including getting up early and getting regular exercise. Before starting my sessions with Dr. Augusto, I was sleeping a lot more than I needed and I had lost most of my appetite. I had lost a lot of weight and ended up about the same size as I had been right before I left Honduras at age 15. Mark and I went shopping for a gym and found one within walking distance of the apartment. It was a locally owned gym in an older building and didn't have air conditioning. The treadmills were fairly new there, and getting to all of the more modern chain gyms would've required us to take a taxi. I started going to the gym every day during the week while Mark watched Isaac. It helped me feel better and reduced my stress and anxiety.

The doctor also recommended that I make more friends. I made an effort to make new friends at church. I started to visit some of the women during the day, when Mark was working. There were several young mothers in the congregation, and I would take Isaac over, and he played with the other kids while the adults would talk.

Mark and I also decided to hire a *muchacha* to help around the house. The apartment was small and didn't need that much help. Besides, we had a washer and dryer, so no one needed to wash the clothes by hand in the small *pila* that was in the apartment's laundry room. We decided to get someone to come a couple days a week to clean the apartment and cook a few meals. We were hoping to find someone who we could trust to babysit Isaac so Mark and I could start going on dates as a couple again.

At church I met Daniela, a woman in her early 20s who was looking for work cleaning or cooking. When I told Daniela how much I would pay her, she looked at her mom with surprise and happily accepted the offer right away, even though it would not be full-time work.

In Honduras, there is a minimum wage that is given in a monthly salary (not in a hourly wage). Because we were looking to hire someone part time, I calculated an hourly wage according to the number of hours the *muchacha* would work. I later found out that the legal minimum wage is only paid to people who have an education and are working in professional careers. Many people paid *muchachas* and other domestic workers much less than the minimum. In addition, because it was considered a salary, the *muchacha* would work the hours dictated by the family and their needs. Going over the number of hours did not always mean an increase in monthly pay. I told Daniela that we would pay her by the hour, and later, when she started babysitting for us, we paid for those additional hours as well.

Daniela soon became part of our family. Having her in the house gave me someone to talk to and helped distract me. She would clean the house and then cook a large lunch (the traditional large meal in Honduras) and she would eat with us. She grew to love Isaac very much. In a short time, I felt confident in her and trusted her to take care of Isaac so Mark and I could go out to dinner or to the movies by ourselves. Daniela was a well-educated and hardworking woman. Hiring her was the best decision I could have made.

As I started to become comfortable with my new routines and was able to get some time alone with my husband, I started to feel better. Honduras, and specifically Tegucigalpa, started to feel like home. I started speaking Spanish like a native Honduran again. Isaac also spoke Spanish all the time because most of his conversations were with Daniela or me. One day after a phone call with Mark's family, which was now the only time I was speaking English, I realized that I was making beginner's mistakes that I hadn't made since I had lived in Miami. Mark, through his big grin, told me that I better start practicing my English, or when we got back to the U.S., I would have to take ESL classes all over again.

In November, we received a notification to appear at the U.S. Embassy in Tegucigalpa the week before Thanksgiving. The lawyer had told us that I would have to present myself at the embassy to demonstrate that I was no longer physically in the U.S. The consulate section of the embassy looked a lot like a DMV. There was a large waiting room with chairs in rows; at the front attendants worked behind a wall of service window stations with speakers mounted in the glass. Ceiling fans moved the hot air around, while a few mounted televisions showed a soccer game on mute.

We arrived at the embassy and checked in at the window where they had to take my fingerprints and picture to prove my identity. Mark and I both thought that we would be done after that because that was all I had to do when I would check in at the immigration offices while in the U.S. The window attendant told us that one of the agents would call us back to their office for an in-person meeting. In the hour and a half that we waited for our interview, Mark and I made the mistake of imagining that the interview would be to tell us that my visa had been approved, and we started to make hypothetical plans on being back in North Carolina for Thanksgiving dinner with family.

When we were finally called back to the office, the agent kindly but quickly brought us back to reality. There was no magic visa available. In fact, he told us that the clock on the potential 10-year penalty was starting that day, and that the three months before would not count. In addition, he walked us through the process of submitting the application for the waiver.

We arrived back home and began to plan our own Thanksgiving dinner based on the ingredients we could find there in Honduras. As it turned out, Mark did get a chance to go back to North Carolina for Thanksgiving. When we first arrived, he had only a 90-day visa to be in Honduras. We spoke with a lawyer to help us with Mark's Honduran residency process, and she recommended that Mark leave and return so that he could get another 90-day visa, which would give us time to complete the application. We made our own small Thanksgiving dinner a few days early, and then Mark flew back to spend Thanksgiving, and specifically Black Friday, in North Carolina.

One day that fall, I was on the phone with Paola, a friend of ours still living in Durham. We had met shortly before I left for Honduras, and we became fast friends. Paola was a photographer. She had taken our family pictures a couple times, and she was the photographer at Gaby's wedding. Paola knew that I had always enjoyed taking pictures, and we had bonded over this previously. Our conversation turned to my plans for when I returned to the U.S. Paola suggested that I use the time away to learn how to use a professional camera, and then we could start a business together when I got back to Durham.

At that moment, it made a lot of sense to me, and I got really excited by the idea. I didn't know why I had never thought of it before, but it made so much sense. I loved taking pictures, but I had never considered it as a potential career until Paola mentioned it. I had found a new goal, and when Mark was in North Carolina, I sent him to buy me the things I would need to practice and learn photography.

Of all the price differences between the U.S. and Honduras, technology was by far more expensive in Honduras than the U.S. When we compared the price of a camera, lens, and a laptop in the U.S., we discovered that we could pay for Mark's airplane ticket and still save hundreds of dollars compared to buying those things at the mall near our apartment.

After Thanksgiving, Mark flew back to Honduras, landing in San Pedro Sula. Mark and I had been asked to be the graduation *padrinos* (godparents) for the daughter of Wendy, one of my mom's friends in La Entrada. *Padrinos* come to the graduation and are expected to bring a gift for the graduation party.

We attended the graduation party at Bernardo Galindo y Galindo, the best public school in La Entrada, and where my mom had once worked. I was thrilled to have my own camera. I spent the whole graduation party taking photos of everyone and everything I saw.

The next day, Mark, Isaac, and I took a bus back to Tegucigalpa. We were so tired from the trip that we decided to travel on one of the local buses leaving directly from La Entrada, rather than take the additional time to drive to Copán Ruinas so we could take the nicer, safer, and more direct bus line. I had my camera out, taking photos of the view and trying to go over all the settings, and I fell asleep with the camera in my hands. Mark put the camera back in the case and stored it up in the overhead compartment so Isaac and I would have more room to sleep.

Upon arriving that night in Tegucigalpa, I reached up into the overhead compartment for the camera bag, but it was not there. Mark and I looked frantically around the seats, but it was gone. I'd had my first professional camera less than a week, and it had been stolen. I knew it was my fault for having it out in front of everyone, but I still hadn't gotten used to having to hide everything for fear of being robbed. It was a nightmare; the camera was gone, and I had lost all the graduation photos.

We both sat silently in the taxi ride home from the bus terminal. We arrived at our apartment, and I went straight to bed. I was heartbroken: I didn't want to eat, play with Isaac, or watch TV. I just sobbed in the dark. The next day, Mark and I went grocery shopping, and when we got the groceries in the apartment, I realized that I had left my cell phone in the cab. My world seemed to be falling apart. The next day was my birthday, and I refused to get out of bed. I slept all day. When I was awake, I couldn't stop crying, so I preferred to remain asleep.

At seven o'clock that night, my husband woke me up and told me he had a surprise in the living room. I walked out and saw that Mark had set up the room for a birthday party. There were sodas, plates, cups, napkins, and a birthday cake. Standing in the living room were our neighbors, and on the two laptop screens were my sister and Mark's family on simultaneous video calls from the U.S. They all sang "Happy

Birthday" to me, and we talked and had cake. By the time everyone hung up and went home, I was feeling a little better.

In truth, losing the camera was a big loss that was hard to take. A short time later, however, we were able to replace it through the credit card company, and my cousin Ana was able to bring the new camera back with her, as she was visiting family in the U.S. The cell phone wasn't that nice or expensive, and I wasn't worried about replacing it. The thing that I was most worried about was my phone being off and whether I would be able to recover my phone number. That week I was expecting a phone call from my father, and I didn't want to miss it.

30

18 Years Later

Ever since Isaac was born, I had grown more and more curious about my father. I wanted to know where he was living and what he had done with his life. I also wanted to introduce him to his grandson and my husband. I began to pray and ask God to help me find him. God answered my prayer when it was time, and I was ready. I could later see that He put me in the right place and right time to find my father. I truly believe it was one of the reasons that I was told to return to Honduras.

The owner of our apartment building, Don Hernán, was an engineer by trade. I remember La Hita telling me that my father had been an engineer with the national electric company, ENEE. One day in the fall, I asked Don Hernán if he had known another engineer by the name of Carlos Humberto Green. He told me that he didn't know anyone by that name but would email the College of Engineers to see if anyone knew of him.

I knew it was a long shot, but I knew that my dad's name was unique, and I figured that he and Don Hernán would be about the same age, so why not try. This wasn't the first time I had come up with a long-shot plan to find my father. Back before leaving Honduras for the first time, I had traveled to Comayagua to attend the wedding of Wendy's daughter, Hadara. I had heard (through my dad's friend Luis) that my father had moved from San Pedro Sula to Comayagua, and I came up with the plan to call the local radio station and ask staff to make an announcement that Don Carlos Green's daughter from La Entrada was looking for him. In the end, I decided not to go through with that plan.

After several weeks, someone replied to Don Hernán's email, stating that he knew a man named Hector Green in San Pedro Sula, and because Green was such an uncommon name in Honduras, perhaps they could be related. Don Hernán shared the email with Hector

221

Green's phone number with me. I couldn't believe that I had gotten this far with the search, and now that I was making progress on the search, I wasn't completely sure I wanted to reopen this door that had been closed for the last 18 years.

I was at the gym near my house one day, and after finishing working out, I took a piece of paper out of my pocket with the number Don Hernán had given me, and I decided to make the call. I felt nervous; I still didn't know if it I was prepared for this call, but I dialed the number anyway.

"Hello, is this Hector Green?" I asked nervously.

"Yes, it's me. Who is this?" a deep male voice answered.

"My name is Keyla Alas. I am Doña Yolanda Alas's granddaughter and Telma Alas's daughter."

"You are from La Entrada, aren't you? I remember your mother and your grandmother."

"I am Telma and Carlos Green's daughter. Do you know anything about him?" I asked anxiously.

"Yes, I am his nephew," Hector replied, revealing some astonishment in his voice.

He told me that he had never known his uncle Carlos had a baby with Telma, but was glad to know who I was and to hear from me. He told me that my father lived in Pespire, Choluteca, about an hour and a half south of Tegucigalpa. We talked for a few more minutes, and right before the call ended, he told me that he would call my father and give him my phone number.

I couldn't believe that I had found a cousin I had never known and that I was so close to finding my father. On top of that, my father was so much closer than I thought he was.

I waited for days for the phone to ring, but Don Carlos never called. I contacted Hector again and let him know that my father hadn't called me back. He got off our call so he could call his uncle. After a couple of minutes, he called me back:

"My uncle told me he will call you soon," he said.

I thanked him and disconnected the call and continued to wait for my father to call me. That was December 2, the day before I lost my phone in the taxi.

After I lost my phone, Mark had gone to the cell phone carrier and had been able to retrieve my number on a new SIM card. He put the new SIM card in his phone so I wouldn't miss a call from my father.

It was on December 5—one day after my birthday—that Don

Carlos Green called me. I was in a supermarket near the house when my cell phone rang.

"Hello, this is your *papá*, Carlos Green," I heard a gruff and tired-sounding voice say.

I felt a big lump form in my throat when I heard the word *papá*. I had never used that word to refer to my father before. To me, he had been my *padre* (father), the man who helped make me in my mother's womb.

"*Papá*, it's so nice to hear from you!" I replied in a quiet and almost fragile tone as I gulped and tried to hide my shock.

The word *papá* felt so empty. It felt odd and awkward to use it to refer to him. Right then, an intense inner debate started in my head. Why did I call him *papá*, and why not refer to him as *Don Carlos Green*? On top of that, why was I even contacting him?

The conversation continued and I told him that I was living in Tegucigalpa, that I was married and had a son. I explained why I had come back to Honduras from the United States. I reminded him about my birthday the day before, but he didn't have any response to that. I told him I would like to see him, and he told me which bus to take and at what stop to get off the bus. We said goodbye, and I finished the call.

I didn't know what to think or feel. Indeed, the call wasn't what I pictured it would be. It was all so surreal. In some ways, it felt like I was calling a distant family member who I hadn't seen in years. In other ways, I felt like I was talking to a stranger. I had no idea what to say to my father after all that time. Plus, I kept calling him *papá*. It was the title he had used, and I didn't want to be disrespectful. He was my parent, and La Hita had always taught me to respect my elders.

A couple weeks later, we boarded the bus for Pespire. The trip on the converted old school bus took a little over two hours. Pespire wasn't that far away, but leaving Tegucigalpa required driving over the mountains, and the mountains to the south were steeper and took more time. When we arrived, my father was waiting for us at the bus stop they called *Las Gradas*.

As the bus pulled up, Mark saw Don Carlos Green standing there, and told me, "You look just like your father, Keyla!" It was true; it was like looking at myself in a mirror. I couldn't deny he was my father. My hands were sweating. My only visual memory of him was an old photo I had in one of my photo albums back in storage in North Carolina. I had always been told that we looked very much alike, but it was still pretty jarring in person.

My father was wearing a white shirt, black pants, and formal shoes. His hair was jet black and wavy, parted on the right side. His skin color was like mine—dark brown. He was tall and slender, and his long legs made him look elegant. His face looked a bit aged, and the wrinkles made him look old. He was exactly as I remembered him, except with the extra years. We got off the bus and walked over to where he was.

"How are you doing? How was the trip?" My father broke the silence with his questions, but there was no hug, or even a handshake. In Honduran culture, the typical greeting among friends, and especially family, was a hug and a kiss on the cheek. My father stood there nervously with his hands hanging by his side. "This isn't a good place to talk; let's go to my house," he added.

We walked to his house, no more than two minutes away, and we hardly spoke to each other along the way. We got to a green and white house with a wooden door and a single window. We walked in, and he immediately introduced us to Doña Socorro, his current spouse, a shorter woman with light-colored eyes. He also introduced us to Daniel, Doña Socorro's adopted son, who lived with them.

Doña Socorro offered us lunch, and we sat down to eat. Sharing a meal didn't help the visit feel any less awkward. I felt like I had been invited into a stranger's house to eat. I kept trying to scan my feelings for that father-daughter bond but couldn't find it. The truth was I was visiting a stranger. I knew he was my father because I had been told that, but I didn't feel like he was my family or even understand what having a father should feel like.

After lunch, he showed me around his house and property. Mark took Isaac to lay in the hammock and play with the cats while I sat to talk with my father.

Our conversation started with small talk and other random subjects, but none of that was what I wanted to hear. He spoke in a quiet voice, as if he were afraid that someone would overhear him. It was so low sometimes that I couldn't even understand some of the things he was saying to me.

I heard no explanations as to why he had abandoned me or pleas for forgiveness. I was sitting with a man who seemed ashamed, but not repentant. I couldn't really read his feelings or even understand my own. I didn't even know if I wanted his apology. What I wanted to hear from him was an answer to the question: What had been more important than my sister and me that made him leave us? I knew that I wouldn't get the answer to that question during this first visit. Doña

Socorro suggested going out to see the town, but my father didn't want to go out; he chose to stay at home. He continued to refuse to leave the house, even when I insisted that he go with us. Doña Socorro took us to see the main square, the river, and the old Catholic church. It was a lovely town with friendly people, though the heat was overwhelming.

Pespire was much smaller than La Entrada, but it was older and had older buildings and a church from the Spanish colonial times. Some of the streets were made of stone, and the houses near the square were old but with a certain charm. Doña Socorro told us that my father had a large family there in Pespire and that one of his brothers had been the mayor of the town a few years ago. Back at the house, I continued my conversation with my father. He told me a little about his life, including his two wives: his first and current wife, Doña Socorro, and a second wife with whom he had lived in Comayagua in between the two separate relationships with Doña Socorro. I told him about my plan to find him in using the radio station in Comayagua when I was 14 years old.

Doña Socorro was my father's main support with her house and her retired teacher's pension. I had no idea what kind of financial situation my father would be in, but I never thought I would see him like that—with nothing.

The last time I saw him was at his job in the fancy office building in San Pedro Sula. As he was an engineer, I had always imagined him with a more comfortable life. In our conversations, though, I found out that he had never been an engineer like La Hita had told me. He had worked at the ENEE, but not as an engineer. I thought how ironic it was that the wrong information about his job had been what allowed me to find him.

The biggest revelation from that first meeting was that he had two children and that I had two additional siblings: a brother, Humberto, and a sister, Karla. They were both living in Comayagua, and he gave me their contact information. The older one was named Humberto and the younger Karla. He also showed me pictures of his parents, and I learned about my grandparents' history. I wanted to know the origin of the Green family name, but he had no idea about it; he only supposed that the name came from Europe. My dad didn't know that Gaby and I had moved to the United States when we were teenagers. He didn't know where we were all that time, nor did he ever tell his current wife or his children about Gaby and me. No one in his family had known about us. Despite being a shock to many, it was a pleasant surprise to most of them. We took pictures, shared with his new family, and in the afternoon, we headed back to Tegucigalpa. I no longer felt as doubtful as before, but neither did I feel any attachment to the man who fathered me.

I called him a few days later, and he invited me to Pespire again for the town fair in January. Mark and I decided to stay one night at a hotel in town because my father didn't have room for us. I enjoyed the experience of talking to him and finally having the opportunity to get to know him better and learn a lot more about him. He introduced me to his brothers and nephews. I never imagined I had so many relatives on the Green side. My father was the youngest of all his siblings. Surprisingly to me, almost all of them were men, and now I have many uncles. Everyone was surprised at how much I resembled my father. They didn't know about Gaby or me either, not until he told them after I visited him just a few weeks before. Everyone was friendly to my family and me. They invited us for lunch, and we even visited one of my uncles' houses.

I visited my father a few more times in Pespire. Once, we traveled together to the country's south, where the heat was even more overwhelming. For Father's Day in March, I brought him a gift, and he gave me some mangoes from the tree he had in his backyard. We went to the cemetery in Nacaome to visit his parents' graves.

Mark and I decided to buy a car after six months of living in Honduras. It was much safer to move around the city if you had your own car. Buying a car was such a blessing. We could then visit my father more frequently and also explore more of Honduras.

We planned to go to Comayagua during Holy Week. It is a city famous for its religious character and the incredible *alfombras de aserrín* (sawdust carpets) created by the locals to decorate the streets during these festivities. The idea was also to finally meet my siblings, with whom I had already spoken to on the phone.

It was better for my father if he stayed with us in Tegucigalpa the night before. Although he rarely left his home, he was willing to go with us. It felt unusual to be with him at my house, but it was a unique opportunity for us to get to know each other better. We talked about many things, and I even told him about that last time I saw him and why I was so embarrassed to hug him.

"My shoes were ripped and worn out, and I was so embarrassed that you saw me like that," I told him.

"What a shame!" he bowed his head and said to himself.

I didn't need anything at that moment: I had a beautiful and healthy son, I had a loving husband, and I didn't need shoes anymore. And here I was, 18 years later, bonding for the first time with my father.

Inadvertently, my father spotted the antidepressant medications I was taking and recognized them right away. I then learned that he had suffered from depression as a teenager and even once thought about becoming a priest.

The following day, we left for Comayagua. We planned to stay one night, so I booked two hotel rooms. We agreed to meet at a restaurant with my half-sister Karla, her young son, and other family members. It was so strange to meet a "sister" I knew nothing about while my sister Gaby and I had basically shared our whole lives together. We both had many questions for each other. She wanted to know about my mom and her relationship with my dad, but I told her I was so young when she died that I never really got to know my mother.

My half-brother Humberto also joined us, though it was only

Keyla and Isaac with Keyla's father, Carlos Green, in Comayagua, April 2009 (family photograph).

for a moment because he had to work. I found it interesting that neither Humberto nor Karla resembled my father as much as I did. Humberto was quite tall, even taller than my husband, and Karla was a little shorter than me. My father was pleased that I had met my siblings.

"It was my responsibility to introduce you to your siblings, Keyla. I didn't want you to come alone this first time," my father told me.

Karla was six months older than me. So I could tell that my father had two women pregnant at the same time. Humberto was quiet and pleasant. He believed that my father seemed happier since we had reconnected again and that I inherited his photography talent.

"When we were kids, my dad used to take pictures of everything, even ants!" he commented jokingly.

Each time I would visit my dad and talk to him, I learned more about his life and everything that happened, even before I was born. Doña Socorro always welcomed me with open arms in her home and loved our visits. One day, she confessed to me that my father loved my mother deeply and that her passing still saddened him. It was vital for me to reopen that chapter of my life. Despite all the years of absence and grief, I was happy to understand why everything happened the way it did. It took so many years to understand my suffering.

I was gradually building a more stable relationship with my father. Although I needed to get used to his personality, and sometimes I had to do my best to understand him, I never expected anything in return, and all the bitterness began to disappear.

Eventually, I understood that the greatest blessing I had in life was La Hita. After learning more about my father's life, I realized that perhaps it wouldn't have been the best thing to grow up around him. I learned to forgive him and let go of my pain.

My life without a father was very tough. I never had a male role model in my home, a man to show us how to make a living, how to love and respect a family. My church was the only example I had to know what kind of family I wanted to build. I now have the family I always dreamed of, and I never hesitate to remind them how much I love them and how happy and blessed I am to have them by my side.

31

Honduras

Little by little, I got used to my life in Tegucigalpa. I had new friends and enjoyed spending time with them. I was going to therapy and feeling much better. I also used to go to the gym and often went out with Mark. Being reconnected with my father was such a blessing, although I still felt awkward around him at times. The time he was absent from my life would never be back, but I tried to get to know him and learn more about him. We started to have a close and beautiful relationship.

In January, we had finished compiling all the documents needed for the application for the penalty waiver. Mark wrote a long, heartfelt letter explaining why he believed I should be allowed to return and live with him in the United States. The attorney had explained to us that approval for the waiver would be based on us demonstrating an adverse impact if I were required to stay in Honduras for 10 years, although she warned us that the disruption of our family on its own wasn't enough for the approval.

The waiver application stated that we had to show an adverse impact on U.S. citizens, so we asked everyone in Mark's and my family who were citizens to write a letter. Mark's parents, his sisters, their husbands, my aunt Rafaela, and even our bishop from our church congregation in Durham all wrote letters. Unfortunately, the rest of my family, including my sister, weren't allowed to submit letters of support, but I knew that they were praying for our success.

In their letters of support, our family justified why they thought I should be allowed to return to live in the United States. They described the kind of person I was, and the impact I had on my family and my community. It was heartwarming and humbling to read that I had made an impact on the lives of so many people. The letters had to focus on me because Mark and Isaac were free to return to the U.S. whenever they wanted according to the law. In reality, that would have been devastating for me. I don't know if I could have handled it.

When our friends in Tegucigalpa found out that Mark decided to go to Honduras with me, aware that he might have to spend 10 years there, they were moved and admired his love for me. Living in a country like Honduras may not be easy for someone who isn't used to insecurity, corruption, and all the problems that are a daily scourge in that part of the world. My love and respect for my husband grew stronger every day. After all that time of being with Mark, I had never doubted his love for me, not a single day. I don't know what my life would have been like if I had faced that all alone.

Once we had everything, we contacted our attorney in the U.S. so that she could submit the full waiver application. After everything was submitted, she told us that the normal processing time was nine months, but that could change. She gave us the website where we could review the status of the application, because written notifications were sent via the Honduran postal service, which was notoriously unreliable. The application was processed, and if the waiver application was approved, the appointment to pick up the visa would be within a few weeks of the approval. If it was denied, the appointment would be November of 2018. All we had left to do was pray, wait, and live our life.

Mark continued his online teaching. As for me, I began to train myself as a photographer. I took several online photography courses and an in-person class at the Alianza Francesa in Tegucigalpa. There I met many Hondurans and foreigners who shared the same passion. I became friends with a young photographer named Rubén, who was a great help to me during my beginnings in that field.

Likewise, I started taking individual classes on editing software such as Photoshop with a guy I met at the mall where I developed my photos. I was so afraid to pursue something new professionally. I didn't know if I would be lucky enough to make that a reliable source of income for my household. I knew I had so much to learn and needed faith in myself to achieve the professional level I wanted so badly.

I started taking pictures of virtually everything: I didn't care about who or what. What mattered was to seize every opportunity to learn. I took pictures of Mark, Isaac, and my new friends, and that's how I built my first portfolio. I started a website and began to advertise my services. I created my business cards and put into practice what I learned in my editing classes. Additionally, I started a small business ordering baby clothes from the United States and reselling them in Tegucigalpa. Even though I was initially hesitant to sell clothes, it turned out to be a good idea, and I was very successful.

Whenever Mark had a break, we would take the opportunity to explore Honduras. Sometimes we would visit the surrounding areas of Tegucigalpa, such as Valle de Ángeles, El Picacho, and El Tigre. On longer school breaks, we would go to La Entrada. A couple times we were able to get out to the Caribbean coast. On one occasion, my cousin Ana took care of Isaac in La Entrada so Mark and I could have a couple days on our own. Although I was afraid to be away from him for two days, I was happy because my family spoiled him a lot.

We visited the Cayos Cochinos, a cluster of coral islands located northeast of La Ceiba on Honduras's northern coast. As a child, I'd never had the opportunity to visit those dream places. I couldn't believe that my country was so beautiful. The water was crystal blue, and I could easily see my feet at the bottom. The sand was white and soft. We snorkeled for more than three miles along the reef, enjoying the fish and other colorful sea life below. Everywhere we went, Mark was fascinated with our weekend getaways and kept telling me how beautiful Honduras was. As for me, I was now able to enjoy my country like never before. Although many people talk about how dangerous it is to travel to Honduras, very few know of the beauty hidden in its beaches, mountains, and colorful sunsets. I certainly cannot deny that it is a dangerous country. We had to adjust some of our own habits, like avoiding driving late at night, which we were used to doing in the U.S.

In June of 2009, Isaac turned two years old, and I decided to celebrate his birthday in La Entrada. My parents-in-law and my sister-in-law Olivia, along with her husband and infant daughter, had talked about coming to Honduras to visit us and to get to know the country. We set it up for their visit to coincide with Isaac's birthday celebration.

Daniela helped me with the preparations for the birthday party. First, we went together to the Comayagüela outdoor market because everything was much cheaper there than in the stores. Anytime I went to an outdoor market, I would go without Mark because I was sure they would give us higher prices when they saw his white face and blue eyes. Without him, I was able to bargain and found excellent deals on the piñata, candy, and decorations. I designed the invitations myself, with my newly acquired knowledge of Photoshop. I arranged for Wendy and Hadara to cook for the party, as their food was the best I have ever tasted. My cousin Ana offered to host the party in the large covered carport at her house.

On the day of the party, we drove our large rented van to pick up my in-laws at the airport in San Pedro Sula. On the way, we were stopped by a policeman who we could quickly tell was looking for a bribe. The officer told Mark that he could surrender his driver's license or he could pay the fine directly to the officer—in cash, of course. The officer told Mark the fine was 50 American dollars.

We showed the officer Mark's wallet so he could see that all we had was a 100 lempiras. Mark and I already knew what was going on when we were pulled over, so when Mark got out of the van to talk to the officer, I pulled all the large bills out of the wallet. When Mark held open his wallet to show how much cash was there, the *sin vergüenza* (shameless) officer dug into Mark's wallet and took all the cash that was there.

I couldn't believe it. We had run into several police officers trying to get bribes, but never had we met one so bold in his corruption. I didn't have time to try and do anything about it because we wanted to be there to meet Mark's family right as they arrived. I was worried that something similar would happen with my in-laws in the car, and I didn't want them to leave with a bad impression of Honduras for any reason.

On our way back to La Entrada, Mark's family couldn't believe all the poverty they saw. Even though the view of the mountains was beautiful, the mere sight of half-naked, shoeless, dirt-covered children standing in their stick and tarpaper houses was too much for them. I immediately noticed the sadness on their faces.

The police stopped us again; I got worried, and my hands started to sweat, but fortunately the officer let us continue on without a bribe. We were already late for Isaac's birthday party. The guests were already there, and we were the only ones missing.

When we arrived in La Entrada, everything was ready to go for the party. My cousin had decorated the tables and hung balloons all over. Hadara and Virginia had prepared *carne asada* (grilled meat), rice, tortillas, and *chismol*, a salsa common in Honduras made of chopped tomatoes, onions, peppers, and cilantro in lime juice.

Almost everyone I invited came to the party, and I was excited to see them there. Isaac's gift table was stacked so high that I thought we were going to need the large van just to get the presents home. I told most of the guests not to buy a gift because I knew they didn't have much money, but many did anyway. I knew it was a large sacrifice for many of them. However, I wasn't surprised that many people brought gifts. I understood that it came from a place of love and respect for me and my son. I was pleased to see that they had such big hearts. Isaac received so many gifts that I didn't know what he would do with them all. Mark's family was delighted and surprised by the friendliness of the people of my town.

The following day, we took Mark's family to explore the Mayan ruins near Copán Ruinas. During our drive up into the mountains, they were both impressed by the beauty of the landscape and shocked by the levels of poverty they saw. It is difficult for people who have never been to a country in the developing world to adequately understand the levels of poverty in Honduras. Looking upwards along our route, we saw lush green hills and mountains covered with a mix of palm, pine, and banana trees. At the base of the hills, we saw a number of small shacks made from a mix of nylon tarp, scrap lumber, and pieces of corrugated metal joined together to form makeshift roofs.

We spent the next couple days touring La Entrada. I showed them my house and the neighborhood where I grew up. We went to the main plaza and the Catholic church where I used to attend mass with La Hita. I was so excited to show Mark's family where I came from.

On Saturday we headed back to Tegucigalpa. I wanted to take my in-laws to see more of my beautiful country—especially to the Caribbean coast to see the Cayos Cochinos—but we had limited time, and they were interested in seeing where we were living in Tegucigalpa. On Sunday morning, we were planning to take my in-laws to our church to meet our friends. However, we woke up on Sunday morning to a political crisis. That morning, the military had removed the president of Honduras in a coup d'état.

Helicopters and airplanes were flying over the city. The electricity was out, and we had no water service, which rarely happened in Tegucigalpa. From the balcony we could see the black smoke of burning tires coming from the area around the presidential palace. The military and national police were clashing with protestors who were throwing rocks and burning tires in the streets. It felt like we were in some kind of movie. My husband's family was very nervous. I had never been in a situation like that before, and I was sorry that Mark's family was there to witness the chaos. The airport in Tegucigalpa was closed that Sunday, and we were concerned that Mark's family would not be able to leave. Thankfully, the airport was reopened Monday afternoon, and my in-laws were able to fly out on Tuesday morning. At the airport, we had a very tough round of goodbyes. Everything was so chaotic, and no one knew how or when it would end. My mother-in-law and Olivia hugged both Mark and me as they broke down in tears. My mother-in-law told us that she felt like she was abandoning us to fend for ourselves.

As we watched his family head to their planes, both Mark and I felt like we were being left behind. It seemed like everyone who could was fleeing to safety back in the U.S. I knew that my life and my family belonged in the United States. I wanted to take my son back "home" so I could keep him safe, but I wasn't allowed to. Mark and I headed back to our apartment, unsure of the future and praying that we would be protected.

The situation in Honduras continued to deteriorate. Street protests, violence, and property destruction led to weeks of curfews. In the middle of July, the focus of the protestors shifted to U.S.-based businesses as chain restaurants and hotels were vandalized, looted, and burned. The nightly curfews started to creep into daytime hours.

One afternoon, Mark and I had just returned from a large grocery store trip when the announcement came that there would be a full lockdown. We were stuck inside for two full days. I felt thankful that we had just purchased milk, food, and diapers. On the third day, the government allowed people back out for a few hours to buy food. Mark went to the store to stock up on food essentials because we did not know how long the next lockdown would last.

There was much uncertainty, and we had no idea what problems the coup, the protests, and the curfews would cause both in Honduran society as well as in the politics with other countries. Both Mark and I were most worried that the U.S. government would suspend consular services in Honduras and the processing of our case would be put on hold until the situation was resolved. Amid so much uncertainty in the capital, Mark and I decided to go to another part of the country to celebrate our fifth anniversary. Many sectors of the economy, such as tourism, were affected over many months, so prices and packages to explore the country were very cheap. We visited Roatán in the Bay Islands; it was one of the most beautiful places I have ever seen.

Daniela stayed with Isaac for a few days in our apartment in Tegucigalpa while Mark and I celebrated our anniversary. I can still vividly recall how crystalline the water was and the whiteness of the sand. I even bought sunglasses because the glare was hurting my eyes. We rented a motorcycle to explore around the island, and I ate the best shrimp I had ever tasted in my life. I shot plenty of pictures and had the opportunity to keep learning and capturing moments with my camera. My husband didn't want to leave the island, and we even talked about living there if we had to stay in Honduras for 10 years. I didn't think it was such a good idea. We would be living in constant heat, and I preferred the cooler climate of Tegucigalpa much better.

After four days on that beautiful island, we returned to the capital. It had already been more than a year since we first arrived in Honduras, and our lives seemed to belong there somehow.

32

Back Home

In early October of 2009, after 14 months in Honduras, Mark logged on to the U.S. Consulate website to verify if there were any updates on the case. We had been checking every month or so since the coup. One reason was to check if the consulate had been closed, and the other was to see if there was an update. The page loaded and Mark checked the screen a couple times to make sure he was seeing it correctly. He then called me over to double-check. The waiver had been approved, and we had an appointment to pick up my immigrant visa from the embassy.

I couldn't believe it. We both shouted with excitement, jumped up, and hugged each other. Because of the ongoing political crisis in the country, I had been mentally preparing myself for an extended wait. After all the waiting, worrying, and stress, I couldn't believe that my nightmare as an undocumented immigrant was almost over.

We called our families and friends back in the U.S. to let them know the good news. Some of them, not used to the slow-moving immigration system, thought that we would be flying back the next week. We let them know that there were still steps in the process and that it could still be a couple months before we got our tickets to fly home.

Mark and I had already started to make plans for our return, and both of us were thinking of staying a few more months. We wanted to spend the holidays in Honduras before we returned. We had a fantastic Christmas and New Year's in La Entrada the previous year. We spent the nights visiting friends and old neighbors, eating amazing food, and lighting fireworks in my old neighborhood.

The other reality was that neither of us felt ready to leave yet. All that time in Honduras had been a blessing for me. Mark and I felt part of a tight group of friends. I had seen more of my native country and discovered the beauty of the landscape and the people. I rediscovered my roots and reconciled with my father. In addition, I had learned so much about myself and strengthened my love for Mark.

We went to the embassy near the end of October for our scheduled appointment and found out that we would have to shift our plans and accelerate our timeline. I was instructed to leave my Honduran passport so the immigrant visa (which was the size of a full passport page) could be pasted in. We set up an appointment to pick up the passport and other entry documents three days later, rather than rely on the Honduran postal service or pay for a private courier service. The consular officer then told us that we had 30 days from that day to report to a U.S. Customs and Border Patrol point of entry in the U.S. We could wait longer, but it would require more applications, money, and waiting. We decided on the way home that we would leave in the middle of November.

We told our friends in Tegucigalpa and La Entrada that we would be leaving in less than a month. They were happy for us, but we could see the disappointment on their faces to learn that we would be leaving. Daniela took the news the hardest. I knew that it wasn't just about losing her job. She had become part of our family and had formed a bond with Isaac especially.

The next three weeks were a whirlwind of activity and preparation. The first stop on our goodbye tour was Pespire to say goodbye to my dad and Doña Socorro. After that, we headed to La Entrada for several days.

I went to say goodbye to my brother, my cousin Ana, and her family. I went on a sort of reverse tour of the El Triángulo neighborhood, this time to say goodbye to my friends and neighbors. I had my camera and took lots of pictures with all my friends. This time I was able to say goodbye to everyone, and I didn't have to hide my plans or worry about not making it to the U.S.

Before leaving, I took Mark to the Berríos School, where I had studied in my childhood. I greeted the new director and saw some of my teachers working there after so many years. I bumped into my fifth-grade teacher, and he recognized me right away.

"Keyla, how nice to see you again!" he exclaimed with astonishment when he recognized me.

I introduced him to Mark, and my teacher told us that he was about to retire. We then recalled the times I performed in a couple of plays during special events at school. I was his favorite student when it came to theater plays. He always picked me and gave me the best roles. I even once thought I might be an actress.

"Do you remember when you played the role of the dark-skinned maid in the play *The Soul Has No Color*?" he recalled.

He seemed to remember it very well. I remembered it was for Mother's Day—which was always a sad time for me—and I played the role of the maid so well that my performance made many people cry.

After visiting the school, I went by the cemetery to say goodbye to La Hita and my mom. I brought them flowers and, with tears in my eyes, told them of the blessings in my life and recounted the plans I was making for my future. That time my tears weren't tears of sorrow but of joy and gratitude.

The afternoon before we left, I took the time to walk through the streets of La Entrada one last time. I wanted to enjoy the landscapes and see the hardworking and humble people from my hometown. La Entrada de Copán is where I started my life, and it was, unquestionably, the basis of my identity. I soaked in the air, the smell of dry soil, the unpaved streets, my old house with the backyard, the schools where I studied, the river where I swam so many times—all of that was me. I was so grateful to God for sending me back to my native country to reconnect with who I was and where I came from.

We headed back to Tegucigalpa for our last week in Honduras. We sold or gave away everything that would not fit in our suitcases. In fact, we had to give away even more than we had planned because I was filling the suitcases with decorations and souvenirs from Honduras—things that would help me to hold on to our time in Honduras and things I couldn't buy back in the U.S. The last Sunday, we said goodbye to the church congregation. We drove up to El Hatillo to visit the Trujillo family and thank them one more time for their support in those challenging first days in Honduras. In the beginning, Tegucigalpa was like a foreign country for me, and they made sure I didn't feel like a foreigner in my own land.

The day of our return flight, our closest friends came to the airport to say goodbye. Tears rolled down my friends' and my cheeks as we wished each other the best for the future. It was time to leave, and Mark, Isaac, and I headed to the security checkpoint by ourselves. I was hit with a wave of feeling homesick for the life we were leaving, and I started to sob.

"Remember that now you can come back and visit them whenever you want," Mark told me with a smile on his face.

It was true. The reality of my new life hadn't sunk in. Going back to the U.S. meant I was no longer going to be a prisoner locked inside the border. The last time I had left Honduras, I knew that it could be 20 or 30 years before I might return—if I was ever able to. That time, I had said goodbye to Leticia thinking that it could be forever. I suddenly felt an enormous peace in my heart, knowing that I could travel wherever I wanted with my permanent residency. I had spent so many years as an undocumented immigrant that I could hardly imagine what life would be like now as a permanent resident. We boarded the plane and took off for Miami, Florida. As I watched the green mountains pass below, I silently said goodbye (for now) to Honduras. Ultimately, I took with me beautiful memories of my country. I will never forget the beautiful view of the mountains from my apartment, the beaches we visited, the historic towns, the food I loved so much, and, most of all, the friends I met. It was as if I had fallen in love again with my land, with my roots. That time I had spent there was to learn, to find answers, to love harder, and, above all, to learn to be grateful for how lucky I was.

Once over the ocean, my mind turned to returning to the U.S. I was nervous about going back to the United States, but it didn't compare to how I felt the first time I left Honduras that morning in November of 2000. I was worried about going through the immigration process, but I knew what life would be like. I wasn't traveling to an unknown place: I was returning home.

I thought about the difference in the type of trip. The first time I had traveled from Honduras to North Carolina, it was close to a six-week journey. This time, it was a half-day trip consisting of a couple of flights to get to my destination. I wouldn't have to walk for long hours, sleep on cold hard floors, or spend an entire day waiting to eat.

More importantly, this time I felt safe with my husband and child. I was not worried about being separated from them or being kidnapped, arrested, or deported. It made me think about how grateful I should be for this dream that finally had come true after so many years of prayers.

We landed and went to the passport control checkpoint. I carried ready in my hand my passport with the immigration visa and a sealed yellow envelope, which I was given at the embassy and was instructed to hand it unopened to the CBP agent when I arrived.

After stopping at the checkpoint counter, we were taken into a room in the back. The room was filled with many people, some detained on suspicion and others, like me, to verify their documents. I heard many people complaining, and others looked scared. That room was a bit intimidating. We waited a long time until an agent finally called my name. We were advised that the wait could be several hours, so we purchased a ticket to Raleigh, North Carolina, with a long layover in Miami. The officer asked me many questions. He wanted to know what I was doing in Honduras, how old I was, my husband's name, etc. He also asked what I did for a living and when I got married. He asked many questions to either verify that the information in the computer was correct or ensure that I was not lying. Satisfied with my answers, the CBP officer stamped my passport.

"Welcome to the United States of America!" the officer welcomed me with a smile.

I walked out of that room with a smile on my face, and we headed for our next flight's boarding gate. Isaac slept, and all I could think about was seeing my family again, my in-laws, and my friends. Upon our arrival, everyone was waiting for us, and it was fascinating to see them again. I felt pleased despite what I left behind in Honduras, and I knew I was back home.

33

A Story to Tell

As we rode in Mark's parents' car back to Fayetteville, everything felt so strange to me. The streets seemed wider and smoother than before; the pine trees were taller; the cars were newer. "Mark, your parents' dog, Maggie, looks pretty fat," I told my husband when we walked into my in-laws' house. Mark turned to look at the dog. "She's not fat, Keyla! You just got used to Honduran dogs always being scrawny." We both burst out laughing.

Being back in the United States felt very different. Being in Honduras as an adult had given me a filter to see my world with a different perspective. There were things I had become so used to in Honduras that when they were not there, it was a shock to the system.

Poverty in the U.S., of course, exists, but it wasn't as severe or as noticeable as it was in Honduras. The wide-open nature of the houses now seemed strange. There were no high walls with razor wire on top dividing one property from another. For the first few weeks, every time I answered my cell phone while on the sidewalk, I felt like I was being unsafe. I kept having to remind myself that I could drink the water from the tap. Overall, I felt even more blessed to live in a country with so many comforts and security.

My family was happy to have us back. We went to visit my aunts and cousins in Durham the same week we got back. We shared stories about living in Tegucigalpa and La Entrada. Now that he had experienced living in Honduras, Mark was better able to relate to my aunts, and he surprised them all by using Honduran slang that he didn't know before. It felt good to be near my family again and to be able to visit them whenever I wanted to.

When we were first married, we lived in Chapel Hill and Durham for school and work. Now that Mark's job was virtual, we had the option to live where we wanted. We decided to try living in

Fayetteville, where Mark's parents and some of Mark's sisters lived, for a little while.

Before leaving Honduras, Mark had started an application for a School Leadership Graduate Program at Harvard University. We decided to rent an apartment until August, in the hopes that Mark would be accepted, and we would move to Cambridge, Massachusetts, in the fall of 2010.

The week after we arrived, Mark and I were out looking for a new apartment. We were eager to have our own space, even though I knew my parents-in-law would be happy to have us in their home through the holidays.

My husband hadn't lived with his parents since he was 18 and went off to college, and he had preferred living on his own. Those cultural differences between the U.S. and Honduras have always been interesting to me. In my culture, children don't leave their parents' house until after they get married, even if they get married in their 30s.

We found a large, three-bedroom apartment, so Mark would have a private place to work. It was so different from our apartment in Tegucigalpa. There was carpet everywhere instead of the hard tile, and we had central AC. The living room was so big, I think our whole Honduran apartment would have fit there. We unpacked everything we had, and I couldn't believe how much stuff there was. We had lived with so much less in Tegucigalpa.

Being that close to my husband's family was a good, though new, experience. They have always been loving and supportive of me. We would now regularly attend the Sunday family dinners, and we had several potential babysitters a short car ride away. Mark and I were able to go to the movies or out to dinner, but not as frequently as when we were in Tegucigalpa. In Honduras, our money went a lot further than in North Carolina.

The most exciting change in my life was the security and freedom I experienced with my new status as a permanent resident. I felt less stress and anxiety, and my bouts of depression were more spaced out. I applied for a new driver's license with my new Social Security card, which no longer said "for work only." I also needed to fill out an application for my permanent resident card (the literal "green card") because what I had been given in the embassy would expire soon. We sent in the green card application with another money order for several hundred dollars. It cost us more than we were planning—we had assumed that the embassy would issue the first permanent residency card when they had granted me permanent residency—but we still had a lot to learn about the inefficient immigration system.

It was a huge relief to have the physical card in my hand a few weeks later. I could now go visit Honduras and return whenever I wanted. I could now travel to other countries, buy a house, get a job, or start my own business, which I was determined to do. I wanted to keep developing as a photographer and establish a successful business.

There in Fayetteville I worked on finding clients. My goal was to become a wedding photographer, but it was a big responsibility, and I did not feel ready yet. Starting out, I took any job that I could get, including boudoir, newborns, and family portraits. I was hired to be the photographer for a *quinceañera* (Sweet 15) of one of the girls I used to babysit. It was an excellent opportunity to practice my art. Through those first few jobs, I realized that I had a passion for photography. I knew it was what I wanted to do for the rest of my life, even if my only consistent "client" was my son Isaac.

In the early spring, we got the good news that Mark had been admitted into a School Leadership master's program at Harvard. Eight months after returning from Honduras, we moved to Cambridge, Massachusetts. We moved into the 13th floor of a high-rise apartment building 10 minutes from the university. I really enjoyed our time in the Boston area. While living in Tegucigalpa, we had become used to living in big cities, and it was nice to be back in a city. While there, I learned to use the public transportation to get around. In Tegucigalpa we would always use taxis, as the city buses were too dangerous. Isaac and I would take the bus to a park or to visit Mark at school. On the weekends we would explore the city on the subway.

Mark was busy with school, work, and his internship and was gone through the day and most evenings. I stayed at home taking care of Isaac and continued planning and working to build my photography business. Moving to a new city meant that I had to start over looking for clients, but I knew that I would find some opportunities if I kept working at it. In the meantime, I took virtual photography classes and then would practice my skills with Isaac in the park and around town.

About halfway through the fall semester, Mark invited me to attend a visiting professor's conference talk on the undocumented immigrant student experience at Harvard. The guest lecturer was Professor William Pérez—a psychologist and specialist in education, immigration, and multilingualism, and an expert on undocumented immigrants. Mark thought that the talk may be relevant to me and my experience as a student. He certainly wasn't wrong because when the professor began to speak, it seemed as if he was narrating my life in detail. Every word made so much sense to me.

"Emigrating is one of the most radical transitions an individual can experience. In the case of immigrant children, leaving their country completely changes how they relate to others, their family patterns. This often leads to a feeling of isolation and the need to adapt to another culture, which frequently results in a loss of identity and anxiety, among other stressors," said Dr. Pérez.

"Through the Hispanic Children's Stress Test, researchers found several stressors such as the feeling of being separated from their parents, pressure to speak only Spanish at home, living in a crowded household, as well as a sense that other children will make fun of the way they speak English. Gradually, these factors will end up triggering psychiatric problems such as depression, anxiety, and constant stress," concluded the psychologist.

I could not stop crying. He was describing exactly how I had felt for years but did not have the words to describe it. As I sat there, my past struggles started to make more sense to me. I knew that I had suffered a loss of identity when I left my country. I had struggled for years to adapt to a new culture and system. In this system, my undocumented status was interchangeable with my identity because I didn't have legal status. Not knowing who I was made me feel as if I didn't exist. This mental and emotional stress was a major source of the depression I had felt and recognizing that helped tremendously during my healing process.

In addition, I learned that the correct term for those who entered the country without legal documentation, or those who remain in this country without legal status, is *undocumented immigrant* and not *illegal*. It is a mistake that I and many others made in the past in ignorance. The term *illegal* is also used by those who want to disparage and scapegoat this community. Either way, labeling someone as "illegal" plays into their feelings of lack of identity, trauma, and depression that Dr. Pérez spoke of.

His words were powerful, not only for me but also for the rest of the attendees. I was excited to see that this message was being delivered at the School of Education, where most attendees were studying to be teachers, administrators, or policy makers at schools around the country. I hoped that they would apply this learning when they encountered undocumented immigrants in their classrooms and schools.

Dr. Pérez's speech touched me in heart, soul, and mind. I was finally beginning to understand the years of pain in my heart. I had spent years believing and time in therapy working on the assumption that my depression and anxiety resulted from my childhood experience. That night my eyes were opened to the fact that my immigration status and my experience in this country as an undocumented immigrant also played a significant role in my mental health.

After the professor concluded his remarks, he presented a few of his students, who told us about their lived experiences as undocumented immigrant students. It was inspiring to hear so many life stories that had been similar to my own. They discussed the shock of moving to a new country with a different culture and language. They talked about the day they realized that getting student loans and scholarships to go to college wouldn't happen for them like their other friends at school, regardless of GPA and SAT scores. Despite their situations, they were still fighting for their dreams, just as I had done for so many years. I did not feel alone, and, most importantly, they still had hope. I knew that many young undocumented immigrant students were, like me, in search of their American Dream.

It was exciting to hear these speakers, who had not given up and maintained their faith and hope despite everything they faced. Some of them were in college, and others had already finished. Although they knew that finding a decent job in their field of study would be impossible, they kept fighting and hoping that the government would pass some version of the DREAM Act (the Development, Relief, and Education for Alien Minors Act), even though the law has been in discussion since 2001, the year I entered the country.

I left that meeting with a desire to share my story. Linda, a young mother friend from my building, was one of the first people I talked to about how I came from Honduras and my journey across the border. She had no idea of all the challenges we face as undocumented immigrants. I told her the reason we had to go live in Honduras was because I had entered the country without a visa. She couldn't believe it. She, like most Americans I talk to, thought that I would automatically become a U.S. citizen by marrying one. Her surprise continued when I told her that the government didn't allow me to work for years, but that I could apply for a tax identification number so I could pay taxes to the government. I described the immigration court hearings, the different immigration petitions and applications I had submitted, and the thousands of dollars that my family and I had spent on lawyers.

"None of that stuff makes any sense, Keyla!" she exclaimed after I told her about all that I had experienced.

It was true; the U.S. immigration system is illogical and full of contradictions and confusing processes. The system is broken, and as a result millions of people are suffering. In our discussion, I realized how uninformed many Americans are about the realities of this country's immigration system. Even other immigrants seemed to be unaware of how it all worked. I once told some Latina friends that I would write about my life as an undocumented immigrant, and they were both shocked. In their minds, like many others, being an undocumented person was a mark of shame that should be kept a secret. I didn't know why it had never occurred to me before to write about my life as an undocumented immigrant. I had a topic, a life experience, and a desire to tell the world what it means to be a *mojada*.

The idea of writing a book had been in the back of my head since I was a little girl in La Entrada. That day as I was talking to Linda, and after listening to Dr. Pérez's inspirational talk, I knew that I would write about my life as an undocumented immigrant and that I would name my book *Mojada*.

In the spring of 2011, Mark graduated with his master's degree, and we prepared for the next change in our lives. At his graduation we had a double celebration because I was a couple months pregnant. After Mark's graduation, we had a few days off and decided to go to Canada to visit Hernán and his wife, our old neighbors from Tegucigalpa, who now lived in Toronto. For the first time, I used my permanent residency to leave the country. Knowing that I could leave the U.S. and return whenever I wanted was a feeling of joy like nothing else.

I continued my photography business part time and worked as a wedding photographer for the first time. I was extremely nervous and prayed that we would have good weather. The photo shoot was a success, and I felt like I was developing my talent as a photographer. The couple, happy with their photos, motivated me to keep improving my art. In the beginning, I was embarrassed to tell others that I was a photographer, but I was gradually gaining confidence and pride in my work.

The time we spent in Massachusetts was enriching for our whole family, and Mark worked on landing a job so we could stay in the area. Unfortunately, none of the positions worked out, so we decided to head back closer to North Carolina. We felt that we should stop in Washington, D.C., to continue the job search. We liked the idea of living in

Washington, D.C., because we had been there to visit Mark's family a few times and we loved it. As a bonus, the pay for school principals in that area was excellent.

The first few weeks, we stayed in a hotel until we had a clear idea of where Mark would work. After living out of hotel rooms for more than two weeks, pregnant and with a toddler, I decided to head down to North Carolina to visit some friends, Liam and Emily. While I was there, my cousin Eva called me and told me that someone had murdered Fausto—Ana's husband—in La Entrada. I was shocked and heartbroken. I called Mark back in D.C., and he was also devastated at the news. Fausto had been so good to us both in Honduras and in the U.S. When I was 13, I finally got to go to the beach because of him. In addition, he had helped Mark drive the U–Haul the 15 hours from Fayetteville to Cambridge the summer before.

I decided to go to Honduras to be with my cousin Ana. She went back to Honduras immediately upon hearing of her husband's death. Ana and their daughters were already permanent residents in the U.S., but her husband was still waiting for the government's response to his application for residency. I couldn't help but think how things could have been different if only his paperwork had been approved.

It was devastating for the family to lose a loved one and the two young girls to lose their father. As I flew back to Honduras, it was heartbreaking to see a country as beautiful as mine was so lost in corruption, lawlessness, and crime that Fausto's family wouldn't be the only one mourning the death of a murdered family member that week. Also at that moment, I felt so blessed to be living back in the U.S. Blessed to raise my children in an environment where I didn't have to worry daily about them being robbed, kidnapped, or killed.

It was the second time I left the United States with permanent residency. My return this time was not as smooth. When I presented my passport at the airport, I was once again taken to that same back room where I was detained when I first entered the U.S. with a green card. The room was full of people in the same situation as me, sitting nervously and waiting to be called.

The immigration officer called me to the desk and interrogated me on the reasons for my trip to Honduras and other information about my life. I didn't understand why I was being questioned, and I became extremely nervous. My fear and anxiety started to flood back in waves.

I later found out that they detained me and would continue to do so at every port of entry because I was put in "deportation proceedings" after turning myself in to U.S. Immigration when I was 16. The official told me that my name had a permanent flag in the system, even though the immigration judge had signed the order dismissing my case when I agreed to voluntarily leave the country with Mark and I was now a legal permanent resident. The only way to have the flag removed from the system, we were told, was to become a U.S. citizen.

34

Dreamer

Mark's opportunity to continue his studies and our move to Massachusetts brought us challenges and blessings we had never imagined. Yet, we were confident because our faith in God has taught us that we could overcome any obstacle. I have always believed that challenges in life bring us spiritual and intellectual improvement. During the summer of 2011, we felt a number of obstacles in looking for a job for Mark and a new home for our growing family. After a month or so of living in hotels, staying with friends and family, and farming out Isaac to different family members while I was in Honduras for Fausto's funeral and Mark was in Washington, D.C., attending interviews, we finally got some good news. Mark had been offered a job at a high school in the D.C. public school system. We found an apartment in Alexandria, Virginia, and started this new chapter of our lives.

I continued with my goal of being an entrepreneur and becoming a successful photographer. It has been a dream of mine ever since Mark bought me my first professional camera. However, my pregnancy and our move to Alexandria forced me to put that dream on hold momentarily. I needed time and energy to dedicate myself to an even more important goal: becoming a mother for the second time.

In December 2011, Isabella was born, and I fell in love with her as soon as she was in my arms. My husband was thrilled; we were parents of a growing boy and a beautiful new girl. I couldn't have been more excited for our now family of four, and I spent a lot of time (both before and after Isabella was born) thinking about our future.

While I was still pregnant, Mark and I discussed the possibility of buying a house. We knew that it was a major decision and in the DC area it would mean a lot of money. This wasn't the first time we had considered buying a house. Ever since I had gotten married, I dreamed of my own house where I could raise my children. Back in 2007, we even went to see a few houses and discussed making an offer. However, it never felt like the right decision, so we didn't continue. Besides, neither of us knew what would happen to me because of my immigration status back then. I never felt that we could make such a long-term commitment with so much unknown.

This time was different. My green card gave me the freedom to make my dreams of having my own home a reality. With the help of a realtor and through a few home-buying programs, we were able to get a loan approved, and after a few weeks of searching, we found a house that we both liked in Washington, D.C. In January of 2013, we signed the contract with the bank and moved into our new house. Moving to this house was great for the whole family. Mark's commute to work was cut by 45 minutes each way! Isaac and Isabella got their own room, and I got an office where I could work on building my business just a few steps away from my children.

In 2014, I decided to work on another dream of mine and resumed my education. I joined a new program, Pathways, supported by our church through Brigham Young University-Idaho (BYU-I). The Pathways program was a one-year online college preparation program focused on math, writing, and study skills at the college level. Upon successful completion, I would be automatically accepted to BYU-I and able to complete my degree online at a subsidized cost.

Right after I started, to both our shock and surprise, I found out I was pregnant with my youngest daughter. It was a busy year, and I was exhausted from my pregnancy, studies, and work to build my business, but I felt the satisfaction that I was finally making my dreams come true. Furthermore, Mark's support and encouragement have always been the fuel I needed when I thought I couldn't do it. Sabina, whose name we chose as a tribute to my paternal grandmother, was born in October, and I completed the Pathways program in December. I was extremely proud of myself for finishing, and even more so because, while raising two kids and having a third right in the middle, I finished with the highest GPA of those in my cohort. Since I was a child, I have always wanted to study, and I embraced that idea for years because I was sure it was a straight path to my intellectual growth. Despite being a mother of two young children who still wore diapers, I completed the program with the highest grades.

I started 2015 with my acceptance letter from BYU-I. I had planned to take a semester off before starting my degree in Business Management and Administration. But unfortunately, those plans were put on hold as my postpartum depression came back for the third time and stronger than I had ever experienced it.

When Sabina was born, I was expecting to go through another round of postpartum depression and asked my doctor to prescribe anti-depressants for me so I could be prepared. As I thought, a few weeks after coming home with Sabina, I began to feel down emotionally. I started the medication, but my depression worsened. Whatever energy I had was barely enough for my husband and three young children.

My depression got so severe that it pushed me to the edge of feeling like I didn't want to live anymore. I felt a profound pain inside that wouldn't let up no matter how hard I fought it. I felt as if I had lost my feminine identity, because I didn't love my new self, my new body. My depression got to the point that I didn't feel capable of taking care of my baby and my other two children. I begged God to give me the strength I needed to make it through this fight again. I wished with all my heart to cease to exist; I thought I would never feel happiness and love life again, and I started having suicidal thoughts. That's when I decided that I needed to seek professional help.

I was hospitalized for several days as a part of my treatment. I never thought I could feel so alone in the world. I felt as if everyone abandoned me, including God. Thanks to prompt, professional support, I was able to feel a little less overwhelmed and the cloud of constant depression began to lift.

The new medications prescribed by the psychiatrist helped me get through those challenging months until I could go back to living without them. It was a slow process, but thanks to my husband's, psychiatrist's, and psychologist's support, I was finally able to emerge from the shadows. No matter how tough it is, you learn a lot about life when you overcome this disease. I had time to think and analyze, and I ended up gaining plenty of knowledge and insight through the process. I learned that the only way to get through is by loving others and genuinely learning to love yourself again. I learned to be more empathetic to those women who struggle to lose weight but fail to reach their goals no matter what they do. I know, from my own experience, why women cry when they don't understand their feelings of sadness, frustration, and depression with the arrival of a new baby, when they think that, in fact, everything should be all smiles and loving tenderness.

My mental health continued to slowly improve, though in total this round of postpartum depression continued for over two years. During the recovery process, I tried to maintain my dream to excel in my business as a photographer. On my path of professional growth, I did not always make the correct decisions. At times, I chose to work for or work with the wrong people. At times, I found myself among people who made me feel that my work wasn't worthwhile and who betrayed my trust. Unfortunately, I sank into such a low state of mind that I decided to take a break from my photography business and accept only former clients.

In all those years of trying and trying, I ended up learning a lot about myself and others and always doing what my heart wanted. I learned to manage my business in such an incredible way that sometimes I didn't know how I did it. God gave me incredible friends and tutors who were willing to share their formula for success with those of us who were starting on that dream.

In 2017, I started in a new business as an independent beauty consultant for Mary Kay. The thing that interested me in working for Mary Kay was helping women discover their own beauty through skincare. Starting in this new job provided me a new challenge in life. Once again, I felt like I had a goal to achieve and a new type of business to learn. Most importantly, working with Mary Kay helped me to stop focusing only on myself and my problems and gave me a way to help others.

During my almost three years in Mary Kay, I learned a lot about business and myself. I had the chance to meet women from many countries and cultures, and I saw that we women had so much in common, no matter our color or language. We all have dreams of excelling as wives, mothers, sisters, daughters, and women. I enjoyed helping other women start in the business and showing them that they could have more control of their own dreams. I loved seeing them step out of their comfort zone, even though I knew, from my own experience, that they carried the weight of the world inside.

While fulfilling my dreams and helping others achieve theirs, I became a stronger person, a stronger woman. I became a woman who looked to serve others and forget about my own problems along the way. Through my work and service, I found that I had climbed out of the hole of my depression, and my struggle had resulted in a wiser woman, with new friends and new opportunities.

Near the end of 2019, I returned to my original love, photography, with more energy and a new focus. In my boudoir and glamour photography, I portray ordinary women who yearn to feel beautiful in their own skin, without changing who they are. My goal is to help them discover how beautiful they truly are. I feel fulfilled working with women like me who dream of a better future every day. Yet, in some ways, I am still in the process of discovering myself, and I never stop dreaming, even if right now, the goal seems impossible.

During those years of struggle, tears, anxiety, and depression, I have learned that I must never stop dreaming despite the circumstance or challenge. I don't shy away from taking chances to achieve my dreams because, for me, the fear of later regret is much stronger than the fear of failure. At the same time, when I make my important life decisions, I have always asked for and worked to follow God's guidance. In that, I maintain the hope that if I don't completely achieve my dream, at least I will learn a lot along the way. Ever since I was a little girl, I have always been a dreamer. While still back in Honduras, I had dreamed of writing a book, finding love, raising a family, and coming to the United States. I couldn't imagine exactly how they all would happen, but in my heart I knew those things would eventually come.

35

U.S. Citizen

To take the final step of my immigrant journey, I decided to file my application for U.S. citizenship at the end of 2018. As it happened, I wasn't the only permanent resident to have that same idea. That was a consequence of the terror and uncertainty spread by the then president's policies and actions on immigration.

There were reports of permanent residents facing problems returning to the country. There were several incidents of people with visas to enter the U.S.—mainly those from majority-Muslim nations, including those with green cards—being denied access at Border Patrol checks in several airports. It was a time of extreme uncertainty for immigrants regardless of status or visa. After the policies attempted against those of the Muslim faith, there were rumors and fears that there be a similar ban for those from Central America.

Watching the political outrage around the caravans of people heading from Honduras to the United States, it seemed entirely possible that we could wake up to a presidential decree that all Hondurans would be denied entry into the country. I was worried, even though I knew that such actions against immigrants were against the law and seemed illogical. Mark was also very worried and suggested that it was better not to leave the U.S. for the moment, thus avoiding any ugly surprises when we decided to return.

Through a program for D.C. government employees and their families, I was connected to the Central American Resource Center (CARECEN), a nonprofit legal organization that helps provide assistance to those who need to fill out their citizenship application (officially known as the "N-400 Application for Naturalization") at a reduced fee. I paid $640 to the Department of Homeland Security for my application and $60 to CARECEN for their work in assisting me to complete the application. When I went to get the money orders, I

Keyla outside the E. Barrett Prettyman U.S. Federal Courthouse, August 13, 2019 (family photograph).

realized that this could be the last time I would have to pay for immigration legal services, and I felt a brief sense of relief.

Although I could fill out the form independently, I didn't dare try this one on my own. The truth is that you don't have to hire a lawyer for most immigration applications. They can be found on the USCIS website, along with the instructions on how to complete them, similar to the tax forms on the IRS website. The USCIS even has a customer service hotline in case you have a question regarding how to complete an application. But similar to tax forms, the immigration applications are long and can be very confusing. The citizenship application is 20 pages long, not including all the documents that have to be attached.

On top of that, the administration was making changes to the rules regarding immigration applications—including immediately denying incomplete or incorrect applications—to discourage people from applying for citizenship. I decided that after living here for nearly 20 years, I wanted to become a citizen and make my vote heard, and if I was going to do so, I would need to get help from CARECEN to ensure it was done correctly.

After submitting the finalized application, I felt a huge sense of relief, even though the official processing timeline said it would take more than a year for the application to be approved. A couple of weeks later, I received a letter from USCIS confirming receipt of my application and informing me that they expected to review my case in March 2020. My green card would expire in December of 2019, and so it looked like I would have to pay another $600 to renew my green card as well. I didn't want to take the risk of being without a valid permit, even if it meant having to spend more money.

To my surprise, in only six months, I received another USCIS letter, this one with a July 2019 date for my appointment for my interview and citizenship test. For the citizenship test, I had to study 100 questions about United States history and government. In the interview, they would pick only 10 questions at random for me to answer. In preparation, I went to a USCIS processing center to have my fingerprints taken and to pick up my question booklet. Looking through the questions, I felt lucky to know many of the answers because I remembered them from my Civics class at Southern High School.

The questions were about laws, citizens' rights, how the government system works, and the type of economy here in the U.S. I had to know how many years presidents, senators, and representatives serve in office. There were also questions related to the Constitution, the Declaration of Independence, the amendments, the rights of the states, and those of the legislative, executive, and judicial branches of government. I was supposed to learn the name of my state representative and senators, but I knew they wouldn't ask me that because Washington, D.C., doesn't have representation in Congress.

In the ceremony I would have to recite the Pledge of Allegiance, which I had known by heart for years, and I had to review and understand the oath I would take when I became a citizen. I had to know the deadline for reporting taxes, the number of original states, the nation's capital (which was easy because I lived there), and the oceans that border the United States (also easy to remember because they are the same for Honduras). I had to know about prominent Americans: George Washington was the first president, Abraham Lincoln was the president who abolished slavery, and Martin Luther King, Jr., fought for civil rights for African Americans.

Mark was a big help, too, because he is a huge fan of history, and if I got stuck on a question or wasn't sure what it meant, I could ask him. Finally, I felt like living in Washington, D.C., gave me an advantage, as a lot of the questions were about people and places that I learned about while visiting the monuments around the city with my family. I had everything I needed to prepare for my interview.

I studied a week before the exam, and although it had been an entire month since the letter arrived, I was confident in myself and quickly learned what I didn't know. In addition, my English was fluent, and despite still having an accent revealing that I wasn't born here, I could easily communicate. Similarly, I could write with ease.

On July 4, I went with my family to watch the fireworks on the National Mall. We had arrived early to get a good seat, and so I used the extra time to study the questions. There I sat, the Washington Monument and the United States Capitol in view, while Isaac read through the questions, quizzing me on information about U.S. history and government. My son was excited to help, and I was grateful to have the practice listening to the questions. I knew the test would be given orally, so the more practice I had in listening and answering in English, the better.

On the exam day, I woke up early and went over the questions one more time. I was starting to feel nervous, but I ate what I could of breakfast. Going to the Immigration offices always caused me a great deal of anxiety, starting back with my first time in 2001. I was sure that today would be different, but I had gone through so many negative experiences that the anxiety came naturally.

I was sure that I knew all the answers to the test, but I was worried that I would be so nervous that my mind would go blank during the test. I also couldn't stop thinking about who would be in charge of my interview and test. Years ago, when my cousin Ritza was going through her citizenship application, the interviewer was rude and treated her terribly. The attitude and impatience of the interviewer made her so nervous that it affected her ability to recall the answers. I was afraid that the same thing might happen and that I might be interviewed by someone in a bad mood that morning.

We arrived at the offices in northern Virginia, about 30 minutes away. I filled out another form, proceeded to be fingerprinted, and then had the photograph taken that I hoped would be on my Certificate of

Naturalization. We then went to a large waiting room on the second floor to wait for my appointment time. The interviewer called my name and invited me back to his office. My husband had to stay there in the waiting room.

The interviewer was a short, younger man with a friendly attitude, who seemed to enjoy his job. When I walked into his office, he noticed that I was nervous and told me that I had nothing to be anxious about.

"I'll ask you the same questions you already answered on your application; you have nothing to worry about," the officer told me with a smile on his face. His attitude made me feel confident. "Think of this as a casual conversation; there's no need to be nervous," he added.

I began by raising my right hand and swearing to tell nothing but the truth. He checked my ID and then began his questions. He asked my name, date of birth, and where I was born. He asked me where I currently lived and how long I had been living there.

As we were talking, I noticed that on his desk was a thick folder that contained every document and application that I and or my attorneys had ever filled out, signed, and submitted from the time I entered the United States at age 16 in 2001 to the present. It was a bit shocking to see 18 years' worth of documents in one place. At the same time, it relaxed me in a way. I realized that he already knew everything about me, as he had it all in front of him.

The interview continued, and he asked me if I was still married and about my children. Besides the official questions, he asked if my children were bilingual, and I told him yes. He congratulated me, saying that it would be an advantage for them as they grew up. He also asked me if I had ever been declared mentally incompetent and if I had ever failed to file my taxes since becoming a permanent resident.

In all the immigration applications I had completed, paying federal taxes was always a question that came up. The one thing every immigration lawyer we had talked to emphasized was to make sure I filed my taxes. In the application for my permanent residency, my husband had to prove that he and I had paid taxes for the previous three years. It was the same for my application for citizenship. That question was easy for me because I had paid my taxes for the nearly 10 years since I became a resident, as well as the years I worked as a nursing assistant and in Bojangles before we went to Honduras.

The interviewer asked me about my profession; I replied that I was a photographer and ran my own business.

"Congratulations, this country needs more entrepreneurs and

people like you who are eager to be successful!" he congratulated me and continued with the questions.

"Have you ever been a member of or been associated with any terrorist group? Have you ever participated in overturning a government? Have you ever forced someone to have sex with someone else? Have you ever submitted false documentation to the government? Have you ever been deported from the United States?"

With that last question, I wasn't sure what to answer, so I told him:

"To process my residency, I voluntarily went to Honduras for approximately 14 months." The interviewer nodded and said, "Yes, I saw it in your file."

He inquired whether I had ever claimed to be a citizen when I still wasn't, as it is a felony to lie about that. Additionally, he asked me if I had ever signed up or voted in federal or state elections.

"Of course not," I replied.

A somewhat unusual question was whether I was of royal descent or lineage from another country's royalty or nobility and therefore a princess. While that sounded like fun, my title as "princess" was only valid with my husband and kids.

"Are you willing to take the oath to the United States, if the law requires it? Are you willing to take up arms to defend the United States?"

I answered all of his questions honestly, unafraid of failing any of them. Despite my imperfections as a human being, I have strived to live a good and moral life, and I felt confident that my answers reflected who I was.

The personal questioning ended, and the interviewer started with the citizenship test questions.

"What's the type of economy of the U.S.?" he asked.

"Market economy," I replied.

He asked me who the president was during World War I, and I answered:

"Woodrow Wilson."

"What is the supreme law of this country?"

I hesitated for a second, but then I remembered that it was the first question in the booklet and answered right away:

"The Constitution of the United States of America!"

As I had answered the first three correctly, I only needed three more correct answers. He asked the next three questions, and I got all of them right. I had passed that part of the test; now came the test of my English reading and writing skills.

He asked me to write the sentence "Columbus Day is a holiday" on the digital screen in front of me. After I finished writing and submitted it, I was afraid that I had messed up, because I wasn't sure if I wrote "Colombus" or "Columbus."

I asked the interviewer about it, and he made a face like he wasn't sure how to spell it and told me it didn't matter. He then asked me to read a sentence that he would record, although I am pretty sure that the entire interview was being recorded.

After I finished my reading, he congratulated me on passing my interview and told me that my application for citizenship was approved, but that I would not be a citizen until I took the oath at a citizenship ceremony.

I asked him about the date of my ceremony, thinking that I would have to wait until March of the following year as the letter I received had stated. To my surprise, he said, "In a week or so." I told him that Mark and I had an upcoming anniversary trip, and I was concerned that we would have to miss the trip. My experience with Immigration up to that point was that everything in your life had to revolve around their schedule, and trying to reschedule an appointment could put you at the back of a very long line. I nervously asked him if it was possible to schedule a later date. He told me it wouldn't be a problem and then asked me which dates were best for me so he could make a note in the file.

I was so excited, and even though I wasn't a citizen yet, I was already feeling a sense of relief and peace. I felt so blessed to have reached that point in my life.

I came out of the interview with a huge smile on my face. Mark was there waiting for me. He seemed to be more nervous than I had been and was looking uneasy. Being at Immigration appointments always brought him a great deal of anxiety as well. He has always been afraid of me being separated from him and our children.

"I passed the interview!" I told him immediately and tackled him with a hug.

He told me he was praying for me the entire time. I told him that it all turned out great because the officer was friendly and made me feel at home. We both left with huge smiles and with a peace of mind that we were almost at the end of this long ordeal.

The next week, we went on a cruise to celebrate our 15th wedding anniversary. The 15 years I had been married to Mark were full of blessings and lessons learned. Before leaving for the cruise, Mark was still concerned that I was considered a resident and would not be a citizen until I took the citizenship oath.

"Don't worry, if I get deported, I'll get a free flight to Honduras, and if you send me money, I promise I'll be fine." We both laughed, as Mark has always loved my sense of humor.

Upon returning home, I received the email with the date of my ceremony: August 13, 2019. We invited family, but because of the brief notice, sadly no one from my family could attend because they had to work. Mark's parents and one of his sisters and her children were able to make the trip from North Carolina.

August 13 arrived, and it is difficult to describe all my emotions that morning. I was happy to have the support of Mark and my three children as well as Mark's family that day. I call them Mark's family, but I feel they are my family, or better said, I feel that I am part of their family. As we left for the Metro train that we would take to the courthouse, I was sure that La Hita and my mother were there by my side as well. I knew that they were happy and proud of the woman I had become.

After getting off the train, we walked a couple of blocks toward the venue of the ceremony, a second-floor courtroom at the E. Barrett Prettyman United States Courthouse. The courtroom was crowded when we arrived. I was assigned seat number 32 on the second to last bench in the middle section of the courtroom, with my fellow immigrants who would all take the oath that day. On both sides of the middle section, in every chair that was available, were the friends and family of the 111 soon-to-be new United States citizens. We were immigrants from countries around the world. During the almost hour-long wait for the ceremony to begin, I started to feel nervous, but having my family there supporting me helped me to feel confident and loved.

The ceremony started with a guest speaker, a reporter who had recently obtained her citizenship. She spoke to us about coming to the U.S. and what she had accomplished since arriving. The presiding officer and the person in charge of administering the oath, Judge R. Contreras, gave a moving speech prior to the oath. He recounted the story of his parents, who came from Cuba on a raft and worked long hours in low-wage jobs to provide a better future for their children. Thanks to the sacrifice of his parents, Judge Contreras and his siblings went to college and then law school, and became judges.

My favorite part from Judge Contreras's remarks was his opinion on not belonging in the country. At that time in the country, there was a growing movement of white Americans telling immigrants (and children of immigrants) to "go back to their country." Judge Contreras looked directly at the center section of immigrants, and with conviction, said:

> "If anyone tells you that you should go back to your country, you tell them that you are a U.S. Citizen, and this is your country!" He continued, "You have as much right as anyone who was born here to be in this country."

To sit there and hear a federal judge proclaim from the bench that the United States was my country and that I had the right and the duty to live here brought up so many emotions that I almost broke down right then.

One by one, the judge called us by our names. I heard "Keyla Osiris Sanders, Honduras," and my heart started pounding. I stood up and looked over at my family. I fought back tears as the waves of excitement and joy washed over me. I saw that Mark had tears in his eyes, and I could no longer contain myself. Tears streamed down my face as I smiled at Mark. He knew better than anyone what it had taken to make it to this day. Not only did he know, but he had been there beside me for a lot of this journey as well. This wasn't my accomplishment alone—we were sharing in the celebration of this achievement.

As I stood there, my mind was flooded with the memories of everything I had gone through to be where I was. I thought about my days as a *mojada*, when I crossed Guatemala and Mexico. I remembered running on the railroad tracks, trying to get to the train car while terrified that I would fall. I thought about the morning I left Honduras, walking to the bus terminal in the dark with my sister and our backpacks. I thought back to the nights sleeping on the hard floors and waking up with flea bites and shivering from the cold because I had no blanket to cover myself.

I went through all the court appearances, the meetings with lawyers, and all the money that I had spent. I thought about all the disappointments and setbacks, and the despair I felt on that first night on our return to Honduras. Finally, I remembered all the prayers and pleas to God that I had uttered those past 18 years to help me get through obstacles and make it to that day. Going through the pain, sorrow, joy, and, above all, gratitude of this journey in that quick of a sequence had me feeling a little like I was on a roller coaster. I had talked to several people that I knew who had been through this process, but their descriptions didn't come close to what it was like to experience it for myself.

Mark and Keyla at the citizenship oath ceremony, August 13, 2019 (family photograph).

Once everyone was standing, we raised our right hands and repeated the words of the citizenship oath after the judge. As I finished the oath, now officially an American citizen, I was hit with a new wave of emotion. This time I felt a calming peace as I felt the weight of all those years lifted off me. I wanted to scream, "I am free!"

After the swearing in, we placed our hands over our hearts and recited the Pledge of Allegiance, and then sat down to wait to collect our packets of documents. When it was my turn, I proudly walked over to the court clerk's table to hand over my Permanent Resident Card and collect my Certificate of Naturalization—the document that proved to the world that I was a United States citizen. I finally had the chance to hug my husband and children and celebrate with them. It turns out that Mark and I weren't the only ones crying: my mother-in-law and sister-in-law both had tears of joy in their eyes as well.

Before we left the courthouse, I walked over to the voter registration table and proudly handed in my completed voter registration form.

Keyla and her family on the day of her citizenship oath ceremony, August 13, 2019 (family photo)

36

Mojados

In 1995, as a young girl still living in La Entrada, I knew that someday I would write a book. In 2010, sitting in that lecture hall at Harvard University, I knew that I would write a book about my journey with my sister, searching for the American Dream. In 2019, waiting in the courtroom to take my oath as a citizen, I felt that I was ready to write my story. I was more than a little terrified to write and publish the account of my life to this point. I was afraid that putting my life on display would open my family and me up to potential backlash and criticism. That fear remains, but my desire to help others find some part of what I have been blessed with outweighs my fears.

In truth, in the years leading up to my citizenship ceremony, my desire to speak out in favor of undocumented immigrants had been growing. First, because undocumented immigrants were once again being unfairly blamed by many politicians for the problems in our country. Also, during that time, I was encountering more undocumented immigrant women through my work. I was amazed by the strength and determination of these women who had to spend so much of their time working multiple jobs and then had to go home to take care of their children. My empathy grew as I learned of their sorrows and triumphs as they fought to accomplish their version of the American Dream for their families and themselves.

I was blessed to find a path to freedom from the emotional and mental strain of the U.S. immigration system. I knew that I had to use that freedom to tell the story of undocumented immigrants so that people could see us for who and what we are: people, human beings who want to be happy, raise their families in security, and contribute to this nation that has been (and is still being) built by immigrants. My hope is to help everyone, and especially those in a position to make changes, see beyond the political talking points, generalizations, and stereotypes and see us for who we truly are.

Unfortunately, people who come to this country have their identity defined by the immigration system. For nearly two decades, both my identity and my self-image were affected by my immigration status. When I first turned myself in to the Border Patrol agents in Brownsville, the government of the United States declared me an "alien," as though I was not human, that I didn't even belong here on Earth. I was even assigned an "alien number" to identify me. That alien number was attached to every form, document, and application I submitted as well as every notification and letter I received back. Even after I received my Social Security number, an immigrant visa, and a green card, I was still officially an "alien" according to the government.

In taking the oath, I was able to feel the freedom from the mental and emotional strain of that system that I was finally leaving behind. I was able to reclaim my humanity. I was free to reshape my identity and my life in any way that I wanted. Most people who are born with this freedom will never understand what that change can feel like.

I am choosing to identify myself as a *mojada*. I claim this title according to my own definition, rather than how it has been traditionally used. More than one hundred years ago, on June 20, 1920, the *New York Times* mentioned, for the first time, the term "wetback" to refer to those who crossed from Mexico to the U.S. via the Rio Grande.[1] The origin of the term had to do with how the migrants crossed. They were observed floating across the river, sitting in inner tubes. Thus, when they arrived on the U.S. side, their backs were all wet.

Since that time, the term "wetback" has been used as an insult used to demean and other-ize those of Latin American descent who are in this country. It falls into the same category as more recent terms such as "illegals" and "invaders" that have become part of the debate around the motivations and contributions of undocumented immigrants. In Spanish, we use the term *mojado* (literally translated as "wet") to describe those who cross the U.S. border without documentation (the official term is "crossing without inspection"), though in Spanish the term is not as derogatory or insulting.

For me, I am *mojada* not from the water in the Rio Grande nor simply because I crossed without inspection. I am *mojada* from the sweat and tears of my journey toward a better life. My journey to the United States was difficult both physically and mentally. I finished many days of walking soaked with sweat. I spent many nights and some days with my face *mojada* with tears. I cried from frustration, loneliness, sadness, and fear. Growing up in La Entrada, the loss of my mother, my father's abandonment, the shame of being abused, and watching my family slowly leave La Entrada were all sources of endless tears.

Along my journey as an undocumented immigrant, although I encountered several challenges and dangers, I was blessed to eventually be reunited with my family. Each year, large numbers of migrants embark on their own quest for a better life. Unfortunately, for many their journey to the U.S. is much more disastrous than mine. These immigrants arrive at the land of the American Dream, but they do so filled with emotional and physical wounds. They are wounded after having been kidnapped, abused, and sexually assaulted, all of which often accompanies them on their journey.[2] They are *mojados* from their tears of so many traumas lived in a short amount of time.

Worse still, every year hundreds of migrants never arrive at their destination.[3] They lose their lives somewhere along the journey. Some are crushed and mangled under the iron wheels of a train or drowned in the Rio Grande.[4] Others give in to the heat, exhaustion, and thirst as they attempt to walk through the desert. Others are "disappeared"— kidnapped and killed by cartels, *mareros* (gang members), or corrupt Border Patrol agents and are never seen or heard from again. Their families and friends also become *mojados* as they mourn the loss of their loved ones on that search for a better life.[5] Then, there are the *desaparecidos* (disappeared)—those who set off but never arrive, and are never heard from again.[6]

The day that I was arrested by Mexican immigration officers, I know that there were angels, both in spirit and in the flesh, that looked over me and kept me safe. Tragically, there is an untold number of young women who, like me, were adolescents and unaccompanied, but who never make it back to Central America. Instead, they are lost to an underworld of sexual violence, sex trafficking, and forced prostitution.[7] These ill-fated *mojadas* and their families' lives will never be the same again.

With the ransom paid and my freedom gained from the kidnappers, my journey as a *mojada* concluded. However, my life as a *mojada* continued as I focused on my dream for a better life. The struggle for the American Dream is one that requires effort, sacrifice, and dedication. That effort is one that immigrants embrace in exchange for the chance at finding success here in this country. They, like me, are *mojados*—soaked in sweat—from the daily struggle to carve out a life and fulfill their potential in the U.S.

I have been a witness to that struggle and sacrifice with my family, friends, and neighbors. These *mojados* who get up early; work long hours, often at multiple jobs; and come home late. They build houses, erect large buildings, and paint houses and apartments all over the United States. Others spend their days washing dishes in restaurants; cleaning houses, offices, public restrooms; or washing cars. There are the *mojados* whose long days play out in fields or in food processing plants, an essential part of our food supply chain. I have seen their sacrifices on frozen winter days and under the blazing summer sun. Many live in small houses or apartments, while others combine several families into one home.

This life of sweat and tears is one that undocumented immigrants take on as a means of accomplishing their American Dream. I use the term "their American Dream" because each *mojada* has their own individual motivations and goals that drive them to come to the U.S. I have talked with many *mojados* who, like myself, dream of running their own business, contributing to their community by providing services and jobs. I have former neighbors from La Entrada who have been able to do just that. There are many more who continue in that struggle, and—God willing—will make it someday.

For others, the "Dream" is to work here in the U.S. to make enough money to improve their life in their home country. They toil, *mojados* from sweat, as they save up enough money to build a house, pay for their children's education, or set up a business that can sustain them and their family upon their return. They are also *mojados* from the tears shed as they anxiously wait to return home to spouses and children left behind. They work and wait for the day when they will have fulfilled their American Dream and can return to their families and lives in their home country.

Still others simply want a better life. They wish to be free from the violence and trauma in their native countries. They want to be able to provide food and shelter for their children. Their dream is to establish a home and raise a family in the relative peace and security available in this country.

Not all those *mojados* will successfully accomplish their dreams. Some will be arrested and deported. Some will be overcome by loneliness and the hopelessness of trying to live and save on the less-than-minimum wages commonly paid to *mojados*. They will return to be with their families before they can earn the money they had dreamed of. Most will continue to get up every morning, with hope that, one day, there will be a happy ending to their struggle.

Thankfully, my journey through the immigration system as a *mojada* had a happy conclusion. Though, my success should be a confirmation of how unfair and unpredictable the U.S. immigration system is. Unfortunately, "success" does not solely come from the talent, effort, and/or determination of an immigrant (though all those are needed).

At my citizenship ceremony, Judge Contreras ended his remarks by saying that attaining citizenship "is like winning the lottery … but it shouldn't be." The simple truth is that success in the U.S. immigration system is more due to chance and being in the right place at the right time. I am grateful for the blessings I have received, and the safety and security granted by my new citizenship. I recognize, though, that this blessing did not come because I am more deserving, more qualified, or have worked harder than any other immigrant who is still struggling, trying to find a way to succeed in the system.

I have family and friends who have been here in the U.S. much longer than I have been. They have spent decades working and sacrificing and building a life here. Most of them have children, and even grandchildren, who are U.S. citizens, yet they are still waiting for that status themselves. I remain hopeful that someday I will be able to celebrate with my family the day they all become U.S. citizens and are able to enjoy the same freedom and relief I have felt.

To all those who read this book, I ask you to step a moment into the shoes of a *mojado* to imagine the pain as a parent, lying in bed not knowing how you will feed your children in the morning. Imagine the fear and violence in your hometown to be so extreme that hiking through the jungle for days, jumping on a moving train, and risking likely kidnapping and assault seem like safer options. I ask you to imagine yourself as a teenager, orphaned by your mother and abandoned by your father at an early age, with the woman who raised you and your entire family in the U.S. Would you make the same decision to come here by whatever means were available? Would you shed the same tears?

I won't ask you to try and imagine working hard, worrying about bills, building up savings, raising kids, or pouring sweat and tears into accomplishing your dreams. In those areas, everyone, regardless of citizenship or where they were born, has a lot in common. What we have in common, you and I—you and a *mojada*—is so much more than what makes us different. Aside from a very important piece of paper, we are the same in our desire to fulfill our version of the American Dream. We all have shed tears of loneliness and despair in that pursuit. We all have poured our sweat into making those dreams a reality. In that way, all of us in this human race—we are all *mojados*.

Epilogue

I enjoy my life in Washington, D.C. Living here has brought my family and me many blessings. I have met many people from different cultures and countries. It is the perfect place for my children to grow up and encounter these many different cultures and learn to have admiration and respect for each one of them. Every inhabitant of this country, regardless of their race, origin, or immigration status, is part of the flavor and color of this great nation. I am grateful for the chance to be here and for having made it to this point. My journey as a *mojada* has been one of the most powerful and most meaningful lessons in my life. I thank God every day for the comfortable bed I sleep in, for the warm food I put in my mouth, for the roof that protects me, for the places I have traveled to. I have learned to appreciate the beauty of this world and to treasure each person who crosses my path.

Counting blessings didn't always come easy to me, especially when I didn't understand the times when I had to struggle and suffer in my journey. For years, I focused on my pain, my depression, and my bitterness because I was unable to understand the blessings that surrounded me.

During those years, every night, I would imagine my own perfect world. In this fantasy, my mother was alive, my father had taken responsibility for raising and taking care of my sister and me, and we lived together in a happy home. I imagined myself introducing my parents to my boyfriends and later the man whom I would marry. Then I imagined the day I became a mom and pictured having my mother present to celebrate the arrival of her grandchildren.

As I have grown through self-reflection, prayer, and therapy, I have learned to see things in a different light. First, I recognize that life is uncertain, and I cannot control the people or situations around me. I do, however, have the power to control how I will act and react to those around me. I have come to understand that it was all part of a perfect plan that God had prepared for me.

Secondly, I recognize that my past, both the good and the bad, shaped me into who I am today, and I should be proud of that. If I were given a chance at a do-over on my past, I wouldn't take it because I wouldn't risk losing those people and experiences that made me who I am.

I still miss my mother every day of my life, but I am grateful to have been raised by La Hita. My grandmother's example of honesty and hard work has helped me throughout my life, and in every step I have taken. She and her teachings played an essential role in many crucial decisions I have made. I would not trade my past, because it is how I learned to love my husband and my children. It is how I have learned to be grateful for what I have.

Finally, I have learned the importance of dealing with and operating in the present. The future is uncertain and not promised to anyone. The past is behind me—and cannot be changed, no matter how much I try. Only in the present can I decide what to do with my life and how to feel.

I owe all I have to God. I thank Him for putting me at the perfect time and age to become a member of The Church of Jesus Christ of Latter-day Saints. The teachings and experiences I have had since the age of 15 have shaped me into a leader, mother, and woman of faith. The church has been and continues to be a space of infinite learning and reflection for me.

There was a specific incident at church that I share because it directly relates to the story I have told in this book, and it was a moment of clarity and liberation for my soul. In my church it is customary for the congregational leadership to ask members to prepare 10-minute talks or mini-sermons on specific gospel topics. In April 2019, a few months before my citizenship ceremony, I had been asked to prepare a talk about forgiveness.

I had prepared my talk using scriptural passages and stories from the lives of others as examples. The Sunday morning for my mini-sermon arrived, and I was sitting in the pews behind the pulpit, waiting for my turn to speak. Right before I got up to speak, a profound feeling came over me. I felt that I should share my own process of forgiveness rather than read the remarks I had prepared. I had the distinct impression that I should share how I was working on healing and forgiving those who had hurt me.

I was momentarily overcome by fear at the idea of standing up in public and talking about my sexual abuse, my father's abandonment, and all the people who had marked my life in one negative way or another. I didn't know how to start talking about something so personal. To that point, I had only discussed these things with my husband and my psychologist. At that moment, I began to cry as I felt the Spirit telling me what I should share. I begged God to give me strength and not to leave me alone. The following is the first part of what I shared that morning:

> At the age of three, my mom died, my dad abandoned me, and I didn't hear from him until eighteen years later. I was also sexually abused as a child. I was so poor that there were times I didn't even have enough to buy shoes.
> For years, my heart was flooded with resentment and unanswered questions, feelings of hatred towards my father for leaving me alone, not taking care of my sister and me when we needed him most, and not preventing others from taking advantage of me. I lived with constant anger and frustration, and I didn't understand how a father could have done something like that to a daughter.
> Many years later, I searched for him and wanted to hear from him. I forgave him, and although it took time to create a father-daughter bond, today I am proud to be able to say that I feel love for him.
> I forgave those who abused me, and I did it not because of them but because I wanted to be at peace with myself. I knew it was necessary to unleash the full potential that my Heavenly Father reserved for me....
> The road hasn't been easy, but it has been full of learning.

As I finished my talk and stepped back to my seat, I felt lighter than ever. As I delivered that speech, I came to the realization that forgiving those who had harmed me wasn't for their benefit, it was for my own. Even though none of my aggressors had asked for forgiveness, it was what God wanted me to do.

After the service, I saw that I wasn't alone. Several women came to find me and tell me about their experiences of sexual abuse, their pain, and how they were looking for healing. It was sad to hear that so many women had been through such pain and trauma, but it was heartwarming to hear that my story had given them strength to carry on.

At the same time, some of the women never had to say a word, but I knew that through my words, their hearts had been touched. I noticed it when a sister who was an immigrant from a country in Africa left the room because she couldn't hold back her tears. She didn't need to tell me anything to know that she had also lived a hard life.

Every time I tell my story, I do it with tears in my eyes, but not with resentment or bitterness toward anyone I have mentioned in this book. They are tears of healing, love, and peace. By forgiving, I don't mean finding a way justify other people's harmful actions. It is a process where I first had to accept that I was not guilty or responsible for what someone did to me. Then I had to recognize that I am the sum of my experiences and had to learn to accept who I am. Little by little over years, I was then able to forgive and later learn to love the person.

I am an example that healing is possible, and one can overcome trauma. This process of learning to forgive has taught me to empathize with other women who, regardless of their background or social status, have had a life full of pain and suffering. I hope to continue sharing my story with other women, girls, and adolescents, so that they know they aren't alone. There is a way to personal healing and a way to find happiness even though the road ahead may currently appear hopeless.

I share all this now not to hold myself up as a perfect example, or as someone who should be admired. I share it because it has been, and continues to be, a hard road, but it is one where I have found some peace and comfort. This is not a quick fix. It is a process that builds gradually over time, like filling a glass of water one drop at a time. Additionally, the process of forgiving others is not a straight line. There will be advances and setbacks.

In truth, the act of writing this book has been a combination of both. Searching through my memories and recalling the details of painful events has been difficult. I have had to increase my mental health treatments and supports as I relive these traumas. To those who are looking to find a path toward healing, or those who are looking to support others in this journey, please understand that it will require the assistance of mental health professionals.

As continue with my life, I will continue to be an imperfect woman who makes mistakes, feels disappointed at times, suffers from anxiety and depression, but knows that God is always with her and guides her in all the decisions she makes in her life. I can feel my grandmother and my mother alongside me in so many moments. I know they help me get back up and continue when I feel like I can't do it anymore. Even though I can't hear them, I imagine their words of love and encouragement telling me that I can.

I feel happy and full of joy with my work as a photographer and blessed to work with people worldwide. My development as a photographer over the last 12 years has been full of constant learning and continuous challenges. At the same time, it has helped me see life differently, to appreciate the beauty of the mornings and the evenings with their full spectrum of different shades. I have learned to see a colorful world, and the beauty that every person has inside them. In this I have been able to leave behind my shadows and darkness.

One way or another, I am still the same Keyla who left Honduras, because I am still dreaming and learning. Although I know that being a citizen brings me more opportunities, having formalized my status doesn't make me a better person or different from who I was before. What has changed me and made me a better person has been the work I have done to drain the poison of bitterness and guilt from my heart. Forgiving and allowing myself to see life with positivity has helped me feel that I have *alas* (wings) to fly anywhere.

Chapter Notes

Chapter 25

1. The United States Citizenship and Immigration Services (USCIS) was the new name for Immigration and Naturalization Services (INS) given after the governmental reorganization after 9/11.

Chapter 36

1. Bretigram, G. (1920, June 20). "Welcomed Mexican Invasion." *The New York Times*, p. 109.
2. Inskeep, S. (2014, March 22). "The Rarely Told Stories of Sexual Assault Against Female Migrants." *NPR*. https://www.npr.org/2014/03/23/293449153/the-rarely-told-stories-of-sexual-assault-against-female-migrants. Zamudio, M. (2014, September 10). "Trail of Fears: Central American women risk sexual violence en route to U.S. for 'a better life.'" *Commercial Appeal*. https://archive.commercialappeal.com/news/trail-of-fears-central-american-women-risk-sexual-violence-en-route-to-us-for-a-better-life-ep-61579-324323771.html/.
3. National Network for Immigrant and Refugee Rights (NNIR) (n.d.). *Stopping Migrant Deaths at the Border*. https://nnirr.org/programs/seeking-border-justice/stopping-migrant-deaths/.
4. Borunda, D. (2021, July 27). "Man struck and killed by train during migrant border crossing attempt in Downtown El Paso." *El Paso Times*. https://www.elpasotimes.com/story/news/immigration/2021/07/27/el-paso-border-migrant-crossing-man-killed-train/5384398001/. Williams, A. (2018, July

21). "Bound for the U.S., migrants gamble with their lives on the 'death train.'" *DW*. https://www.dw.com/en/bound-for-us-migrants-gamble-with-their-lives-on-the-death-train/a-44763721. Timmons, P. (2019, June 29). "'People with no names': The drowned migrants buried in pauper's graves." *The Guardian*. https://www.theguardian.com/us-news/2019/jun/29/migrants-drowning-rio-grande-river-deaths-us-mexico-border.
5. Missing Migrant Project (accessed 2022, July 27). https://missingmigrants.iom.int/region/americas?region_incident=4076&route=3936&incident_date%5Bmin%5D=&incident_date%5Bmax%5D=. Diaz, L. (2022, May 12). "Migrant disappearances quadruple in Mexico in 2021, says report." *Reuters*. https://www.reuters.com/world/americas/migrant-disappearances-quadruple-mexico-2021-says-report-2022-05-11/.Biörklund, L. (2022, June 9). "Central America's caravan of mothers: Personal grief and political grievance." *The Conversation*. https://theconversation.com/central-americas-caravan-of-mothers-personal-grief-and-political-grievance-183793.
6. Srovin Coralli, A. (2021, May 20). "Mexico's Search for Disappeared Migrants has Evolved, but Challenges Remain." *Migration Information Source*. https://www.migrationpolicy.org/article/mexico-search-disappeared-migrants.
7. United Nations Office on Drugs and Crime (2012, September). "Trafficking of women and girls within Central America." *Transnational Organized Crime in Central America and the Caribbean: A Threat Assessment* (pp. 53–57).

Index